URBAN
CYCLING

URBAN

how to get to work, save money, and use your bike for city living

CYCLING

MADI CARLSON

SKIPSTONE

Published by Skipstone, an imprint of Mountaineers Books
Printed in the United States of America
18 17 16 15   1 2 3 4 5

Copy editor: Nancy W. Cortelyou
Design and illustration: Heidi Smets
All photos by the author unless otherwise noted

Library of Congress Cataloging-in-Publication Data
Carlson, Madi, author.
  Urban cycling : how to get to work, save money, and use your bike for city living / by Madi Carlson. — 1st edition.
      pages cm
  Includes index.
  Summary: "A how-to guide for getting around by bike in lieu of a car, with special attention to route-planning, cycling with children, and bicycling infrastructure"—Provided by publisher.
  ISBN 978-1-59485-943-4 (trade paper) — ISBN 978-1-59485-944-1 (ebook)
1. Cycling—Handbooks, manuals, etc. 2. City traffic—Handbooks, manuals, etc. 3. Bicycle commuting—Handbooks, manuals, etc. I. Title.
  GV1043.7.C37 2015
  796.6—dc23
                    2015028113

 Printed on 30% PCW recycled paper

ISBN (paperback): 978-1-59485-943-4
ISBN (ebook): 978-1-59485-944-1

Skipstone books may be purchased for corporate, educational, or other promotional sales, and our authors are available for a wide range of events. For information on special discounts or booking an author, contact our customer service at 800-553-4453 or mbooks@mountaineersbooks.org.

Skipstone
1001 SW Klickitat Way, Suite 201, Seattle, Washington 98134
206.223.6303
www.skipstonebooks.org
www.mountaineersbooks.org

LIVE LIFE. MAKE RIPPLES.

For Brandt and Rijder, may you inspire the next generation of urban cyclists

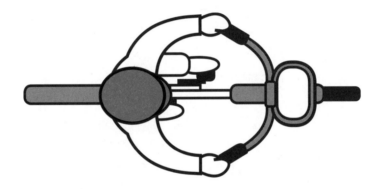

Contents

Acknowledgments 11

Chapter 1
Benefits of Bike Commuting
Save Time 14
Save Money 15
Save Your Health 16
Save the Environment 19
Profile: Bicycle Benefits, Various Cities 20

Chapter 2
The Bike
Commuter Bikes 25
Other Types of Bikes 34
Buying New 39
Profile: Samantha Arnold, Chicago, IL 40
Buying Used 42
Testing and Adjusting Bike Fit 43

Chapter 3
Bike Parts and Components
Tires and Inner Tubes 47
Brakes 51
Pedals 52
Saddles 54
Gears and Shifters 55
Profile: Elly Blue, Portland, OR 58
Handlebars 62

Chapter 4
Gear and Accessories
Reflectors 65
Lights 66
Locks 67
Helmets 72
Profile: Momentum Mag,
  Vancouver, BC 73
Clothing 75
Bags, Racks, and Baskets 79
Profile: Adonia Lugo, Washington, DC 80
Fenders 85
Pumps 86
Kickstands 87
Front-Wheel Stabilizers 87
Mirrors 87
Chain Guards 88
Bells 90
Music 90
Drink Cages and Cup Holders 91
Cell-Phone Mounts 92

Chapter 5
Urban Bicycle Infrastructure
Sharrows 94
Bike Lanes 99
Multi-Use Trails 99
Neighborhood Greenways 99

Profile: Seattle Neighborhood Greenways 100
Bike Boxes 101
Left-Turn Box 102
Bicycle-Specific Traffic Lights 104
Wayfinding Signs 106

Chapter 6
Riding Techniques
Riding Defensively 108
Riding Predictably 110
Vehicular Cycling 112
Signaling and Turning 114
Traversing Intersections 117
Profile: The League of American Bicyclists 118
Avoiding the Door Zone 119
Passing 120
Crossing Rails and Avoiding Obstacles 121
Riding on Sidewalks 122
Salmoning 123
Sharing Multi-Use Trails 124
Dealing with Aggressive or Unsafe Motorists 125

Chapter 7
The Route
Evaluating a Good Bike Route 127
Finding Your Route 128
Profile: Cascade Bicycle Club, Seattle, WA 133
Taking Your Route to Go 135
Profile: Nona Varnado, Los Angeles, CA 136

Having a Backup Plan 138
Taking a Practice Run 140
Go for It! 141
Your Evolving Route 141

Chapter 8
Less Than Ideal Conditions
Rain 143
Cold, Snow, and Ice 148
Heat and Humidity 151
Profile: Patrick Stephenson, Minneapolis, MN 154
Illness 156
Saddle Sores 156
Injuries 157

Chapter 9
Basic Maintenance
Basic Bike Check 162
Tires and Tubes 162
Brakes 170
Chain 172
Build Your Repair Kit 174
Keep Your Bike Clean 176
Learn Bike Maintenance 177
Profile: Bikes Not Bombs, Boston, MA 179

Chapter 10
Multimodal Bike Commuting and Bike Share
Car 181
Park and Ride 184
Bus 184
Commuter Train 188
Ferry 189

Transit Bike   190
Bike Lockers   190
Bike Transit Centers   191
Profile: David Katzmaier, New York, NY   192
Bike Share   195

Chapter 11
Commuting with Kids
Selecting a Bike, Seat, or Trailer   199
Family Bikes   203
Profile: Dorie Apollonio,
San Francisco, CA   214
Helmets   216
Methods, Tips, and Tricks   217
Riding with Bicycling Kids   220

Chapter 12
Laws, Theft, and Collisions
Bike Laws   223
Bike Security   226

Profile: Alliance for Biking & Walking
  Washington, DC   228
Collisions   229

Chapter 13
Next Steps
Go on Group Rides   233
Lead Group Rides   234
Start a Group   235
Race   236
Profile: CycloFemme, Nationwide   237
Go on a Bike Tour   238
Randonneur   239
Use Bikes When Traveling   239
Profile: Barb Chamberlain, Seattle, WA   240
Be an Advocate and Volunteer   242
Work in the Industry   243

Resources   245
Index   248

Acknowledgments

Thank you to the many people named in this book—your contributions mask the fact that I'm just the muscle behind this operation. Riding all the bikes is a lot easier than writing about them! Extra special thanks to my eight profiled urban cyclists from around the country: Dorie Apollonio, Samantha Arnold, Elly Blue, Barb Chamberlain, David Katzmaier, Adonia Lugo, Patrick Stephenson, and Nona Varnado. I often refer people to you and am ecstatic to introduce a new audience to your inspiring and helpful bike-related exploits.

Several bicycle mechanics allowed me to ask tons of questions and take zillions of photographs while they demonstrated specific repairs and maintenance jobs I requested; many thanks to Edward Moore of Ride Bicycles, Johnny Latenight of R+E Cycles, and Ben Rainbow of Back Alley Bike Repair. I'd still rather have you fix my bike's flats than do it myself, but I am a more confident home wrench for having spent so much time with you.

I owe a debt of gratitude to several friends whose bike knowledge has now become my bike knowledge and whose anecdotes have made their ways into this book: Jolene Carpenter, Linette Demers, Alyssa Smith, and Kath Youell—thanks!

Kent Peterson, thank you for proofreading and fine tuning! No bike book should hit the streets without your stamp of approval.

Thank you to Kate Rogers, Margaret Sullivan, Kirsten Colton, and Mary Metz of Mountaineers Books and Skipstone for your patience, encouragement, and working of editorial magic. And, at a most basic level, thank you to Chris Saleeba for connecting me with Kate and starting this whole thing.

Finally, thanks to the many Seattle bike organizations and groups with which I've spent time, not only for teaching me bike maintenance, urban riding, and racing skills, but even more for sharing the wonderful community that bicycling begets: Bike Works, Cascade Bicycle Club, Menstrual Monday, Point83, Recycled Cycles Racing, Seattle Kidical Mass, and Seattle Neighborhood Greenways—you rock!

CHAPTER 1

Benefits of Bike Commuting

FROM MIDDLE SCHOOL ON, I had been an on-again, off-again bike commuter, but when I moved to Seattle, I was a daily car driver. The weather in my new town—the cold, not the famous rain—was a shock to my thin Southern California blood, but as soon as I adjusted, I started to bike again. At first traveling on two wheels only to the closest destinations, I ever so gradually replaced driving with biking. It helps immensely to live in a metropolitan city. While there are improvements I'm eager to see in Seattle's bicycle infrastructure, it's the most bike-friendly city I've ever lived in.

Until recently, I still had my car, which although in wonderful working order and fairly fuel efficient, never inspired flights of fancy. But my bike—I can wax poetic about it all day long. I'm stronger, I'm healthier, I'm happier, I feel more in touch with my community, and I spend zero money on gas.

For most, transportation cycling is surprisingly efficient. That stoplight that takes three cycles to get through during rush hour in your car is a mere 15-second pause on your bike thanks to the free-flowing bike lane . . . or likely isn't even on your route anymore. The financial savings are most immediately apparent if you've shed the need for parking passes or road tolls, but there are still daily savings for choosing to leave the car at home even for "free" commutes. You might not be surprised that riding your bike even a short distance is good for your health, but the benefits go far beyond physical fitness, which you'll notice as your happiness quotient rises. And while bettering your own health, you'll also positively affect the well-being of your community and the world as a whole.

There are also the less predictable benefits. Traveling from home to work and other destinations slow enough to really see the city—and with the ability to stop and quickly park anywhere and everywhere—will reveal a new layer of life. Maybe you'll sniff out a new favorite restaurant, find a life-changing book during a 30-second pause at a Little Free Library, or become the hero of the office when you stop by a tree bearing the sign "Free Plums, Limit 10."

Whether you get around on two wheels out of necessity each and every day, or opt to ride just once a week in a conscious effort to lessen your carbon footprint, you'll discover there are numerous benefits to traversing your city by bike. It's efficient, saves you money, boosts your health, improves your mood, and has a positive impact on the environment.

SAVE TIME

My friends often take issue with my terminology when I declare that bike commuting feeds into my innate laziness. How can providing the energy to move a bike around town be lazier than getting behind the wheel of a car? So glad you asked! My bike is always within reach—kitchen, basement, or carport. Those with dedicated car parking spots won't appreciate the easy-accessed bike, but retrieving *my* car usually required a game of hide-and-seek since I didn't drive frequently enough to remember where I had last parked it! And the bus is even harder. Although there's a bus stop right across the street from my house, grabbing my bike as soon as I'm ready to head out the door is so much simpler than adjusting to a bus schedule.

The only part of my bike commute that feels slow is waiting for red lights, but that downtime rarely feels wasted, as it can in a car. And that's because I'm out in the fresh air, can talk to neighboring cyclists, and sometimes even discuss biking-related questions through open car windows.

Freedom of movement feels different on a bike too. In a car there's often another vehicle right in front of you that feels more like a blockade than a commute buddy. Even when a car's average speed is greater than a bike's, a commute feels faster by bike. This perceived speed may not get you to work faster, but it can get you to work happier.

And, surprise, biking *is* faster in certain scenarios. According to Arizona's Maricopa County Department of Transportation, bicycling is quicker than other transportation modes door to door for distances under three miles. In congested situations, it is often faster for distances up to five miles. Longer distances might not be faster by bike, but while a ten-mile commute could realistically take 10 extra minutes by bike (say 50 minutes versus 40 minutes by car—likely enough on congested streets in many cities) that's just 10 extra minutes on either side of your commute that contributes to your physical health and

Bicycle Speed	Time to Travel One Mile
8 mph	7.5 minutes
9 mph	6.7 minutes
10 mph	6 minutes
12 mph	5 minutes
15 mph	4 minutes
20 mph	3 minutes

Travel time by bike

mental well-being, and saves you gas money.

Once the pedaling part of the trip is over, there's more time to be saved in parking. Many workers bring their bikes into their offices or office parking garages. Otherwise, on-street bicycle parking is generally right by the front door. That means no walking from a parking spot you invariably searched and circled to get, and avoiding a parking lot full of impatient drivers doing the same.

SAVE MONEY

While I'm a fiercely proud, born and bred *frugalist*, saving money is not my main motivator for commuting by bike. It might even be last on my list, with happiness, greenness, efficiency, and health all vying for first place. But it's often the first question a person considering a bike commute asks: how much money will I save?

Cars are anything but cheap. From the 2014 AAA *Your Driving Costs* study, the cost per mile and per year for an average sedan, based on fuel, maintenance, tires, insurance, license, registration, taxes, depreciation, and auto loan finance charges, as well as an average of 15,000 miles per year, is $0.592 per mile, or $8,876 per year.

In *The Basics and Benefits of Bicycle Commuting*, car-free author and bicycle commuting advocate Chris Balish calls the bicycle the most cost-efficient mode of human transport ever devised. Walking is technically cheaper, but he points out that if you factor in the time saved by covering ground more quickly, bicycling can be considered the all-around cheaper choice.

The awesome efficiency of the bicycle makes it difficult to calculate the per-mile cost of biking. Most figures calculate an actual savings of $0.05 to $0.15 per mile with a *net savings* of even more when factoring in canceled gym memberships or health-care savings from a less sedentary lifestyle.

The IRS 2014 Standard Mileage Rate for business miles, which covers the fixed and variable costs of fuel and wear and tear, is $0.56 per mile. Using $0.10 per mile as our average bike cost leaves us with $0.46 saved per mile when you choose bike over car—and that's not even including tolls and parking fees. If your workplace is two miles from home, that quickly adds up to $9.20 per week—or

	Small Sedan	Medium Sedan	Large Sedan	**Sedan Average**	SUV 4WD	Minivan
Cost per Mile	$0.464	$0.589	$0.722	$0.592	$0.736	$0.650
Cost per Year	$6,957	$8,839	$10,831	$8,876	$11,039	$9,753

How expensive is that car? (based on driving 15,000 miles annually. Source: AAA Your Driving Costs)

more if your trip is longer, though most bicycle commutes are five miles or less.

The numbers are very impressive on the national level. In *Pedaling to Prosperity*, the Sierra Club shares that 40 percent of all trips using any mode (car, public transportation, bike, feet) in the United States are within two miles of home. If each person replaced just one four-mile round-trip each week, using a bicycle instead of the car, it would result in a national savings of almost two billion gallons of gas and $7.3 billion a year.

SAVE YOUR HEALTH

The American Heart Association recommends 30 minutes of moderate exercise five days a week for overall cardiovascular health. Those 30 minutes of exercise are beneficial even when broken into two or three segments. That means a 15-minute bicycle commute twice a day will help prevent heart disease and stroke, the nation's number one and number four killers.

Bicycling for transportation is an excellent moderate-intensity activity. The Centers for Disease Control and Prevention (CDC) rates bicycling slower than ten miles per hour as moderate, but assuming you don't have a speedometer on your bike (yes, there are speedometers for bicycles, called bike computers, and we'll cover those and other fun accessories later on—see Chapter 7: The Route, Taking Your Route to Go), use the Talk Test for Exercise Intensity:

> › Moderate-intensity activity: You can talk, but not sing.
> › Vigorous-intensity activity: You cannot

say more than a few words without pausing for a breath.

A moderate-intensity bike ride is great for arriving at your destination healthy and fresh-faced, but not dripping with sweat. If you prefer to change your clothes before work, can arrive a bit on the sweaty side, or want extra intensity on the way home, consider getting vigorous. A 30-minute moderate-intensity ride to the office is great for *preventive health* and a vigorous-intensity ride home can lower blood pressure and cholesterol. To *improve your health*, the American Heart Association recommends 40 minutes of moderate- to vigorous-intensity aerobic activity three or four times per week. This might mean finding a longer or hillier route home, but it's still a convenient way to get healthy.

////////////

THE BICYCLE COMMUTER ACT OF 2008

Does your employer know that a bicycle commuting reimbursement was added to the IRS list of qualified transportation fringe benefits? If you're not already receiving another tax-free commuter benefit (such as up to $115 per month for public transportation or $210 per month for parking) and your employer is willing, you can be reimbursed up to $20 per month for reasonable expenses related to your bike commute, including equipment purchases, bike purchases, repairs, and storage.

////////////

Anne and Tim King of Ride Savvy lead healthy and happy bike-filled lives.

WEIGHT LOSS

You *might* lose weight from bicycling for transportation, but you probably won't. I include this section because bicycling is associated with health and becoming healthy is often associated with weight loss. The more I bicycle—ever increasing distances and, on my cargo bike, with ever larger children—the stronger and healthier I get, yet my weight doesn't change ... or if it does, it's slightly in the upward direction.

Bicycle commuting will get you in shape and help you maintain your *current* weight, but you'll probably also experience an increased appetite. It's common to think bicycling means you can eat more since you're hungrier. And you can ... just not if the goal is to lose weight. Unless you make the effort to not increase your caloric intake to match your increased appetite, you probably won't lose weight. However, your shape is likely to change for the better as your body becomes healthier and stronger, even if this doesn't mean dropped pounds.

THE AIR WE BREATHE

On a bike, you're not contributing to air pollution—a wonderful thing, but that doesn't mean you're not affected by the pollution generated by others. Fortunately, it's not as bad as you might think.

Bicycling alongside a truck's belching exhaust pipe might make you worry that you're doing your lungs more harm than

PRESCRIPTION TO PEDAL

If you have any health concerns, check with your health-care provider before your first ride.

■■■■■■■■■■■■■

good, but a 2013 study in New Zealand published in *Environmental Pollution* comparing air quality for car drivers, bus riders, and bicyclists found the air inside *cars* is the most polluted. The air inside buses was less polluted than the air in cars, but bicyclists fared the best, and bike commuters using separated paths breathed even cleaner air than their road-sharing mates.

If you're worried about air quality on your route, consider switching to quieter roads or changing your schedule to ride before or after peak commute times. Even moving out in front of the line of cars when stopped at a red light can lessen the amount of pollutants inhaled. This is most easily accomplished using bike boxes (the holding areas that are meant to position bikes in front of cars at red lights) but also works with bike lanes (lanes parallel to car travel lanes).

Having normal-functioning lungs, I don't feel the effects of riding on congested roads, but I know people who cannot ride near highways because it triggers their asthma. I often see people bicycling with a bandana tied over their nose and mouth. The cloth of this makeshift air filter will block large particles, but a true antipollution face mask will block more. Any extra layer can cause discomfort and/or extra sweat, but a face mask could be a worthwhile solution if changing your route isn't possible.

MENTAL ACUITY

You'll notice your body will feel energized from the physical exertion of biking to work, much different than the sluggish feeling you get from sitting in a car or bus for a comparable amount of time. The same goes for your brain. A March 2014 *Bicycling* magazine article, "Your Brain on Bicycling," on the mental effects of cycling calls the "sweet spot" for sharpest brain function at right after 30 to 60 minutes of riding at 75 percent of maximum heart rate.

In the *Mass Experiment 2012*, nearly 20,000 Danish children between the ages of five and nineteen were studied to look for links between diet, exercise, and concentration. It was concluded that walking and bicycling to school increased their power of concentration for the entire morning, on par with kids six months older. Granted, the study refers to school-age kids, and the difference in brain power between an average thirtysomething and a thirtysomething-*and-a-half* is negligible, but sitting down to work or school after an invigorating bike ride through the city certainly makes for a clear-headed start to the day.

I find the mental acuity doesn't have to wait until after the bike ride. I get my best ideas *while* riding and I know countless other people for whom this is true. There's just something magical about the parallel between turning the pedals with one's feet while the gears in the brain spin at the same rate, generating brilliant ideas—and all this while still scanning traffic, making split-second handlebar adjustments, and lightly squeezing the brakes.

HAPPINESS

Back when I was biking some days, but not all, I found myself ill-tempered on my nonbiking days. It took me an embarrassingly long time to notice the correlation, but I've since heard similar reports from others. I've never been diligent about exercising for the sake of exercising, so my experience might not mirror that of a dedicated gym goer; however, the daily exercise provided by biking around town at a reasonable speed is all it takes to keep me happy year-round. If I skip biking for even one day, I find myself a bit down—or at least sluggish—so I can say I'm a much happier person because of bike commuting. Yes, these same benefits might be found through riding a stationary bike at the gym or any other sort of daily exercise, but for me, the combination of exercise with utility is key. For one thing, it wouldn't happen otherwise, but I also love the dual purpose: transportation and well-being rolled into one simple act.

As a native Southern Californian transplanted into the gray Pacific Northwest, I worried about the effects of the gray skies throughout the winter (and throughout most of the summer too, to be honest). My first couple years in Seattle, I spent 30 minutes each morning in front of a sun therapy lamp and carefully planned vacations to sunny destinations in the winter. However, all that became unnecessary once my bike exposed me to fresh air and exercise on a daily basis. I haven't left for the winter in two years now (other than to visit similarly gray Portland and Vancouver) and it's not a problem. The self-proclaimed Biggest Weather Wimp surviving the Gloomiest Fall/Winter/Spring without a complaint—I can't think of a better argument for bike commuting than that.

The aforementioned *Bicycling* magazine article cites studies that show that as little as 20 to 30 minutes of any daily exercise staves off depression in the long term and boosts feel-good serotonin and dopamine levels in the short term. Exercise beyond 30 minutes causes your body to create endorphins for more mood-lifting feelings. At the same time, regular riding helps lower adrenaline and cortisol, decreasing stress and making it easier to bounce back from anxiety-filled situations.

SAVE THE ENVIRONMENT

Many people who make a conscious effort to swap car for bike are doing it for the health of the planet, and their own improved well-being is just a happy side effect.

Despite periodic accusations that bicyclists produce more emissions than drivers of cars due to increased carbon dioxide from their extra-heavy breathing—most recently by Washington

Bicycle Benefits

Various Cities

If you need more incentive to bike around town, check the window of your favorite coffee shop or local business. See a Bicycle Benefits sign? Just by having your bike and a $5 sticker on your helmet, you can get up to or more than 10 percent off a purchase—like a coffee on your way to work!

Ian Klepetar started Bicycle Benefits in Saratoga Springs, New York, in 2006 with the support of local businesses that believed in what he was working to create: a way to encourage commitment to cleaner air, personal health, and a more sustainable community by offering a financial benefit or reward when you bike to a shop or restaurant. All you have to do is purchase a $5 sticker at a participating business and show the affixed sticker on your helmet when you arrive on your bike. Ian believes these financial incentives will motivate reluctant city bicyclists to use their bikes for short trips to their local merchants.

Each participating business, which is easily recognized by a Bicycle Benefits sign in the window and a discount displayed on the counter inside, can choose its own benefit, although Bicycle Benefits encourages discounts equivalent to or greater than 10 percent off a purchase. Among my circle, the most popular Bicycle Benefit in Seattle is "Buy one, get one free" at Mighty-O Donuts. The free $2 token at most Seattle farmers markets is also a hit, drawing many of us to the weekly market, rain or shine.

Ian, now the director of the Bicycle Benefits team, hopes these small trips might lead to longer rides and a more bike-oriented culture. He travels across the country, mainly by bike, to promote the program, staying in some cities for three or four months in order to get a new program up and going. In fact, he received the 2012 Pacesetter Award from the Adventure Cycling Association for demonstrating extraordinary commitment, dedication, and service to the advancement of Adventure Cycling's mission of inspiring and empowering people to travel by bicycle. Today, some 50,000 program stickers have been distributed to individuals and nearly 1,500 businesses are on board in dozens of cities throughout the country.

Volunteers can launch Bicycle Benefits programs in their own cities and use the concept as a tool to increase awareness and ridership. The website has an interactive map that lists all participating businesses and allows interested businesses to easily sign up online.

State representative Ed Orcutt in March 2013 (he later apologized)—biking is a zero-emissions endeavor while cars emit four different exhaust pollutants:

› **Hydrocarbons** react to create ground-level ozone, a major component of smog. Ozone irritates the eyes, damages the lungs, and aggravates respiratory problems. It is our most widespread and intractable urban air pollution problem. A number of exhaust hydrocarbons are also toxic, with the potential to cause cancer.
› **Nitrogen oxides**, like hydrocarbons, contribute to the formation of ozone and additionally are a component of acid rain.
› **Carbon monoxide** reduces the flow of oxygen in the bloodstream and is particularly dangerous to persons with heart disease.
› **Carbon dioxide** is a greenhouse gas and contributes to climate change.

Personal vehicles are nowhere near the largest polluters in the world, but driving a car is probably a typical citizen's most "polluting" daily activity, per the Environmental Protection Agency *Automobile Emissions: An Overview* fact sheet. Each gallon of gas used while driving creates about 20 pounds of carbon dioxide, which might roughly translate to one short trip every day for a week. So cutting out just one trip makes a huge impact.

The 2008 report *Active Transportation for America* from the Rails-to-Trails Conservancy states that increasing the total share of all trips made by bicycling and walking from 12 to 15 percent would reduce greenhouse gas emissions by 33 million tons per year, not to mention a savings of 3.8 billion gallons of fuel a year.

NOISE POLLUTION

Have you ever noticed how quiet the city seems very early in the morning or late at night, or when a blanket of snow has kept cars off the road? We're so accustomed to the near-constant hum cars add to city life that noise pollution goes unrecognized until we get a break from it. However, it does real damage. Nonprofit Culture Change shares that vehicle noise pollution causes everything from high blood pressure and stress to migraine headaches, hearing loss, and birth defects. Not a surprise when you consider that the sound of a heavy truck hits 99 decibels from a distance of ninety feet, and cars missing mufflers or with damaged tailpipes blast over 105 decibels.

However, when you're rolling down a side street, greenway, or bike path instead of sitting in traffic, your ears aren't experiencing the prolonged exposure to noise above 85 decibels that can cause permanent hearing loss. Not to mention that replacing more and more car trips works toward a cumulative lessening of noise pollution.

When so much of our days are spent shuttling from point to point, when that time is spent closed up in a single-occupant vehicle, fighting for space on a crowded road, it's no wonder we're harried, stressed, and distracted. When you instead spend that time actively commuting, surrounded by (hopefully friendly, or at least amusing) people, with time to release the reins and watch the world roll by, you just might find new dimensions sneaking into your transit time: the sense of accomplishment you get from pushing the pedals hard to get up that last steep hill, the feeling of euphoria as you coast down the other side of said hill, the biting wind in your face while racing along the flats, the camaraderie of giving a thumbs up or a wave to another bicyclist.

Exposed to the elements and observant of so much more while out on a bike, instead of ensconced in the warm box of a car, you can't help but feel alive and joyful.

DO IT FOR THE CHILDREN

From the December 2008 publication *Safe Routes to School: Steps to a Greener Future*, about a quarter of children live very close to school (within one mile) but only half currently walk or bicycle. In 1969, 85 percent of all children living within one mile of school walked or bicycled to school. If we returned to these levels, we would save 3.2 billion vehicle miles, 1.5 million tons of carbon dioxide, and 89,000 tons of other pollutants—equal to keeping more than 250,000 cars off the road for a year, according to the Safe Routes to School National Partnership.

The same organization warns that one-third of schools are in "air pollution danger zones"—and that the children exposed to traffic pollution are more likely to have asthma, permanent lung deficits, and a higher risk of heart and lung problems as adults. However, schools that are designed so children can walk or bike to school provide opportunity for measurably better air quality. If you have kids, biking or walking with them to school will not only improve their health—it also improves the quality of the air *you* are breathing.

My family is typical of our neighborhood: school is very close to home (two blocks in our case) and work a few miles away. My children don't yet walk to school alone, but it's feasible to bike (or walk my bike) alongside them to school and then continue along to work. The kids get their dose of concentration-boosting active transportation and I expose all the students who see me to the concept of bike commuting, hopefully helping grow a future generation of nonpolluters.

CHAPTER 2
The Bike

I'VE OWNED A VARIETY of bikes over the years: a handed-down ten speed, a new ten speed that was recalled by the manufacturer and returned to me as a hybrid, a beach cruiser I discovered unlocked by my apartment, presumably left by the person who accidentally took my hybrid of the same color, another beach cruiser, a mountain bike. I don't remember ever thinking that any of these bikes was inadequate or uncomfortable—I thought "a bike is a bike."

When I got back into biking after having a baby, I planned to put the toddler seat on my then commuter—a beloved beach cruiser with martini glasses painted on the fenders and bowling pin valve covers on the inner tubes—but the angle of the stem proved incompatible. Instead, I attached the seat to an unused beach cruiser in my garage. It was a couple sizes too big for me, but with the seat lowered all the way I fit comfortably and used it happily for a close to a year. When I eventually replaced it, the reason was simply because we'd moved to a hillier city and I wanted more than the beach cruiser's single gear.

Nowadays, I own multiple bikes and use them for different purposes. My cargo bike is great for carrying two kids and a week's worth of groceries. My commuter bike is better for rushing to a meeting ten miles away or putting on the bus, and my mountain bike is great in our occasional snow. Which tells you I've moved on from my "a bike is a bike" philosophy—especially after riding my mountain bike six miles along a bike path made me realize that, while full suspension is great for off-road riding, it makes for tiring travel in the city. All that said, if a bike moves when you want it to move, stops when you want it to stop, and fits your body how you want it to fit, you've probably found the right bike.

If you have a bike of any sort already, use it. Or if someone has offered to lend you a bike, take her up on it. (And if that neighbor with extra bikes in the garage hasn't offered, why not ask?) Keep in mind that basic bicycle design hasn't changed drastically since the late nineteenth century. If you have access to a working bike, you may not need to invest in a brand new steed with "Commuter" emblazoned on the side. Unbury that neglected, ill-fitting bike of unknown origin from the back of your

BIKE ANATOMY

Do you know your seat stay from your chain stay and your stem from your head tube? It's not a big deal—you should be safe calling your saddle a seat and your tire a wheel—unless, say, you're trying to describe something to a bike mechanic over the phone. But becoming versed in bike anatomy is simple.

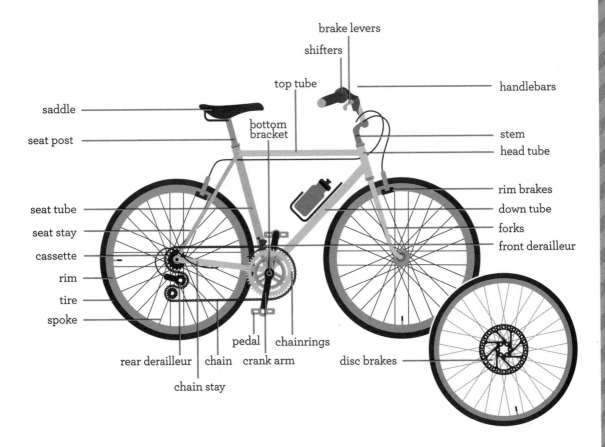

garage and pedal away. In her "Everyday Rider: My Five Best Bikes for Beginners" column for *Bicycling* magazine, Elly Blue recommends that people start riding bikes they can have modest expectations of. "I'm here to tell you that your first bike doesn't matter. Bikes aren't like cars—they break way less, and when they do break you're usually looking at a $20-or-less fix. And if you get the wrong bike, the stakes of selling and replacing it are pretty low. Worry less about the brand or model and instead make sure you meet your first bike with a spirit of curiosity and experimentation rather than anxiety and attachment." You can test out biking for transportation on any bike—you can invest in a new bike later if you feel the need.

If you do decide to purchase a bike, whether new or used, you'll find a plethora of options. The descriptions that follow will help you narrow down some of your preferences before you even put hands to grips and feet to pedals. When in doubt, test ride it. You'll probably be able to tell right away if you like a certain bike or not. And if you can't tell, ride more: ride uphill, ride downhill, navigate potholes, and imagine yourself hunched over the handlebars in a sudden downpour.

COMMUTER BIKES

If you're in the market for a new or used bike, keep in mind that while certain bikes are more useful and comfortable for urban riding, it all depends on your preferred style of riding and your specific commute. Watch the bicyclists in your hometown. You may notice trends based on the character of the area: light road bikes in your hilly, well-paved city; single-speed beach bikes in your small, flat community; or thick-tired mountain bikes in your pothole-riddled, broken-glass-strewn bustling urban metropolis.

Noting the trends is a good starting point, but don't feel pressured to ride the bike du jour. Trust your instincts and find the bike that's right for *you*. Many people ride performance bikes for daily short, flat trips or workhorse bikes for hour-long, uphill-both-ways commutes . . . by choice!

Searching for a lightweight bike for long-distance rides on paved surfaces or a burly shock-resisting bike for off-roading is easy because they're categorized as "road bikes" and "mountain bikes," respectively. However, there's no consistent term for the bike built to accommodate fenders, racks, and baskets that you'll use to ride through town while carrying a briefcase or a bag.

Here are some descriptors you might find in bike product listings that will signal a bike is suitable for commuting: city, comfort, commute, hybrid, path, town, urban, utility. Many of these terms—especially "city" and "utility"—are used to describe fairly different types of bikes. This can make shopping more difficult. Don't overlook bikes labeled "comfort" just because it more typically describes beach cruisers, evoking slow, cushiony rides along a flat waterfront path. That "comfort" bike may very well be just the perfect urban commute bike for you.

upright city bike

commuter bike

road bike

Comparison of body positions on different types of bikes

We can lump the most popular good-for-commuting bikes into two types: **upright city bikes** and not-as-upright **urban commute bikes**.

UPRIGHT CITY BIKES

Upright bikes position the rider to sit with his back just slightly bent forward or at a 90-degree angle to the ground (the latter also called "ultra uprights"). These bikes are designed for slow, comfortable travel. That's not to say you can't pedal harder to move faster, but an upright city bike is for enjoying the ride, not rushing to your destination. The stylish lines of upright city bikes speak to many riders, but their safety and comfort really make them commute winners.

Safety

The upright body position makes for some terrific safety boons. By sitting upright, you create a taller shape for other road users to see. You can see more too because your field of vision is greater when you are sitting at 90 degrees. Try this out by leaning forward 45 degrees or so and noting how your perspective shifts. Now glance back over your shoulder: the 45-degree angle obstructs part of your backward view. Also, having more weight on your saddle and less on your handlebars means it's easy to take a hand off the handlebars for signaling turns or stopping.

Features

Many upright city bikes come with fenders. Some even come with a rear rack, lights, and a bell. Most don't have front

Upright city bike

derailleurs (pronounced "dee-RAIL-ers"), the part of the bicycle that moves the chain from gear to gear, which means they can—and usually do—have chain guards (see Gears and Shifters in Chapter 3 for more information). This metal or plastic shield covers some or all of the front chainring and the top of the chain as it travels back toward the rear of the bike to keep your clothing (or bare leg) free of oily stains. Comfortable saddles, such as sprung saddles (saddles with springs underneath) are common, as are ergonomically shaped handlebar grips.

Upright city bikes are usually available in diamond versions (with a high top tube) and step-through versions (with a low top tube or no top tube at all). Step-through frames are traditionally thought of as ladies' bikes, but they're truly for anyone who doesn't want to contort his body to get on the bike.

TUNE UP THAT OLD BIKE

If your found or borrowed bike doesn't go when you want it to go or stop when you want it to stop, take it to a bike shop for a tune-up. Even if it does work like you want it to, consider making an up-front investment in its well-being anyway. Tune-up prices vary from city to city and shop to shop, ranging from $30 to $150 (plus parts). If you don't have a trusted local bike shop (LBS), call around for price quotes and availability. Availability might end up being more of a deciding factor than price—if it's the beginning of spring, you might need to schedule your tune-up a week or two out.

DUTCH BIKES

Dutch bikes, a special category of upright bikes, are exceptionally beautiful and exceptionally useful. Designed to live outside year-round, through rain and snow, Dutch bikes are virtually maintenance free. Most Dutch bikes come standard with the following:

1. *Dynamo lights.* Attached to the frame and theft-proof, these lights are powered by pedaling so no batteries or chargers are needed.
2. *Fenders.* Full fenders hugging a Dutch bike's wheels protect your clothing from the water your bike would otherwise channel up from the ground.
3. *Fully enclosed chain.* More than a chain guard, Dutch bikes have a chaincase that protects both the chain and drivetrain from the elements and your clothing from the chain.
4. *Internally geared hub (IGH).* Yes, most have gears. IGH provides maintenance-free gears that can be shifted at a stop (see more in Chapter 3).
5. *Built-in rear rack.* The rack is part of the frame and strong enough to support an extra rider.
6. *Two-legged center stand.* A double kickstand holds the bike steady while you load your panniers with heavy wheels of Dutch cheese.
7. *Skirt guard.* Thin panels shield the sides of the rear wheel where your skirt, coat, or other clothing could otherwise get caught in the moving spokes.
8. *Wheel lock.* After you've depressed the lever to push a steel shackle between the spokes of your wheel, and removed the key, your bike cannot be pedaled or rolled away. This doesn't prevent your 50-pound companion from being shoved into a canal or lifted into a pickup truck, thus the nickname "café lock," as you should only rely on this lock when your bike is in your line of sight.

Urban commute bike

Weight

Upright city bikes are made for comfort, not speed, which means they tend to be heavy—up to 50 pounds.

What about Hills?

In city-cycling meccas like Amsterdam and Copenhagen, upright city bikes are the bikes of choice. The bike lanes in both cities are separated from automobile traffic, so there's no impetus to keep pace with cars (unlike in most American cities). Their flat topography is conducive to using heavy bikes that don't favor hill climbing.

But don't be turned off from upright bikes if your city isn't flat. Lighter equivalents have more generous gearing and can be used to travel your city's ups and downs in upright fashion. Just be sure to first determine your personal threshold for uphill minutes on this frame, as the nonaggressive position still won't feel ideal for riding uphill.

Some models have front derailleurs for a larger range of gears, making hills easier, although it comes at the expense of the front chain guard. Pricier rear gears can also increase gear range and still allow for the front chain guard. (See Chapter 3 for an explanation of internally geared hubs.)

Cost

New upright city bikes can start as low as $300—more likely those with just one speed. The fully decked-out models may cost as much as $2,000. But between $500 and $800 is a reasonable medium.

Pros:

› Long wheelbase makes for a stable ride.
› Bike comes with matching fenders (which means they fit well and will complement the color and style of the bike, for those especially concerned with aesthetics).

> Chain guard protects your clothing from grease (usually).
> Saddle and grips are comfortable.
> Upright position creates less strain on your neck, wrists, and back.
> Easy to see and be seen.
> Easy to perform hand signals.

Cons:
> Heavy—about 50 pounds
> Slow
> Hard to ride uphill

URBAN COMMUTE BIKES

Urban commute bikes, with a more traditional road or mountain bike diamond-shaped frame, put the rider in a bent-over position for more aggressive riding, although not to the degree of a road bike. These bikes can move fast and climb hills, and this combination of comfort and speed makes them common go-tos for bike commuters.

Features
The handlebars are similar to a mountain bike's—flat bars that rise up slightly from their attachment point or sweep back toward the rider. This keeps your body position upright enough for a good field of vision, just not to the degree of an upright city bike.

Urban commute bikes usually come with commuter essentials such as fenders and a rear rack. Models that don't come standard with these parts will have the small metal mounts, called eyelets, that make it easy to attach aftermarket ones.

Weight
Urban commute bikes weigh around 30 pounds, light enough for most people to lift onto a car rack, but still strong enough to carry your gear and provide a smooth ride—albeit not as smooth as a 50-pound Dutch bike.

Cost
A good price for a solid commuter bike is $500, and many more can be found in the $500 to $1,000 range.

Pros:
> Relatively fast (compared to an upright city bike, but not like a road bike)
> Good for hill climbing

Cons:
> No chainguard so no protection from chain grease or chainring.
> Less upright means less comfortable.

FOLDING BIKES

Folding bikes are just what they sound like—bikes that fold. The amount of fold varies—some bikes simply fold in half, making them easy to store in a half-bike-size spot, but not so convenient to carry around. Bikes with smaller wheels can more easily be carried downstairs to a subway station and stowed in the smallest bike stowage spot. No matter the size, folding bikes are excellent for commuting. They're easy to store in an office as well as carry inside grocery stores and the like. More expensive models tend to ride more like regular bikes and are comfortable to ride for long distances and are

Folding bike

Folding bikes come in a variety of gear ranges, which means (1) you don't have to pedal more to make up for having smaller wheels and (2) they are capable of making it up any hill.

Weight

Folding bikes can weigh as little as 18 pounds but may run into the 30-pound range depending on their material and components. A titanium folder with no racks or fenders, and a single speed can weigh a svelte 18 pounds but will cost more. Aluminum and steel models weigh between 25 and 30 pounds before the addition of racks and fenders. This makes them portable, but probably not something you'd want to carry for long distances.

equipped to carry cargo, but simpler ones are just for short trips.

Features

Folding bikes usually have small wheels—16-inch, 20-inch, and sometimes 24-inch. Some folding bikes have full-size wheels, but since the size of the wheel usually dictates how small the bike can fold, smaller wheels are usually considered more practical. Smaller wheels may take some getting used to, and some folding bikes are designed for short distances only, but many feel just like regular bikes.

Folding bikes can be equipped with racks, fenders, kickstand, and lights. This is most easily done using parts that are designed for the specific folding bike, since they're ensured to fold up correctly, but in many cases, aftermarket pieces can be added.

Cost

There are a lot of different folding bikes to choose from, with over a hundred manufacturers. Some folding bikes cost less than $200, but high-quality models designed for regular riding are over $1,000 and on upward to $3,500.

Pros:

› They fold! Easy to store and carry.
› Low step-over means easy to mount.
› They can be used for extensive city riding.

Cons:

› Smaller market than traditional bikes means higher price.
› Many are not designed for heavy, repetitive use or long-distance cycling.

Electric bike

ELECTRIC BIKES

The electric bike, or e-bike, is a game changer for many bicycle commuters. For some, that electric push means steep hills and long distances are no longer barriers to bicycling. For others who need to arrive at work sweat free, e-bikes are the *only* possibility for bike commuting. E-bike technology is developing quickly, with bikes getting better each year and prices dropping.

Features

E-bikes come complete (factory-built) or as an add-on kit to your existing bike. Either way, your e-bike will feature a motor and a rechargeable battery. Factory-built e-bikes are appealing because they are built for use as e-bikes—the frames are made to hold the weight and shape of the battery and often integrate the battery and motor in such a way that it's hard to tell they're not regular bikes. As long as you're taller than five feet and shorter than six feet five, and don't weigh more than 250 pounds, you can buy a ready-made e-bike. Add-on kits are easy for upgrading the bike you already own and can result in higher speeds than factory-built models.

Pedal Assist or Throttle

E-bikes come with pedal assists, throttles, or both. Pedal assist works with your pedaling, giving more power depending on how hard you pedal. You're definitely still bicycling, just receiving some help. The throttle makes the bike go whether or not you're pedaling, which uses more battery power. Many e-bikes have both: the throttle is useful for starting from a full stop or quickly clearing an intersection, and the pedal assist gives you a boost for the bulk of your ride.

Types of Assist

There are different types of electric assist—a motor in the front wheel, a motor in the rear wheel, a motor in the pedal cranks, or even a trailer hooked up behind your regular bike to propel you. They all feel different, so test ride what's available, and see which system appeals to you.

Batteries

E-bike batteries have a range of ten to over forty miles. This is very dependent on the terrain, the amount of pedal assist used, the amount of throttle used, and the weight your e-bike is carrying.

The battery detaches from the bike, so you can carry it inside to charge it up. It will take two to eight hours to fully recharge, depending on quality. Lithium ion batteries are the highest quality generally available, recharge quickly, and last longer than nickel metal hydride (NiMH) or sealed lead acid batteries. If you have a long commute you may want to bring the charger with you. It might be simpler in the long run to buy a second charger for the office.

Riding E-Bikes in the City

Before you buy an e-bike, check what laws, if any, apply to them in your state. As e-bikes become more commonplace, these laws will change, so check often, but here is a sampling:

› Many states have a maximum speed of 20 mph.
› Alabama requires a class M driver's license.
› California requires power output of less than 1,000 watts.
› Boulder, Colorado, bans e-bikes over 400 watts from bike lanes.

› Washington, DC, requires e-bikes to be registered and insured.
› E-bikes are currently illegal in New York State, though several bills (none successful yet) have tried to change this.

You'll probably be precluded from traveling with your e-bike on the bus as well, depending on your local transit authority rules—but ideally the assist will make using the bus unnecessary. Besides, your e-bike might be too heavy to lift onto a bus bike rack.

Servicing Your E-Bike

Since the bike parts of your e-bike are like any other bike, it can be serviced by any bike shop. Generally speaking, though, you'll need to work with an electric bike shop for anything battery or motor related. Finding a local shop for ongoing maintenance is helpful. However, many people without local support ship broken parts back and forth for service. If an e-bike would make your commute doable, don't let the lack of a local shop keep you from looking into this great option.

Weight

E-bikes are heavier than regular bikes, as you may suspect, weighing 55 to 65 pounds. You won't want to lift it up any stairs.

Cost

A commute-worthy e-bike will cost between $1,000 and $3,000. Recharging your battery overnight might add a little to your electric bill, but this will be just pennies a pop.

Pros:

> Electric assist makes hills and long distances manageable.
> E-bikes are easy to recharge.
> The regular bike parts of an e-bike can be serviced at local bike shops.

Cons:

> E-bikes can be an expensive up-front investment.
> E-bike riders may have to follow stricter rules and regulations than regular bicyclists.
> If specialty maintenance doesn't exist in your city, you'll have to mail broken parts to the manufacturer.
> E-bikes are heavy. This is negated by the motor while riding but can be an issue when carrying up a curb or a couple stairs for storage.

OTHER TYPES OF BIKES

Bikes built for specific purposes, be it recreational or other, can be commute bikes too.

ROAD BIKES

Long, hilly, well-paved commutes might be most comfortable on a quick and nimble road bike. If you need to portage your bike at either end, such as up a couple flights of stairs, a sub-20-pound bike can spell commuting success.

On a road bike, with saddle higher than handlebars, you'll be leaning forward at an aggressive degree, over drop handlebars. This aerodynamic position, along with the lightweight frame, makes road bikes speedy. However, drop han-

Road bike

dlebars can take some getting used to. Be sure to try out this position before settling on your bike. Shifters are usually integrated with the brakes, though they can also protrude from the ends of the handlebars, called bar-end shifters. If you find this too uncomfortable, a local bike shop can replace the handlebars with swept-back handlebars and the bar-end shifters with twist or trigger shifters.

Road bikes are not automatically equipped to handle fenders and racks, but there are inventions for this!

Clip-on fenders. These will keep you dry in rain (although I'll admit my road bike's clip-on fenders tend to work a bit loose and rub on something—annoying, although not unsafe).

Clamp-on or seat-post-mounted rack. If you don't want to wear your belongings on your back, use a road-bike-friendly rack. The weight limit is around 20 pounds. (Note that you might be surprised by how quickly a laptop, your lunch, and maybe a change of clothing can add up to this weight limit.)

Front basket. A small basket up front can work on your road bike, but too much weight on the handlebars will compromise your steering—there's already a lot of weight from your body on the front of the bike, so you don't want to add much more.

MOUNTAIN BIKES

Even though mountain bikes are built to perform best in off-road conditions, you still might enjoy your street commute while riding one. And some commutes feature off-road cut-throughs, ideal on a mountain bike. If your mountain bike has knobby tires and off-road riding isn't part of your daily route, change those tires to smooth ones for a less sluggish ride.

Rigid mountain bikes have no suspension. Hardtail mountain bikes have suspension in the fork that holds the front wheel to the frame—essentially a spring that absorbs bumps. Full-suspension mountain bikes have the same fork as a hardtail as well as suspension built into the frame for cushioning the rear wheel hitting bumps.

Full-suspension mountain bikes tend to cost more and have more parts that require maintenance, and are more comfortable used for mountain biking over city riding. However, a rider with a bumpy commute and an aching back might find a hardtail or full-suspension mountain bike a comfortable ride.

Mountain bikes can be outfitted with seat-post–mounted rear racks or mountain-bike–specific racks for commuter duty. Mountain bike fenders don't perform as well as full-coverage fenders on smaller bikes, but they'll protect your clothes to a certain extent.

TOURING BIKES

Touring bikes are built for spending long days in the saddle while carrying supplies. At first glance, they look like road bikes with their flat top tubes and drop bars, but they're equipped with fenders, racks, and thicker flat-resistant tires. Their geometry is also a bit different from road bikes, featuring a longer wheelbase for a more comfortable ride and a less hunched-over angle. You might like the drop bars and bar-end shifters (common on touring bikes because they're easier to perform maintenance on in the middle of nowhere), especially if you travel longer stretches without a lot of shifting. If you don't, swap them for swept-back handlebars and twist shifters

Full-suspension mountain bike

Recumbent trike

to turn a touring bike into your perfect urban commuter bike.

RECUMBENT BIKES

Recumbent bikes are also built for long rides but have reclined seats for a completely different body position. There's less stress on the neck and back and no pressure on the wrists. Many recumbent riders find this position helpful if pain (especially prostate pain) makes riding a regular bike impossible.

Recumbent bikes come in many different shapes and sizes, with varying degrees of recline and length of wheelbase. They take a bit of getting used to, but there are only a few differences from a regular bike:

› Recumbents give you a shorter shape so you are less visible. Most city riders attach a high-visibility flag to address this.
› Checking behind is done with mirrors, not by glancing back over your shoulder.
› Recumbents are geared for seated hill climbing. Hill climbing isn't harder, but since you can't stand up in the saddle, you'll lose the uphill race to your regular-bike-riding peer.
› "Recumbutt" is exactly what it sounds like: sore gluteal muscles as a result of riding a recumbent bike. It's usually remedied by reclining the seat.
› Since they're not mass-produced like regular bikes, recumbents can cost twice as much. Heavy, entry-level bikes can be found for $500, but lighter ones will be $1,000 or more.

CARGO BIKES

Many commuters need to transport more than what fits on a regular bike and might use a cargo bike to do so. A cargo bike is any bike specifically designed to carry a load. They come in many shapes and sizes, designed to carry cargo both in front and behind the rider. Some are no wider than normal bikes, just a foot or so longer to accommodate extra bulk. Those that do have wider areas for carrying large loads tend to fit in the same spaces as regular bikes, making them just as maneuverable through your city's bicycle facilities.

Cargo bikes are especially great for commuters carrying kids. For the full scoop on cargo bikes, see Chapter 11.

TRIKES

Yes, they make tricycles for adults too! Trikes provide riders with an extra wheel for better balance and open the world of bike commuting to people with balance issues. There are two main types of trikes:

› Delta trikes have one wheel in the front and two wheels behind, often with a big basket for cargo between those back wheels.
› Tadpole trikes have one wheel in the back and two in front, usually with a large cargo box in the space created between the two front wheels.
› Recumbent bikes come in three-wheel forms too, in both delta and tadpole varieties.

Trikes shouldn't perform high-speed turns, be taken on sideways-tilting roads on which they might tip over, or rolled down curbs where the two parallel wheels might not stay in line. Most are not built for climbing hills, but with those words of caution in mind, they make biking possible for many people. Prices are similar to recumbents, starting around $500, though high-end hill-climbing recumbent trikes will run into the thousands.

WOMEN-SPECIFIC BIKES

Many bikes come in women-specific models. Sometimes this means a step-through frame rather than a flat top tube to more easily accommodate our voluminous petticoats. But especially with road bikes and mountain bikes, there are some slight differences that might make a women-specific bike a better fit for a female purchaser.

In general, women have narrower shoulders, shorter arms, shorter torsos, wider hips, and longer legs, so women-specific frames and parts are designed to accommodate this. It's not a gimmick and women shoppers—and men with short torsos and long legs—should consider test riding women-specific bikes. (Be warned: women-specific bikes tend to come with small swirls and/or flowers on the frames. I find this either cute or annoying, depending on my mood.) Tall women may have trouble finding the right women-specific bike, but if the gender-neutral models don't fit correctly, changes to handlebar, stem, and saddle can mimic the differences found in the women-specific frames.

BOX STORE BIKES

Box stores (also known as big-box-stores, supercenters, superstores, and megastores) sell bikes that are temptingly cheap. For $200, you can buy a city bike that looks just like the $1,800 sturdy original from the Netherlands. But the low price belies its durability. According to Sheldon Brown, the average department store bicycle is ridden about seventy-five miles in its life span from showroom floor to landfill. The website of one box store displays their adult bikes in the "Toys" category, in fact.

The problem with big-box-store bikes is twofold: (1) they use exceedingly cheap components, and (2) they're assembled by store staff rather than by trained bike mechanics. It's not uncommon to find box store bikes with forks installed backward, handlebars or pedals not firmly attached, or unconnected brakes.

If you do buy a box store bike, extend its life span by taking it to a local bike shop for a tune-up. The added cost of the tune-up ($30-$100) will still be cheaper than a new non-box-store bike. When tallying the added cost and extra effort, however, it might just tip the scales in favor of looking for a bike with a better reputation.

BIKES FOR ALL SIZES

Mass-produced bicycles are made for riders who weigh up to 250 or 300 pounds and are between five feet and six feet five. Bikes do exist outside this zone, though.

Over 250 Pounds

Some manufacturers make bikes to accommodate riders up to 500 pounds. Above that, custom bikes can be built to fit any person. People who are close to the upper weight limit of their bikes can also choose to replace their rear wheels with strong, double-walled rims, stronger spokes, or more spokes.

Shorter Than Five Feet Tall

Some manufacturers build smaller than average bikes, and bikes can be custom ordered from many frame builders. It's OK to shop in the kids' section too. If adult bikes are too big for you, try a 24-inch kid bike (a measurement that refers to the wheel diameter). Brands vary, but if your inseam is between 24 and 28 inches, a 24-inch bike might be a good fit.

Taller Than Six Feet Five

Extremely tall people usually choose to custom order a bike. Some riders make do with changes to handlebars and seat posts to try to make an XL frame work for an XXL rider. If you don't feel any discomfort doing so, this is a cheaper and quicker way to get biking.

BUYING NEW

New bikes are big business in the United States. Over 11 million bikes with wheels bigger than 20 inches sold in 2013 according to the National Bicycle Dealers Association—and that was considered a soft year. Your new bike will probably cost between $500 and $1,500, depending on type, material, and components. And figure on spending more for an electric model.

Buying new puts countless bikes, from basic commuter models to the latest in folding or specialty designs, at your test-riding disposal. The easiest way to get started is to head to your closest bike shop and start riding bikes. Different shops are dealers of different brands, so you might find yourself test-riding bikes at several shops—including stores that specialize in folding bikes and e-bikes.

A local bike shop (LBS) is a small business specializing in bicycle sales, maintenance, and parts. Generally these are independently owned, although they can include small chains. Your LBS may not necessarily be the closest independently owned bike shop, but rather your shop of choice.

Only 15 percent of bike shoppers purchase their bikes from an LBS, but it's a great way to go—your bike will come professionally assembled and you'll get help with fit as well as making changes, like a different saddle or handlebar grips.

Other options for buying a brand-new bike include chain sporting goods stores, outdoor specialty retailers, and online.

Samantha E. Arnold

Samantha Arnold

Chicago, Illinois

Samantha Arnold has been biking to work for twenty years, off and on, starting back as an adult in graduate school and then slowly easing into city riding upon moving to Chicago—mostly along the lakefront trail and long recreational rides outside the city. But as she got to know the environment, she slowly switched from mostly public transit plus some biking to mostly biking plus some public transit.

Samantha bikes her 4.5 miles-commute every day, year-round, with occasional bus or cab trips depending on weather or client meetings. Her route takes her through residential neighborhoods, a light industrial district, the edge of an entertainment district, and straight across downtown Chicago and Michigan Avenue to her office building along Millennium Park. She loves Chicago and finds she experiences it more on a bike—not to mention avoiding stressful high-traffic driving and enjoying much better parking, especially at the grocery store.

BIKES

Samantha's primary everyday bike is a WorkCycles Omafiets Dutch bike. It's a big, heavy, sturdy, steel bike and perfect for Chicago's flat, urban environment. It weighs about 50 pounds, and her lock weighs an additional five pounds. She's kept her hybrid bike, a diamond-frame mountain bike, from grad school in great shape for longer rides and vacations. And she utilizes Divvy, Chicago's bike-share system too.

CLOTHING

Samantha chose her Dutch bike so she wouldn't have to make any changes to her wardrobe—it's a step-through, with full-coverage chain guard and internal gears, so pants and skirts never get caught. She puts more thought into layers in winter than before her bike-commuting days, but since she stays pretty warm while biking, she goes for windproof and/or water-resistant outer layers and breathable inner layers. She likes winter coats that look nice but are not too long or bulky. Performance bike gloves and chemical heat-pack toe warmers make her winters—even the "Chiberia" winter of 2013–2014—manageable by bike. In summer she likes long sundresses, which work great on the step-through Dutch bike but also work in a pinch on her diamond-frame mountain bike.

BIKE SECURITY

Samantha's bikes are safe in the basement at home and never stay the night outside elsewhere. Heavy-duty ABUS chain locks keep them safe when they are outside, and like many Dutch bikes, Samantha's main bike has a built-in wheel lock. She is very cautious about what she locks the bike to.

ROADSIDE REPAIR

Samantha keeps a repair kit on her mountain bike to patch flat tires but often finds it just as easy to walk to the nearest bike shop or bus stop to return home. On her Dutch bike, which doesn't have quick-release wheels, it's harder to fix a flat, but thanks to flat-resistant tires, she's only had one flat in four years of daily riding. The Dutch bike doesn't fit on Chicago's bus bike racks, so when she got that one flat, she walked the bike to the bike shop closest to her office and had the flat repaired there.

ADAPTIVE BIKES

Samantha maintains a robust page on adaptive bikes and a listing of adaptive bike recreation programs and resources on her blog, *Ding Ding Let's Ride* (see Resources). When researching bicycles for her stepson, who has cerebral palsy, she discovered a wealth of options for children and adults with disabilities or special needs and has created the premier resource for sharing her knowledge and findings with others.

Her adaptive bike experience has primarily been with children, but as her stepson grows into bigger bikes—now a cool tricycle built from a conversion kit that can turn a standard kids bike into a three-wheeler—she's talking to more adults who see his trike and instantly think of uses for themselves, friends, or family members.

SAMANTHA'S TIPS FOR NEW BIKE COMMUTERS

"What if there are no showers at my office? This is a question that seems to come up often. I'm all about smelling good, but really, a little sweat never hurt anyone. Longer ride but no showers? Take a shower before you leave, don't forget the deodorant, pack a change of clothes, pack some body wipes, allow yourself some time to cool down, and you're good to go. Keep in mind that you don't *have* to shower just because you rode your bike to work. If you take public transportation, you probably do some walking, and if you're walking to work, my guess is you get sweaty some days, and it's not the end of the world."

BUYING USED

Buying a used bike is a great way to save money and resources. Some LBSs sell used bikes in addition to new, and that's a surefire way of finding one in good working order with support at the ready if things go wrong. Craigslist and similar online forums or local online community groups are also good ways to find access to used bikes.

BUYING A USED BIKE:

1. **Make sure it's not stolen.** The serial number is usually under the bottom bracket—where the pedals connect to the bike. Not all bikes are registered, but enter the number in the Bike Index search box at https://bikeindex .org and you've done your due diligence. Sometimes you can tell from a listing that the bike might be stolen— the price is much too good to be true and/or the description doesn't match the pictures. Steer clear.

2. **Check for frame damage.** Carefully inspect the frame to make sure it's not bent, dented, patched, cracked, or rusty.

3. **Check the brakes.** Squeeze the brakes and try pushing the bike forward. Brakes are usually cheap and quickly repaired, but if the bike is not road ready, you may be able to negotiate a lower purchase price.

4. **Check the wheels.** Lift the front of the bike with one hand and spin the wheel with the other to watch for wobbles. Do the same to the back wheel. Check all metal parts—rim, spokes, hub—for rust. A new wheel, tire, and tube will run $100 new— although two of the three may be salvageable and used parts are easy to find for much less.

5. **Check the tires.** Look for obvious holes, cracks, or fibers poking through. Bring a bike pump along and fully inflate the tires so you can see if the inner tubes are functional when inflated. Tires and tubes aren't expensive to replace, but find out now if they've got some life left in them.

6. **Test ride to check size.** Bring a multitool along. Adjust the saddle to the correct height (see Testing and Adjusting Bike Fit, below) and see if the bike is comfortable to ride.

7. **Bring the bike to a bike mechanic.** If you've looked for obvious problems and the bike checks out, go for it! But if you're not sure, bring it to your LBS and have them look at it before you buy.

TESTING AND ADJUSTING BIKE FIT

It usually doesn't take a lot of riding to tell if you like a bike or not, but it's smart to take your time. Work through all the gears, find a hill to ride up, both seated and out of the saddle, and test the brakes for sudden stops and for slowing while coming down the hill. Have the seat height adjusted multiple times if it's not right, and ask all the questions you want.

FRAME FIT

Often you can tell from riding a bike if it's too big or too small, but you can also measure yourself to the frame with a couple of tricks:

› **For bikes with flat top tubes,** like road bikes and some upright city bikes, you should have one inch of clearance ("standover height") when straddling the bike in front of the saddle. If it's hard to tell how much room you have between you and the top tube, lift the frame until it makes contact with your body and see if there's one inch between the tires and the ground.

› **For urban commute bikes,** with sloped top tubes, you should have 2 inches of clearance when you straddle the top tube.

› **For step-through upright city bikes,** the measurement is not as straight-forward, so you'll instead rely on your reach from saddle to handlebars. Adjust the saddle to the correct height for 80 to 90 percent leg extension at the bottom of your pedal stroke. Reach to the handlebars and check that you have just a slight bend at the elbows.

If the shop doesn't have a bike in your size for testing, you can still take a bigger or smaller version for a spin. Some shops don't have every model of bike assembled in my "small" (five foot five) size, but I can still get a pretty good feel for a bike, its brakes, and shifting by riding a size off. If you like the bike, feel confident about purchasing one in your size.

BIKE FIT ADJUSTMENTS

If your bike isn't comfortable, you'll be less likely to ride it. Many parts of your bike can be adjusted, and it's pretty simple to tweak a few things yourself. Get out your multitool and go for it. Start with your saddle.

BIKE MATERIALS

Bikes are made from many materials, such as aluminum, steel, carbon fiber, titanium, or even bamboo. Most commuter bikes are aluminum or steel. Carbon fiber is light and expensive and great for road bikes, but precludes add-on pieces like a rear rack for panniers. Titanium is also light, but stronger than carbon fiber, and even more expensive. Bamboo is somewhat new to the scene, sustainable, and will hopefully become more commonplace. It is very strong and features great vibration damping for a smooth ride.

You probably won't choose your bike solely based on the material—steel bikes supposedly have more flex for a more comfortable ride over rigid aluminum, but it's often hard to tell the difference. Aluminum is lighter and cheaper, but frames are made of thicker tubes to equal the strength of thinner steel tubes. At the end of the day, there's often not much of a weight or price difference between these two materials.

Adjust Your Saddle

There are several bolts on the seat post and saddle that allow you to change the saddle height and angle. The smallest change can have quite an effect, so make little changes and ride for at least 10 minutes to see how each tweak feels. After loosening the bolts to make adjustments, be careful to retighten sufficiently, but not overtighten. Tighten just until it feels snug, not beyond that, so that you can loosen it again when the time comes, as well as avoid the risk of stripping the threads. You're better off undertightening and stopping to tighten a bit more than putting too much muscle in it to begin with. Keep an Allen wrench with you when you test ride so you can adjust the saddle as necessary.

It's not too fine a science, but if gauging bolt tightness by feel sounds too intimidating, you can use a torque wrench instead of an Allen wrench. You'll need to know the desired torque setting for the bolt you're tightening, most likely found in the manual. Adjust the tool to the proper setting, and it will let you know when you've reached that level of tightness.

Saddle Height

Your saddle height can make a big difference in bike comfort. Proper seat height means your legs should almost straighten completely (80 to 90 percent) at the bottom of your pedal stroke.

Incorrect saddle height is a very common problem and is easily addressed. Many seat posts have a quick-release lever you can loosen by hand. Otherwise you'll need the appropriate size Allen wrench. Loosen the bolt, pull up (or push down) the saddle, and retighten. Take care that your saddle is still facing perfectly forward. If you can't get your saddle high or low enough, you will need a longer or shorter seat post . . . although this might very well be a sign that the entire bike is not the right size.

If you're recently back on the bike, a low saddle may feel safer, as you can easily get a foot flat, or nearly flat, on the ground at stops. Just keep in mind this can strain your knees over time.

Saddle Angle

Your saddle should be flat. If it's even slightly tilted forward, you'll put more weight on your hands to keep from sliding forward off the saddle. If you suspect this might be a problem, find the bolts at the top of the seat post under your saddle, loosen them, slightly tilt the nose of your saddle up, and retighten.

Saddle Forward or Backward

Your saddle can slide forward or backward along its rails. A slight adjustment here can make for a better reach to the handlebars or a better angle between knee and pedal. Find the bolts at the top of the seat post under your saddle (the same bolts for saddle angle adjustments above), loosen them, move your saddle forward or backward to suit you, and retighten.

Adjust Your Handlebars

There's not much you can do to your handlebars, save for replacing them with a different shape. If you have straight mountain-bike–style handlebars, adding bar ends is an option that can open up more hand positions. Some people find grasping onto bar ends a more comfort-able way to climb hills or start from a stopped position.

Some bikes have adjustable stems so you can raise and lower your handlebars. Experiment with more upright versus more aggressive body positions.

PROFESSIONAL BIKE FITS

If you don't want to attempt a bike fit yourself, let the professionals take over. This is not the same as a quick fit performed in a bike shop to select the correct size bike for you and make small adjustments over the course of a few minutes. A bike fit is a comprehensive, session with a specialist often sought out by bike racers— but they work equally well for commuters.

Bike fits are offered both by trained bike fitters in bike shops and by some physical therapists. A professional bike fit will take at least an hour and cost $100 or more—it's not usually a free add-on service when you buy your bike. Sometimes insurance might cover a bike fit provided by a physical therapist. Get referrals from friends or call around to find someone you feel comfortable with. Bicyclists with multiple bikes can often translate the results of a bike fit to their other bikes.

CHAPTER 3
Bike Parts and Components

I **HAVE A FRIEND** who's fond of saying, "The best bike is the one you already have." The tires hold air, the brakes stop the bike, the pedals propel you forward, and the gears shift up and down. Best of all, it's yours, and you're ready for a lifetime love affair with transportation cycling.

I don't entirely agree with that—I've owned quite a few bikes that weren't good fits, and now I wish I had swapped out uncomfortable parts right away. My cargo bike's first pedals were powered by an internal generator and blinked—the front white, the back red, and the side yellow. But the weight on the bottom, which was supposed to keep the pedals in their correct position, didn't always work. I didn't change the pedals until one of them gave out. Now the basic, flat pedals don't blink, but I can use either side of them. They're great. For that particular bike. For now. The options—for pedals and more—are nearly endless.

Perhaps you need to change old, cracked tires and want to know your options … or your pedal broke and you've been thinking about trying the style of pedals your friend uses wearing cleated cycling shoes. Knowing the variations of the different parts is both useful and a good way to narrow down what you're looking for, whether you want to revamp your current bike or search for a new one.

As with many things relating to bikes—or anything, for that matter—some parts span quite a price range. The more expensive versions might equate to easier use and no maintenance, but you may also want to factor in weight-saving materials or simple aesthetics.

TIRES AND INNER TUBES

Tires are especially important, since they can affect the comfort of your ride, stability, traction on slick roads, and speed. A flat tire immediately spells the end of a ride until fixed. Which, granted, is a mere five minutes for the proficient flat changers, but for many of us is a hassle we'd rather avoid.

Inner tube valves: Presta (left) and Schrader (right)

VALVE TYPES

Inside your tire is the inner tube. You insert air through the valve that pokes through a hole in the rim. There are two types of valves: Schrader and Presta.

Schrader valves are thick and the same style as found in cars (to remember this, think "there's a c-a-r in Schrader"). They have a pin blocking the hole in the center that the pump will depress when engaged to enable air to pump in. This is probably the type of valve you had on your childhood bike and reinflated at the gas station back when air was free. For grown-up bikes, they're typically found on mountain bikes.

Presta valves are narrow and therefore found on road bikes, which have narrower tires and rims. This type of valve features a locknut you must unscrew to add or release air. This adds a step, but makes for easier pumping. For many bicyclists, this benefit alone is reason to use inner tubes with Presta valves. However, Presta valves are also easier to break. I am par-

ticularly skilled (or unskilled, as the case may be) at wrenching my pump off at an angle and bending the skinny valve head. A slightly bent valve head will often work just fine, but too much force will completely pull off the locking nut.

Most newer bike pumps (see Chapter 4) will work with both valve types. But if you already have a single-style pump, you can buy an adapter. It's about a dollar for a Presta-valve-to-Schrader pump adaptor and a bit more go in the other direction.

TIRE INFLATION

Printed on the side of your tire is a range of tire inflation in psi (pounds per square inch). Narrow road bike tires use a high pressure, 100 to 140 psi. Balloony mountain bike tires use much lower pressure, 30 to 50 psi. Typical commuter bikes are usually somewhere in the middle, 60 to 80 psi. Your bike should always be within the recommended tire pressure range, although you'll choose the upper or lower end depending on a few factors:

Weight. If you plus your cargo are on the heavier side, say 250 pounds or more, you'll want a higher pressure.

Rain. Very wet conditions call for 10 psi lower than your normal pressure.

Temperature. For each 10-degree-Fahrenheit drop in the temperature, your tire pressure drops by about 2 percent. Stay near the upper end in winter. If you keep your bike inside a 70-degree-Fahrenheit house and go outside into 30-degree-Fahrenheit weather, the psi could drop from 70 to about 64, which might mean you should add some air before riding.

Do you really need to vary your tire pressure over the course of the day as temperatures and weight change? Not unless your tires feel noticeably low as conditions change. Potholes and even smaller bumps can easily pop an under-inflated tube. Tires with too little air also run the risk of a pinch flat (often called a "snake bite" because of the double hole left in the tube during the pinching)—the underinflated urban rider's common woe.

Wider tires hold air longer, but riders of all types of tires should get into the habit of routinely checking their tire pressure. For some commuters, a tire check is part of the morning routine, but if a daily test isn't appealing to you, aim for once a week. The best way to check your pressure is to use a tire pump with a built-in gauge. A bit of air will escape while you attach the pump, but you can reinflate while reading the gauge. Squeezing the sides of your tires—a better way to check air than pressing directly down with a thumb—will alert you if you're running dangerously low. Of course the best first step is to squeeze your tires when they're fully inflated to know what they should feel like.

TIRE TREAD
A tire's tread (the grooves in the rubber) provides your wheel with traction. The knobby tread of mountain bike tires is terrific for loosely packed gravel, logs, and rocks but can feel needlessly slow and tiring while traversing the typical American city. Smooth tires—or "slicks"—are the more common choice for biking in cities. Tires with treads that fall in between these two types do exist, but they are more of a gimmick. If you're looking for a more stable city ride, choose wider tires instead, which will provide more contact with the road, offering better traction on both flat and uneven surfaces.

TUBELESS TIRES
Tubeless tires are just what they sound like—tires without an inner tube. They're mostly used by mountain bike and cyclo-cross racers since their advantage is being able to run extremely low tire pressures, providing better traction. Their price keeps them from being the ideal commuter setup. However, tubeless tires do not get flats and so may be worthwhile if your commute seems to be particularly flat-incurring.

FLAT-RESISTANT TIRES
I was an incredibly proficient flat-tire changer in college. For the least costly repair job possible, I would either borrow two spoons from the dining commons to use as tire levers (to pry the tire off its rim), buy a cheap patch kit and borrow a passerby's pump, or walk to the off-campus bike shop.

But that was then. Now I sport tires that cost $50 each (versus $15 or so for regular tires) that offer flat protection. They're purportedly slow and not cushiony, but not dealing with flat tires is a priority I seem to share with many of my peers who sport similar tires. And you can go years of heavy riding between flats.

TIRE SEALANTS

Most bicyclists put just air in their tires, but sealant is an additional tool in the fight against flats. You can buy inner tubes with sealant already injected in them, or add it into your own tubes. This is easier for Schrader valves, into which the sealant can be directly squirted; you'll need to purchase a two-part valve for injecting it into Presta tubes.

The sealant, which stays in viscous form inside the tube, oozes into and blocks any small holes instantly. But it can be messy. Sealant can get into your pump, or leak between the inner tube and the bike tire if there are bigger holes. Sealant wipes off bikes and washes off clothing, yet recipients of exploded sealant-filled tubes may not find cleanup as easy as advertised and so return to regular tubes. For some bikers with particularly debris-ridden routes, especially in areas where the most common cause of a flat is a thorn, sealant makes all the difference, but a flat-resistant tire is often enough.

TIRE SIZES

Tire size is printed on the side of your tire, with both outer diameter and width indicated. Look for something like this: 26x1.5 or 700x35c.

If you can't read the side of your tire or your bike is tire-free, you'll have to get creative. Check the manual or online for archived specifications, or bring the bike to your local bike shop. I find measuring the rim too difficult to be reliable, but of course that's an option too.

Diameter

The first number is the diameter, most commonly 26 inches or 700c. (The "c" no longer represents what it once did—it's not centimeters!—but manufacturers still use it.) Found on most mountain bikes, 26-inch tires are on the smaller side, at 559 millimeters (22 inches) in inner diameter. Usually found on road bikes, 700c tires are bigger, with an inner diameter of 622 millimeters (24.5 inches). Upright city and commuter bikes can come with either size tire.

Width

The second number represents the width. Road bikes are typically narrow at 23 millimeters, touring bikes wider at 35 millimeters, and mountain bikes the widest—2 or 2.5 inches.

Moderately thick tires are the most comfortable for city bicycling. There's more surface area in contact with the road, making for better stability. Upright city and commuter bikes with 700c wheels will use tires of 35 millimeters or more. Upright city and commuter bikes with 26-inch wheels tend to run tires that are 1.5 or 1.75 inches wide.

Your rims will accommodate a range of widths, so it is possible to change your tires to wider (or narrower) ones. Be sure to match the diameter of your current tires. The limiting factors will be your brakes, forks, or frame.

Inner Tube Sizes

Inner tubes are sold in the same sizes as tires, so buy ones that match. In a pinch, a too-big inner tube can be inserted and not be fully inflated. I've dealt with flats that way, but it's not a good long-term solution.

BRAKES

Your bike should have front and rear brakes, the front brake operated by your left hand and the rear by your right. The two most common types of brakes are disc brakes and rim brakes, and both are activated via brake cables that connect the brake to the brake lever.

There are pros and cons to each system, and many people have vehement opinions about which is better. I am partial to disc brakes. They work well in the rain and I'm not bothered by the loud squeals they often emit for no reason. However, I also ride bikes with rim brakes and am able to survive wet conditions without mishap. Any well-maintained high-quality brake will stop your bike.

RIM BRAKES

Rim brakes come in several different styles including caliper, cantilever, and V-brakes, but they all stop your bike in the same way. When you squeeze the brake lever on your handlebars, rubber brake pads contact the wheel's rim, causing the wheel to stop turning and the bike to stop moving. Simple!

Pros:

› Simple and inexpensive
› Don't interfere with accessories like rack, trailer, and rear-mount kickstands

Rim brakes (direct-pull cantilever brakes)

Disc brakes

> Easy to maintain for the average rider
> Easy to visually inspect pads for wear

Cons:
> Create wear and tear on the rims
> Don't work as well on untrue (bent) rims
> Require more force (longer squeezing of brake levers) on wet roads or steep hills
> Debris on the rim reduces stopping power.
> Not always as strong as disc brakes

DISC BRAKES

Disc brakes feature a disc rotor on the left side of the wheel, with small calipers that wrap around it and press the brake pads against each side of the rotor when the brake lever is pulled. Disc brakes come in two varieties: mechanical and hydraulic. Mechanical disc brakes are more common on entry-level bikes with discs. They're cheaper and require less-complicated maintenance, but since they operate with cables, like rim brakes, those cables require maintenance in the form of tightening and replacing periodically. Hydraulic disc brakes provide superior stopping power and use hydraulic fluid in a closed system of hoses to push the brake pads into the rotor. The closed system is maintenance-free; with only the pads needing replacement.

Pros:
> Don't create wear and tear on rims
> Work fine with warped rims
> Less affected by wet conditions and mud than rim brakes

> Long lasting!
> Have stronger stopping power than rim brakes (when comparing high-quality versions, that is)

Cons:
> They are more expensive than rim brakes.
> Their brake pads are much harder for the average rider to replace.
> Bike frame must have disc brake mounts to accommodate disc brakes.
> They may not be compatible with some accessories, like rack, trailer, and rear-mount kickstands.
> It's not uncommon for them to squeal for no reason, even if they've just been readjusted.
> The disc's relatively smaller braking surface can heat up more easily when heavily used, which reduces braking power. (This can be avoided by feathering the brake and is usually only an issue on long, steep hills.)

PEDALS

Pedals are mostly one of two varieties: flat, the kind you remember from your childhood bike, and clipless, the kind that couple with special cycling shoes. I use and like both types of pedals. My mountain bike and road bike both came with clipless pedals. I found them intimidating at first, but am happy to report that in ten years, I have always been able to unclip in time when coming to a stop. However, I don't like finding somewhere to sit down and change footwear when

I'm commuting, so now I use pedals that are flat on one side and clipless on the other. Best of both worlds, right?

Most new and used bikes come ready to be pedaled away from the purchase transaction, but some bikes come without pedals. This is usually the case with road bikes—they often come with extremely cheap flat pedals, with the expectation that you will immediately swap them out for clipless pedals.

Pedals are easy to change if you want to try different styles. Don't feel stuck with slippery pedals that don't work well with your favorite shoes or pedals with such sharp pins for gripping your shoes that they routinely cut up your calves when you miss your pedal. Rain will make your pedals and/or shoes more slippery and might dictate your choices.

PLATFORM PEDALS

Platform pedals, or flat pedals, don't require special footwear, and you can use them even in high heels! They're well suited to city riding, which involves routine removal of foot from pedal while stopping in traffic. Flat pedals come in a variety of surfaces with varying amounts of grip.

Smooth Pedals

Smooth pedals work great if you ride in treaded shoes, but if your foot often slips off, you'll want to consider either switching to different pedals or not bicycling in certain shoes.

Grippy Pedals

Grippy pedals—not an industry term—have sandpapery, bumpy plastic, or rubber surfaces that help grip the sole of your shoe.

Pinned Platform Pedals

Pinned platform pedals are popular for mountain biking and BMX biking, where it's very important not to slip off the pedals while biking technical terrain or performing tricks. For this same reason, commuters are also drawn to them. Some have plastic pins that are easy on the soles of your shoes and your skin, should you have a mishap. The grippiest ones have metal pins that will really grab hold of your shoe, possibly tearing up the bottoms of delicate shoes and most definitely doing damage to your shin and calf if they get in the way.

Clipless pedals and shoes

Toe Clips and Toe Straps

Toe clips and toe straps attach to many flat pedals to help keep your foot from slipping off. Toe clips are cage-like baskets that hug the toe of your shoe. Toe straps are one or more straps of varying widths that cross over the top of your foot. Both work with most normal shoes.

The benefit of toe clips and toe straps is that your foot is held in the proper position, cutting down on a lot of extra movement. Another benefit is utilizing your upstroke, although there is some debate about this. If you're pedaling steadily, you're probably getting sufficient push with your other foot's downstroke. If you're not pedaling steadily, such as when you're heading uphill at the end of a tiring day, the upstroke pull is noticeable.

Practice with the clips or straps in the grass if you've never used them before—you might tip over as you get used to pulling one foot free upon stopping.

CLIPLESS PEDALS

Clipless pedals are special pedals that connect to a compatible cleat on the bottom of your shoe. The physics is similar to toe clips and toe straps, but to a much larger degree. They provide much more power by keeping your foot centered in the most efficient spot on the pedal plus provide upward pulling power—although remember that's debatable (but I can feel it!). With most clipless systems, your foot is able to rotate ever so slightly as you perform a rotation of the pedal, which helps to prevent knee injuries.

Why are they called clipless? Toe clips were widely used by bike racers before clipless pedals were invented, so the absence of the clip or cage led to the name.

Cleats attach with either two, three, or four bolts, so your shoes must have properly placed holes. You don't necessarily have to buy special shoes, though. Even high-heeled shoes with a sufficient wooden platform in which to recess the cleat can be adapted, either through a service or as a DIY installation.

Recessed Cleats

Clipless systems designed for mountain biking have recessed cleats—the cleat is buried within the sole of the shoe to better shed mud. The shoe is easier to clip into the cleat and easier to walk in as well, since the slippery metal cleat doesn't make much contact with the ground.

Clipless-to-Flat Adapters

It's not very comfortable to ride clipless pedals with regular shoes, but people do so for short distances. A better solution is the pedals that are platforms on one side and cleated on the other. Another solution is an adapter that clips in the same way the cleated shoe does to create a platform.

SADDLES

The wrong saddle can make for an awful commute, so plan to spend some time finding the right one. While reading reviews or comparing amongst friends can be helpful, saddle choice is really a personal preference learned through testing.

It's tempting to think a squishy saddle will be the most comfortable, but too soft a saddle will probably cause discomfort. Your sit bones, or *ischial tuberosities*, are designed to bear your weight when seated. If you sit down with your back straight, you should be able to feel these two bony protrusions. Bicycle saddles are designed to provide contact at these two points, essentially protecting the softer area in between, which would otherwise feel too much pressure against the saddle.

A saddle that correctly makes contact with your sit bones will be the most comfortable. In general, a woman's sit bones are spaced more widely than a man's, so women-specific saddles are slightly wider. This doesn't mean all women will fit women-specific saddles best, but they're a good place to start.

SADDLE MATERIAL

Most saddles are stretched leather, synthetic leather, or padded plastic. There's no real advantage of one material over the other, just preference developed through trial and error. Leather and synthetic leather saddles flex while in use, alleviating the need for added padding, and are porous for breathability in hot weather. They are designed with depressions created for the sit bones and other parts and break in to the exact shape of their riders over the first couple months of use, provided the saddle was the right width to begin with.

Plastic saddles are lightly padded with foam or gel and covered with a layer of material, such as leather, vinyl, nylon, or rubber. These saddles are not designed to break in and shape themselves to the specific rider but are rather comfortable right off the bat.

SPRUNG SADDLES

Sprung saddles are saddles with springs built in for cushioning bumps. They're often found on fully upright city bikes and beach cruisers because your sit bones are taking your full brunt. But these saddles would prove uncomfortable—causing pain and chafing—if used for any extended amount of time on a bike that isn't perfectly upright.

CUTOUTS AND NOSELESS SADDLES

Some people cannot comfortably ride regular saddles, even with proper adjustment and their weight carefully centered on their sit bones. If you know your saddle is a good fit and properly adjusted, but are experiencing soft tissue pain or numbness, there are other options to help you ride in comfort. Many saddles come with a "cutout" or hole in the middle to keep pressure off the soft tissue between the sit bones. Noseless saddles provide a platform for the sit bones but don't make contact with as much surface area as traditional saddles.

GEARS AND SHIFTERS

Gears change the cadence of your pedaling. They're numbered; I'm in nice and easy low gear number 1 for climbing steep hills and in my highest gear, 27, when running late with an empty trail ahead of me.

Just as downshifting into a lower gear when climbing up a steep hill is useful, so is starting from a low gear to quickly gain speed when crossing a street.

Geared bikes have either external gears with derailleurs to guide the chain between cogs and chainrings or internally geared hubs with the gear change happening hidden from view in a metal cylinder.

EXTERNALLY GEARED HUBS

"Derailleur" describes the cable, guide, and pulleys that "derail" the chain from one sprocket to the next when you shift gears on a bike with external gears. Rear derailleurs have between 6 and 11 sprockets, more commonly called gears. Bikes with two or three chainrings (or rings) on the front have a front derailleur too. This doubles or triples the overall number of gears.

Shifting with an external gear cannot happen at a stop. If you've been riding quickly in your highest gear and hit a red light, you should quickly downshift and pedal a few times while the derailleur moves the chain before you come to a stop. If there isn't time or space for this to happen, you'll be stuck in a gear that's hard to start from.

INTERNALLY GEARED HUBS

Internally geared hubs (IGH) have multiple gears (ranging between 2 and 14) on the back wheel, but they're hidden within the hub at the center of the rear wheel.

Internally-geared hub

The most noticeable functional difference from external gears is that shifting can happen at a stop—and for some makes of internally geared hubs you should in fact cease pedaling while changing gears, although it's fine to coast along. This is very convenient for the stop-and-go reality of city bicycling. As you might imagine, many upright city bikes come with this setup.

IGH replace the rear sprockets and are not compatible with a front derailleur because the chain doesn't move. They require very little maintenance: since all the parts are safely enclosed in the hub, and since the chain doesn't move from sprocket to sprocket, the system doesn't wear and stretch.

Gears normally have numbers. However, internally geared technology makes a couple of interesting variations possible.

Infinite Gearing

Infinite gearing has a range, but there are no stops or clicks as you twist the shifter. Pedaling gets easier and easier if you're downshifting to head uphill, or harder and harder if you're shifting up for increased speed.

Automatic Shifting

Automatic shifting can be likened to cruise control in a car. Rather than shift to a certain number, you choose a cadence—slow, medium, or fast—and the gears will shift with changes in terrain or speed to keep your pedaling at a consistent rate.

Belt drive

BELT DRIVES

In place of a metal chain, some bikes can use a belt drive made of rubbery material that requires little to no maintenance. They don't get dirty, operate more smoothly than chains, are quieter, and last much longer. A belt drive can't stretch from cog to cog like a regular chain, so it must be paired with an internally geared hub or go on a single-speed bike.

Belt drives aren't incredibly common nor available everywhere yet, having only been around a couple of years, but I like to point out the maintenance-free options, especially as a rider who has broken a chain or two (due to my lack of upkeep, mind you).

Aaron Cynic

Elly Blue

Portland, Oregon

Elly Blue is a writer and publisher in Portland, Oregon, who has been biking for transportation for over fifteen years. As a twenty-year old in New Haven, Connecticut, Elly relied on an unreliable bus system for transportation—which made for a lot of time walking and waiting—until the day she pulled her old bike out of her parents' garage on a whim. Like many, she's never looked back.

Since she's self-employed with a home office, Elly doesn't have a regular commute, but she bikes almost every day, either to meetings across town or to the grocery store. And beyond grocery shopping, a bicycle is the obvious choice of vehicle for free-box shopping. Elly's bicycle is equipped to carry large loads from free boxes—clothes, books, or household items Portlanders put on the curb for passersby to take. Since Portland is fairly small, it's rare for her to ride more than five or six miles in a day.

BIKES

Elly's primary bike is an old mountain bike with an Xtracycle longtail cargo bike conversion. She can carry everything (or anyone) she needs to with no special planning. For travel, Elly brings her Brompton folding bike. Although it is much smaller than her Xtracycle, she can carry almost as much, when paired with a backpack, thanks to a large Swift Industries front rack bag and rear saddlebag.

CLOTHING

Elly rides in regular clothes, but she's made a number of changes over time to make her wardrobe more bike-friendly. She went through a lot of trial and error and some hilarious wardrobe malfunctions before she stopped buying pencil skirts, polyester shirts, or jackets that were tight across the shoulders, and started rolling up a pant leg.

BIKE SECURITY

Elly uses and recommends U-locks.

ROADSIDE REPAIR

Elly has a refreshingly realistic and relaxed handle on on-the-go bike repair. She doesn't usually carry tools, and since switching to flat-resistant Schwalbe Marathon tires five years ago, she doesn't often get flat tires. The few times it's happened, she's been within walking distance of her home or a bike shop. Were she to get stranded, she'd call a friend or flag someone down, but it's not high on her list of worries.

TAKING THE LANE

Elly Blue Publishing, an imprint of Microcosm Publishing, produces books and a quarterly zine, *Taking the Lane* (see Resources), about bicycling from a feminist perspective. Besides writing for her own label, Elly writes articles for various publications, including an extremely popular regular column for *Bicycling* magazine's website called "The Everyday Rider." Her books are guidebooks for getting started with biking for transportation and for saving the economy—with bikes.

Elly's folding bike gets a lot of use on her annual Dinner and Bikes tour, which inspires guests across the country to use bicycle transportation via short films about bicycle activism and culture, presentations from local advocates and sponsors, and a Bikenomics presentation.

ELLY'S TIPS FOR NEW BIKE COMMUTERS

Not one to share all her tricks for free, Elly refers new bike commuters to her books, but she offers her favorite thing about biking for transportation: "It's fun. What else in daily life is just 100 percent fun?"

SHIFTERS

Shifters come in a variety of types and positions. I find twist shifters and trigger shifters the two most logical choices for city riding. Since these shifters are located close to the handlebar grips, you don't have to move a hand away from your brake to shift. It's convenient and safe for the stop-and-go of urban commuting.

All shifters are connected to a cable that moves the derailleur (or does its magic inside the hub for IGH) with each click, shift, or other adjustment. Your right hand controls the shifter that operates the rear derailleur, or rear IGH (right/rear). If you have multiple chainrings in the front, your left hand controls the front derailleur.

Twist Shifters

Twist shifters are common on upright city bikes and urban commute bikes. The shifters are right next to the grips, just to the inside of where your hands rest while riding. Numbers are marked on a stationary ring, and your conveniently located fingers twist the adjacent grip to point the arrow at the gear number you desire.

Trigger Shifters

Trigger shifters feature two levers, each located just below the handlebars, so you never have to move your hands from their riding position. One lever is pushed with the thumb to move gears in one direction and one is pulled with the forefinger. Trigger shifters are common on urban commute bikes and mountain bikes.

Thumb Shifters

Thumb shifters are also positioned between your hands on the handlebars, but situated above the handlebars. You'll need to shift your hands to reach them.

Other Shifters

Levers for shifting can also come out the ends of the handlebars (bar-end shifters) or down by your knees (downtube shifters). Both of these locations feature straight levers than you manipulate up or down—like a large light switch with many settings for lack of a better example—to move through the gears.

Bikes with curly drop bars, like road bikes, usually have combined brake levers and shifters. Your right hand pushes the entire brake lever to the right to change the rear derailleur to a lower gear and pushes a smaller lever tucked under the brake lever to return to higher gears. As with other shifting systems, the left hand is in charge of operating the front derailleur.

SINGLE-SPEED BIKES

The chain on a single-speed bike wraps around one chainring in the front and one cog in the rear with no shifting necessary. In this case, the rear cog is *not* fixed to the wheel as it is for a fixed-gear bike, so if you stop pedaling, the rear wheel will continue to rotate independently. There are fewer parts to maintain, and the chain doesn't gradually wear down and stretch out the same way it does on a geared bike.

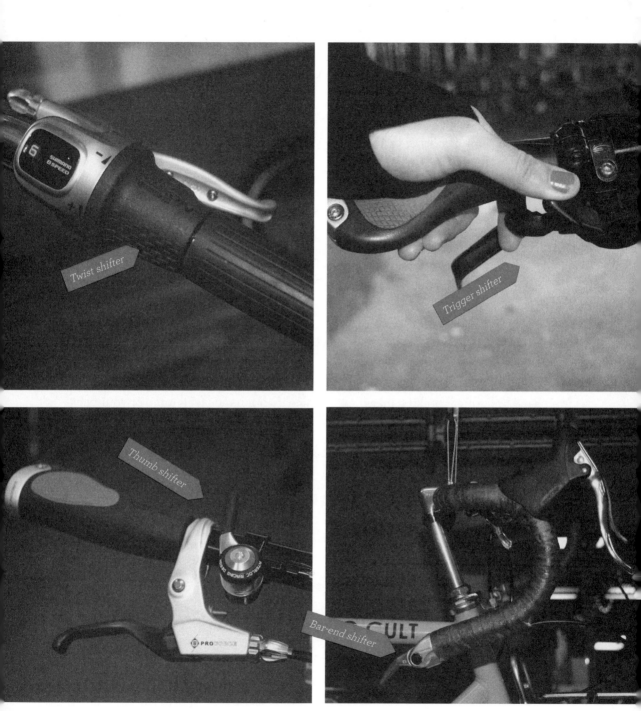

Twist shifter

Trigger shifter

Thumb shifter

Bar-end shifter

FIXED-GEAR BIKES

You've probably heard the term "fixed-gear bike" or "fixie." Like a single-speed bike, it has just one chainring in the front and one cog in the back, but the cog is connected (fixed) to the wheel, which means the rider must pedal continuously to keep the bike in motion. There is no coasting on a fixed-gear bike! These bikes are used in track racing, and since they have the unique ability to be pedaled backward, appeal to artistic cyclists who perform elaborate tricks.

In the city setting, fixies are popular with bicycle messengers and are sometimes used by commuters. Generally, fixed-gear bikes used in cities have a front hand brake. Rear braking takes more technique: cease pedaling while holding the pedals in place (clipless pedals or toe clips necessary!), leaning forward and skipping the bike to a stop, or—more quickly—by skidding sideways to a halt.

In addition to having fewer parts to maintain, fixed-gear bikes are popular for their style of ride. An experienced rider is adept at varying his or her speed by changing pressure on the pedals, and skilled at shifting through traffic to avoid hazards—which probably sounds as frightening to any new commuter as it sounds to me.

HANDLEBARS

Handlebars come in all shapes and sizes. The slight variations in width and angle make them hard to translate from rider to rider—your friend's long-researched favorite handlebars might be extremely uncomfortable for you. If you're feeling any discomfort while riding, especially in your wrists or hands, handlebars are a good place to make an adjustment or consider a complete change.

FLAT BARS

Flat bars come standard on most urban commuter bikes and mountain bikes. They provide a fairly upright riding position and work great in the crowded city, creating a taller shape for others to see. Grips and bar ends can be added to provide additional hand positions. This is nice if your hands feel numb or your back gets stiff while riding. Some people prefer climbing hills out of the saddle with their hands on the bar ends.

SWEPT-BACK BARS

Swept-back handlebars are similar to flat bars, but bend to place your wrists at a more natural angle. I have replaced flat bars on my cargo bike with swept-back bars for a more comfortable ride. Many city bikes come with swept-back bars, but there are a lot of choices! Some rise up from the stem and sweep back far enough to put you at a completely upright angle, while others provide just a small bend at the ends for a 30-degree twist to your hands.

Riser bars with bar ends

Swept-back bars

The bends in swept-back bars also create more room to attach light(s) and a bell.

DROP BARS

Drop bars are the curly handlebars that are found on road bikes and touring bikes. They provide for many hand positions, but your body is canted forward quite a bit in all spots. I prefer to ride with my hands "on the hoods"—holding onto the covering of the brake and shifters so I can easily brake and shift. However, when I'm tired, it's nice to move my hands to the middle of the bars and stretch out my back.

A lot of bike commuters with drop bars happily ride around the city, and I am often one of them. However, I really prefer being on a more upright bike for ease of seeing and signaling, although it's at the expense of a bit of speed, as I'm not tucked in as aerodynamic of a position as drop bars allow.

OTHER BARS

Other examples of common handlebars include:

› *BMX bars.* Rise up quite high with just a bit of sweep back and can turn a mountain bike into a more upright vehicle.
› *Bullhorns.* Essentially backward, upside down swept-back bars that point away from the bike with a small rise at the end.
› *Moustache bars.* Curve forward and then back, like drop bars that have been flattened into a horizontal plane.
› *Riser bars.* Very similar to flat bars, but angle up a little bit close to the stem and then flatten out.
› *Trekking bars.* Similar to moustache bars, but have one additional curve toward the stem for a close-in hand position.

CHAPTER 4
Gear and Accessories

YOU CAN ADD MANY bells (literally) and whistles to your bike to make it the most comfortable and useful vehicle imaginable. One of my bikes sports pedal-powered lights, the sturdiest kickstand on the market, three bells (five if I count the kids' bells on the back), a radio/MP3 player, handlebar smartphone holder, big front basket, travel mug holder, pouch for my keys and other little treasures, and surely many other add-ons I'm forgetting to mention. Of course, as long as your bike starts and stops, you're good to go (and stop going, as needed). But if you want to leave your bike unattended, you'll need a lock. If you want to ride in the dark, you'll need a light. Some bicyclists, obsessed with "light" and "fast," focus on acquiring only the most sensible components. It's fine for fenderless speedsters to worry about the added grams of this water-bottle cage over that one, but it's not a concern for those of us just trying to get to the store comfortably. Bike accessories are for safety, comfort, and fun, and the modern-day bike commuter deserves to enjoy all three.

What follows is a list of both necessary items and extra stuff. If you opt to add accessories to your bike, choose ones that fit well and you like the look of. You don't need to fill your handlebars with oodles of stuff like mine, but you might add an accessory here and there over time to help create the bike you want to ride more often.

REFLECTORS

Don't take the reflectors off your new bike! I say this having watched well-meaning friends "do me a favor" by stripping the reflectors off my bike, stating they're not cool. For many states, reflectors are part of the riding-in-the-dark laws for bicycles (see Laws Regarding Bicycle Lights, below).

A lot of bikes come with a front white reflector, rear red reflector, and yellow reflectors on the wheels and pedals. Some tires come with reflective sidewalls. Plus there are a slew of safe and decorative reflective stickers that can help you personalize and brighten your frame.

High-visibility triangles and flags can be attached directly to your bike. Yellow and green are common colors for high-visibility bicycling items, but you'll also find amazingly bright oranges, reds, and pinks.

LIGHTS

There's nothing better than biking through town on a bright day: sun sparkling off the pavement, exchanging smiles with passersby as the vitamin D soaks into our skin. But riding in the dark is sometimes unavoidable for commuters, especially in the winter. Maybe you even enjoy riding in the dark, once rush hour has ended or the temperature cools down. Enter bike lighting.

A light is a relatively simple and inexpensive way to make your commute safer in a lot of conditions, and a must-have at night, often required by city law. It's good practice to always run both front and rear lights while riding in the city, even during the day. Your opinions on lights might change as you ride more. I've seen a lot of friends add more and more lights to their bikes, although I'd imagine it goes the other way too. If you feel safest being covered in lights, go for it—although pay attention if people shield their eyes from you.

LAWS REGARDING BICYCLE LIGHTS

Laws vary from state to state, but most require a front light and a rear reflector when riding in the dark. They're part of the vehicle code. California's vehicle code, for example, requires:

› A white light visible 300 feet in front of you
› A rear red reflector visible from 500 feet when a car's headlights shine on it
› A white or yellow reflector on your pedals, shoes, or ankles, visible for 200 feet
› A white or yellow reflector on both sides of the front half of the bicycle, and a white or red reflector on both sides of the rear half. Note: if your tires have reflective sidewalls, you're covered!

Here are some popular examples of auxiliary lights:

› Wrap lighted flexible tubes, connected to battery packs, around your frame.
› Attach small lights in a rainbow of colors to the side or bottom of your frame. I ran pink Down Low Glow on my bike for quite a while and thought it was pretty cool.
› Attach lights to your spokes, which are nice for side visibility because they create a larger shape as your wheel spins—some are even programmable to create different patterns.
› Add lights to the sides of your pedals, which like spoke lights will also cast a larger light as your foot spins.

Even non-bike-specific lights are nice to string on your bike. I go for cheap battery-pack-powered holiday lights in winter, although I have to tuck the battery packs into plastic bags on rainy days.

A well-locked bike

LOCKS

Even if your bike splits its time between the inside of your home and the inside of your office (a great way to keep a bike from being stolen!), you'll want a lock for the occasional side trip. Hopefully, you never have to deal with bike theft, and your recorded serial numbers and bicycle photo shoots prove a big waste of time. (See Bike Security in Chapter 2.) Of course there's no guarantee, but smart locking will go a long way in preventing your bike from being stolen.

Just like choosing what to wear and where to ride, how you choose to lock your bike depends on your comfort level. Some people spend ten minutes removing tires and applying multiple locks in their theft-free assemblage; others stash their unlocked bike behind a tree and hope for the best.

My locking behavior often depends on where I park and how long I intend to be there. If I've heard about a bike theft at a certain spot, I deem that area "high theft" and lock with care. Sometimes it's just a feeling that encourages me to lock carefully. Yet at the same time, I've gotten lazier as I've gotten older. In college I removed my front wheel every single time I locked up—several times a day! I never do that nowadays and rarely see bikes locked as such. Use the bikes around you as a cue; if they're locked more securely than yours, consider upping your game.

HOW TO LOCK YOUR BIKE

Ideally, you'll always lock your bike to an immovable object, even inside a garage or while transporting your bike in a car. Most locks come with brackets for mounting them to your bike or a rack when you're not using them. Stowing your lock in a pannier works, too, as does burying it at the bottom of a basket, although a lone lock in a basket is bound to rattle around.

The Bike Index, which cites that over a million bikes are stolen every year in the United States, offers the following recommendations on their website:

› Cable locks should never be used as a primary means of locking a bike in a city. Cheaper and older U-locks can often be broken without any tools. Use a U-lock that costs at least $40. (See U-lock and Cable Lock, below.)

› Aim to have the hardest bike to steal on the rack. Two U-locks, or a U-lock and one heavy-duty cable, are considered to be the minimum required in large cities to keep a bike secure.

› Don't rely on foot traffic to keep your bike safe; years of reports have taught that many thefts, particularly those involving cutting cable locks, occur under the cover of crowd activity or in front of bustling cafés or restaurants.

› Don't rely on the presence of cameras to keep your bike secure. Security footage is rarely of much use once a bike is gone, and thieves know this.

› Tug on whatever you're about to lock to make sure it can't be easily removed. Signposts in particular can be easily removed by unbolting them, and some are already unattached.

› Many bicycles are stolen from garages and store rooms. Lock your bike securely to an immovable object even if in a "secure" place.

On top of locking your bike, you can take a piece with you to essentially disable it. Carrying most of a bike away from the scene of the crime isn't as appealing to a thief as riding it quickly away. Your seat post and saddle are easy to take along with you, but even a front wheel is portable . . . though dirtier.

TYPES OF LOCKS

Bike locks can be expensive, and it's a big hurdle for many who've just spent what feels like a lot of money on a bike to then spend even more money on another accessory. But what a shame to lock your $1,000 bike with a thin $10 combination lock, never to see either again. Some people pay more for a new lock than they paid for their used bike. That's OK! They've accurately imagined what an inconvenience it would be to lose their bike, and acted accordingly. But odds are you will not drop more cash on your lock than you did on your bike.

It's good practice to lock with two different locks, ideally ones that require two different tools to defeat. Also avoid leaving any lock in such a position that it can be moved to the ground and bashed with a hammer.

Key or Combination?

Many locks are available in either a keyed or a combination lock version. The locking mechanism of a cheap combination lock is probably easier to break than the locking mechanism of a cheap keyed lock, but high-quality (remember: expensive and heavy) locks will be safe in both keyed and combination varieties.

A variety of locks. Top row: folding lock, heavy-duty U-lock with cable, two heavy-duty cable locks. Bottom row: light-duty cable lock, extremely light-duty cable lock, light-duty U-lock, light-duty combination cable lock.

Consider the following before choosing a keyed or combination lock:

› Keyed locks require you to *not* lose the keys. Although most come with multiple keys, and if you register your lock upon purchase, you can request replacement keys if needed, that's not much help when you're standing next to your locked bike with no key. Some keyed locks can be ordered so that one key fits multiple locks.

› Combination locks require you to memorize the combination and are hard to use in the dark.

U-lock

U-locks—so called because one of the two pieces is shaped like a U—are heavy and strong. While buying the biggest one is tempting, as it makes gathering the bike rack, frame, and front wheel into the U possible, you want to avoid extra space—that's where a bike thief can squeeze in a car jack. Tiny U-locks fit just the bike frame and rack in the U; these rate great at theft resistance, but work better paired with a second lock if your wheels are quick release.

Chain Lock

Thick chains make suitable bike locks, but again, the more secure, the heavier they are. Many chains are covered with sturdy fabric or rubber to keep the metal from scratching your bike frame.

Cable Lock

Cable locks are light, but not very secure. They are useful as secondary locks or if you don't live or park in a high-theft area. Some stretch very long, making it easy to get both wheels and frame secured to a bike rack.

Many bike shops won't sell cable locks. The *Chicago Sun-Times* reported in 2013 that a cable-lock-locked bike was more likely to be stolen than if it had not been locked at all! That's not to encourage you to leave your bike unlocked; perhaps the would-be thieves of Chicago assumed those bike owners were within sight of their bikes or planning to return momentarily.

Wheel lock

Wheel Lock

Also called a "café lock," this lock is built onto the bike, usually at the rear wheel. When engaged, a metal pin blocks the wheel from turning. It's useful as a secondary lock and in fairly secure settings, within your sight. Wheel locks are safer on heavy bikes that most people wouldn't be willing to carry away. My 20-pound road bike isn't the best candidate, but my 75-pound cargo bike isn't going anywhere if the wheels don't turn.

Another way to wheel-lock your bike is to run a U-lock through the frame and front wheel. No one could ride your bike away, although it's still possible that someone could carry it away. I often lock my aforementioned 75-pound bike to itself when I'm spending time outdoors, not expecting to leave sight of my bike but wanting a bit of security just in case.

Other Locks

New locking technology is being released all the time, like products that use your smartphone for recognition instead of a key. Other lock shapes include:

› Heavy-duty folding locks, newer to the market, that are very secure.
› Strong and light titanium locks.
› Handcuff locks—exactly what they sound like—are designed as bike locks. They're strong, small for transporting, and provide a certain look that appeal to some.

Locking Skewers

These aren't for locking your bike to a bike rack, but rather for locking the pieces of your bike to your bike.

Locking skewers replace quick-release parts such as wheels, seat posts, and even lights, hubs, and brakes with theft-proof skewers. Useful in high-theft areas, they come with a coded key if you need to remove them. You should still combat complete bike theft with a strong lock, but you don't have to worry about the little pieces vanishing.

THE SHELDON BROWN LOCKING STRATEGY

Sheldon Brown, world-renowned for his encyclopedic knowledge of all things bicycle, suggested this method to be sufficiently safe: lock with a very small U-lock around the rear rim and tire, somewhere inside the rear triangle of the frame. Hacking through the frame and tire to steal the bike would render the bike unusable. This simple method works if you don't have a quick-release front wheel. Sheldon also recommended:

1. Instead of carrying your heavy U-lock around, leave it fastened to the rack at work. Use a cable lock for quick trips around town.
2. Use a U-lock and a cable lock at work, since both require different tools to break.
3. Secure your quick-release seat post with an Allen head bolt.

I agree with Sheldon that no one will take a hacksaw to my rear wheel. However, this method *appears* less secure than one that involves locking the frame, and it's best not to draw the wrong kind of attention to your bike. Upon closer examination, the would-be thief might deem the frame and rear wheel secure, but go for other parts, like front wheel or saddle. Since most bikes these days have quick-release front wheels, wrap a cable through the U-lock to secure the front wheel as well.

HELMETS

Most states do not have a blanket law requiring all adults to wear helmets. Children must, though. Check your law at the city level as some cities have stricter rules, such as in Seattle. Washington State does not have a mandatory adult bicycle helmet law, but the City of Seattle does.

If your city requires you to wear a helmet, wear a helmet! And consider wearing a helmet even if you're not lawfully required to do so. Helmets aren't expensive, and they are effective at preventing life-altering head and facial injuries.

HELMET STYLES

I know for a lot of people it's important to like the look of their helmet in order to be encouraged to wear it. If this sounds like you, rest assured there are a lot of fun options to suit your personal style and personality. And even more than aesthetics, an uncomfortable helmet might dissuade you from wearing it—and possibly from riding period!

An uncomfortable helmet can be a case of bad fit, which is important to fix for safety and comfort. Or it can be a ventilation issue, in which case you can change to a different style of helmet with more vents.

I clump bike helmets into two categories: very vented aerodynamic recreational cycling helmets and shell-like round urban helmets with few, if any, vents. I like the look of the urban helmets, but due to my thick hair, find them too hot to wear in the summer. All helmets are adjustable, but the aerodynamic ones tend to be more adjustable.

Beyond initial comfort, there are options that you'll find in some helmets, but not others.

Visors

Both vented and round helmets have versions with visors, which are very useful for keeping sun out of your eyes, useful even when wearing sunglasses. Some visors are part of the helmet; some are removable. And they are made from a range of materials, from easy-to-wipe-down plastic to easy-to-stain-with-bike-grease cloth.

Ponytail Hole

I've seen many longer-haired people utilize the wider gap of a ponytail-friendly helmet for keeping tresses neat and tidy (and off the neck), so if this feature speaks to you, find a helmet that accommodates your mane in this way.

HELMET FIT

If you wear a helmet, make sure it fits you well and that you wear it correctly for both comfort and safety.

Follow these tips from the League of American Bicyclists:

› To find the right-size helmet, put one on your head without fastening the straps.
› The front of the helmet should be level and two fingers' width above your eyebrows.
› Shake your head from side to side: There should only be a little movement.

Momentum Mag

Vancouver, British Columbia

"Smart Living by Bike" is the tagline of the magazine, *Momentum Mag*, and its articles make cycling look fun and stylish too. A resource for the North American urban bicyclist, the magazine runs product reviews, buying guides, and articles on everything bike related, from infrastructure to fashion. *Momentum Mag* strives to normalize bicycling by influencing a shift in the transportation culture in North America away from car-centricity.

Gear reviews cover mainstream products—such as lights, helmets, and bicycles you've probably seen at your local bike shop—but also stylish panniers, baskets, clothing, and more unique bikes you might not otherwise discover. The Style category contains articles such as "Riding a Bike in a Suit Made Easy," with a lot of practical tips for riding comfortably in a suit.

All categories feature profiles of interesting companies and people, embedded with tips and advice for adopting an urban cycling lifestyle.

The magazine encourages reader participation through numerous contest giveaways and reader submissions to "We asked, you answered," in which readers submit photos and tips. Submit a photo if you see an applicable "ask" come up via the magazine's social media avenues—it's fun!

Print editions of the magazine are published five times a year and are available for free at many bike shops in the United States and Canada, for purchase at many newsstands, and of course, by subscription. Digital editions are available for purchase as well and readers can subscribe to free weekly newsletters.

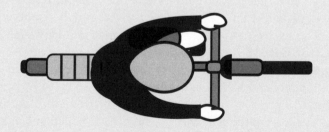

> The side straps should come to a point just below your ears—move the small tabs on the side of these straps up or down until they are a half an inch or less under your earlobe.
> The chin strap should be about half an inch below your chin when your mouth is closed.
> Wearing a bike helmet with loose straps is the same as not wearing a bike helmet at all.
> After a crash or impact on your helmet, it should be replaced.

My chin strap tends to work itself loose every few days, so I take care to tighten it as necessary when I don my helmet in the morning. I measure my "about half an inch below the chin" by seeing if I can fit only two fingers between my chin and helmet strap and verifying that my chin makes contact with the strap as soon as I open my mouth.

And to check the "two fingers' width above the eyebrows" to make sure my helmet isn't sitting too far back on my head, I simply look up and verify I can see my helmet. If I can't see it, it's slid too far back and won't protect my head.
A helmet that fits properly is snug, but not uncomfortable; it is easy to ignore once you're off and pedaling.

HELMET ACCESSORIES
Helmet accessories can make your already good-fit helmet even more comfortable or serve a double duty.
> *Helmet covers.* These keep the rain and cold out of vented helmets. Most have reflective details and are available in high-visibility colors. Some have bills or brims and are made of attractive fabric to create a more hat-like look.
> *Earmuffs.* Your ears might get cold without bike-helmet-specific earmuffs.
> *Wind blockers.* Use these to block out wind noise.
> *Aftermarket visors.* If you find yourself squinting in the sun, you need not buy a new helmet with a visor, just add an aftermarket one. Many sizes are available through shops that cater to recumbent bikes, especially, because the reclined angle makes sun exposure more of an issue.
> *Lights.* Your helmet makes a great bike light mount, much better than your bare head.
> *Video camera.* Some urban bike commuters record all of their rides in case of a crash; others just for the joy of sharing scenic bike-ride footage.
> *Reflective stickers.* I've got black flowers on my white helmets. One of my kids has yellow puppies on his helmet, and the other has blue stars.

HELMET HAIR
Having never been in a profession that demands carefully coifed hair, I don't worry too much about how my helmet affects my hair. However, I tend to wear a ponytail while riding and remove the rubber band as soon as I've reached my destination, hopefully before it can put a dent in my hair. That and not having bangs that will display a helmet mark right across the middle (which I learned

the hard way) are the only two hair tricks I use. Other popular strategies are covering your head with a silk scarf before donning your helmet or using dry shampoo to restyle at your destination.

CLOTHING

The popularity of bicycling as sport and recreation leads many to believe it must be done in cycling-specific clothing, even when it's a two-mile, flat ride to work. That's not the case, especially if your steed is an upright city bike with fenders, wheel skirt, and chain guard. Even on an urban commute bike with a front derailleur and exposed chain, only slight changes to wardrobe—if any—are warranted.

Starting a bike commute shouldn't be reason to purchase an entirely new wardrobe, although you might opt to phase out certain styles. I'm too lazy to deal with rolling up a pant leg or two (my right pant leg gets dirtied by my chain and my left pant leg catches on my drink cage if there's no water bottle in it), so I've switched to wearing midcalve-length pants (capris) with wool socks if it's cold or more often, midlength skirts over leggings. The slight forward lean of my body position on my commuter bike makes for a couple inches of bare back in certain shirts, which is annoying, so I've phased out shorter shirts from my wardrobe. Top layers are all zip-up so they can be added or removed quickly without wrestling them over my helmet.

I haven't made any changes to my footwear—I tend to invite more outfit comments for riding in flip-flops than in flowing skirts. I'll admit that on three occasions in as many decades, I've had a flip-flop fly off my foot while biking. On none of these occasions has it come close to getting lodged in my spokes or causing a crash, so I live with the knowledge that in ten years I'm due to once again park my bike and jog a few feet to retrieve a flip-flop from the gutter. Of course, there are shoes made for both comfortable bicycling and everyday wear, featuring firmer soles for effective pedaling and sometimes even with reflective accents.

You can find accessories that make your regular clothing work. Not all pant legs stay rolled up—and not all pants wearers want to roll up—but straps to hold nontapered pants in place do the trick. Some straps are reflective, some are fashionable, and there are a lot of options—do an online search to see for yourself.

It's easy enough to find regular clothing that addresses my preferences for comfort while biking, but many bike-clothing retailers have introduced "lifestyle" clothing lines and new labels just for the urban bike commuter.

And, of course, it's not imperative to ride in your regular clothing. Many people are most comfortable riding in cycling-specific clothing made of Lycra or wool and changing at their destination. Most cycling shorts and bibs (shorts connected to straps that go over your shoulders) are padded and worn without undergarments. This provides comfort for long hours in the saddle. Nonpadded cycling shorts are harder to come by, so if padding sounds bulky rather than comfortable, look for other types of athletic shorts for commuting. For cold commutes, wear longer cycling pants, or pair shorts with knee or leg warmers. Jerseys come in short- and long-sleeved versions, and the short-sleeved ones can also be paired with arm warmers. Cycling apparel—especially bottoms with padding—should be changed out of as soon as is practical and washed after every use.

▰▰▰▰▰▰▰▰▰▰▰▰

CYCLE CHIC

The phrase "cycle chic" was coined by Mikael Colville-Andersen in 2007, author of the *Copenhagen Cycle Chic* blog started that same year. It refers to cycling in everyday clothing, with an emphasis on fashionable everyday clothing. The term has become a bit corrupted or misinterpreted, especially in America, and applied to bicycling in *very* fashionable clothing. This makes it almost not worth mentioning, but I like its original concept—dress for your destination, not your journey—and hope it will survive in that mien.

There are brands using the term cycle chic to sell fancy bike accessories, and that's not a bad thing—the more useful accessories out there, the better! But it does serve to confuse the meaning and accessibility of biking in what you're currently wearing *without* having to make special purchases.

▰▰▰▰▰▰▰▰▰▰▰▰

HIGH-VISIBILITY CLOTHING

As far as I'm aware, high-visibility clothing isn't required by law in any city, but many commuters opt for bright apparel in the form of neon-colored, high-visibility jackets, helmet covers, shoe covers, or gloves. If you don't want to buy a new jacket, you can make your clothes dazzle with reflective accents instead, such as iron-on reflective patches and pinstripes, or reflective ankle straps.

A friend of mine told me that when she drove to work she noticed that "acid green and fluorescent yellow" popped out at her amidst the sea of bicyclists in normal clothing. She has since added a bright yellow vest to her commute (as well as a tall flag and helmet lights).

BIKE-COMMUTER WEAR

Aldan Shank and Juliette Delfs are cofounders of the Seattle "cycle commuter boutique," Hub and Bespoke. Their mission is to support the current urban bicyclist as well as entice the city-wary bicyclist to commute by bike. It's their dream to live in a city where bicycles have transformed the streets into quieter, more social byways. They hope that by offering clothing and accessories that are functional for biking and designed for city life, they will normalize the activity of riding a bike and simplify the decision to take to two wheels. Here they provide some valuable clothing advice:

For Women, from Juliette

Here's what I say: if you can high-kick in it, you can bike in it! Women really do have it easy. We get to wear tights or leggings and still be office/city appropriate.

Juliette's urban "kit," from head to toe:

› *Headwear.* Under a helmet, a headband is nice in summer or winter. In the summer it catches sweat; in the winter it covers your ears for warmth. Off the bike, you have an accessory to mask "helmet hair." If you are commuting to the office, stash a cordless flatiron or curling iron at your desk to respruce your hair.

› *Upper body.* I look for apparel items that allow for a comfortable, arms-forward reach. If not sleeveless, then it's usually made from a knit material. You will hear people who sport-ride say that cotton's no good. Pshaw! In the summer, cotton is lovely; in fact, it's great at not holding body odor. Look for lightweight jerseys, as they will not hold as much moisture and dry quickly. A wool jersey is a definite must for the winter.

› *Below the waist.* I choose skirts and dresses that I can dance in and, of course wear with tights or leggings. Nothing too long and flowing, because that can get in your way. If you have a skirt that you need to hold down, use a simple elastic hair tie or a sweetly designed skirt clip. In the winter months, fleecy tights are quite delicious and still quick to dry if you get wet. Anecdotally, and verified by our female customers, a skirt on a bike seems to get you some friendly attention. If your preference is for pants, again, women are lucky. We

easily find fashionable offerings that have suitable stretch. For rainy, winter riding, a pair of trousers made with a nylon or poly blend will dry quickly.

› *Footwear.* I love to wear my clogs. The stiff footbed makes pedaling very comfortable. Of course, heels also have stiff arches that make them great for riding (but not so comfortable for walking). I have a pair of waterproof overshoes that make a huge difference in the winter and let me wear any shoe I choose.

› *Hands.* Gloves make holding onto the handlebar a little more comfortable, allowing for a little more relaxed grip. Also, if you do fall, it's a good way to protect those hands. Use fingerless gloves in the summer. While it's hard to find a style that is sort of pretty, the gloves with the cotton-crochet back are pretty sweet. In the winter, if I'm not dealing with big rain, my fashionable water-resistant, fleece-lined leather gloves work swell at keeping me warm. I applied a decorative iron-on reflector to the back of the gloves so I can be seen signaling at night.

› *Rain.* The type of rain you experience along with your terrain affect suitable rainwear. No matter what they say, waterproof fabric acts as a barrier to venting your body heat. Look for a garment that allows you to adjust and accommodate for airflow. In warmer climes, or if you tend to be warm, ponchos can be a nice alternative.

› *Effective safety apparel* is eye-catching, but that doesn't mean you have to look like a road worker. In the winter, color is not that helpful to make you visible. It's simply too dark outside for that to make a big difference—it takes lights and reflective details. Keep in mind that reflective details that move while you ride (attached to your wheels or pedals) are more eye-catching than ones that are more static.

For Men, from Aldan

In Seattle, we're lucky to have many workplaces with fairly relaxed dress codes. This makes it easy to find apparel that's both functional on the bike and suitable for the day. Those who are required to wear a suit will most likely find changing clothes upon arrival a necessity, but for everyone else, there are many wardrobe options that are comfortable and don't scream, "I rode my bike here!"

A few items Aldan recommends from his personal experience:

› *Headwear.* In the cooler months, I don't leave home without my wool headband. It's a small thing but it . makes a big difference in my personal comfort. Without it, I get that inner ear ache that comes from cold air rushing past bare ears. Since it's wool, it keeps my ears warm even when it's wet, and still lets heat escape from the top of my head during the ride, which keeps me from overheating.

› *Hair care.* "Helmet hair" tends to be less of an issue for guys with shorter hairstyles, but sometimes a little grooming at the destination can be helpful. I use a dry clay that adds a bit of volume to hair that's been flattened by a helmet. The trick here is to wait until your hair is dry (from rain or sweat) before applying any product, so you don't end up with the Greased Lightning look. The adage "a little goes a long way" also applies.

› *Upper body.* Lightweight wool shirts are the real winner here for their temperature regulation, moisture resistance, and odor control. These are not just for the dead of winter; thinner, lighter fabrics make wool shirts great on warmer Seattle days too. Furthermore, the newer garments from modern wool-apparel producers are far less itchy than you might think; many are mistaken for cotton at our shop. Speaking of cotton, I don't shy away from wearing cotton shirts when I bike. I find that I'm not really riding fast or long enough to warrant sportier fabrics or tops, and the cotton doesn't hold odors like synthetic jerseys. Even when it's cold and wet out, I can put a wool sweater for warmth over a cotton button-down, and then a waterproof or water-resistant shell to protect against the drizzle. I arrive dry, warm, and not smelling like I just finished the Tour. Because, you know, I didn't; I just rode a few miles to work.

› *Pants.* This is one area in which I think some specialization make sense. I've spoken with many male customers at the shop who tried to make their regular pants work for the ride only to have them "blow out" over time. I think this is mainly due to the fact that, unlike many women's pants, men's pants usually aren't made of stretchy fabrics. Your typical jeans, chinos, and slacks often lack materials like elastane that make a trouser more flexible. In contrast, the pants we carry at Hub and Bespoke are built for movement, with features like stretchy fabric and gussets that reduce tension on important seams. These trousers perform similarly to hiking pants, but lack the dozen or so pockets you'll find on those—because you'll probably make it to work without having to dip into your gorp supply.

> *Shoes.* This will be controversial for some, but I say for urban commutes, ditch the clipless pedals (and the shoes with them). Clipless makes great sense for longer rides and races where efficiency over many miles is important. But if you're only riding a few miles to work or play, I say let efficiency take a backseat to convenience. Regular pedals let you wear regular shoes rather than pack them (it's amazing how much room a pair of shoes takes up in a bike pannier). From a style perspective, I'm of the school of thought that if there's one clothing item that can make or break an entire outfit, it's the shoes. So if you're looking great otherwise, why disrupt the look with sporty shoes? If oxfords are too much of a stretch for

you (I wear them on the bike all the time), then dressy leather boots work wonderfully and look terrific too.

BAGS, RACKS, AND BASKETS

Odds are you already have a bag that will work well for carrying your stuff while biking. I rely on one—sometimes a backpack, sometimes a messenger bag—for my small daily items. (Pockets work, too, as long as the items won't fall out and aren't uncomfortable, but odds are you'll occasionally need to transport more than your phone and keys.) There are many options for transporting your stuff; pick the one that feels the most comfortable and stylish to you.

I've done my share of biking with a purse slung over one shoulder, but bags that swing around and/or need the aid of an arm to keep them in place aren't the best bets for biking. A swinging bag can be a major distraction if it slides off your shoulder. Your handlebars might seem like a good perch; I see people using this method nearly every day. However, the heavier the bag, the more it threatens to affect steering. You also risk getting the bag caught up in your spokes. With anything you carry, wear, or attach to your bike, take care that it can't dangle, fall, or blow into your spokes, where it will get tangled up in your wheel and cause you to crash. There are lots of ways to carry things on your bike that won't make the seasoned bike commuter flinch as you pass by, worried you're running the risk of spoke entanglement.

Ben O'Donnell

Adonia Lugo

Washington, DC

Adonia Lugo has been transporting herself by bike for ten years, most recently around Washington, DC. A bicycle anthropologist, a cultural anthropologist who studies how bicycling influences social structure, Adonia studies the diversity in bicycling today. She started her bike commute with a $10 bike from the Goodwill Outlet . . . although when she upgraded to a bike with better gears soon after, she found on-street riding much more enjoyable.

While she now works from home, Adonia's full bike commute when she worked for the League of American Bicyclists, which she rode about once a week, was four and a half miles each way. Most days she used Capital Bikeshare to ride a mile and a half down a path near her house to reach a train that took her into the city center.

BIKES

Adonia has been riding the same 1980s Panasonic road bike since 2007—a reliable, pretty lightweight bike. She really likes the feeling of bending over on her drop bars when climbing hills and doesn't mind choosing clothes that allow her to straddle the flat top tube. If she absolutely had to wear a pencil skirt or clothes that would similarly restrict her movements, she says she would utilize a bike with a step-through frame through Capital Bikeshare.

CLOTHING

Adonia doesn't usually buy clothes without thinking about how they'll work with her bike. A capable seamstress, she frequently alters her clothes to make them bikeable, primarily by removing sleeves and lowering necklines to make clothes more suited to DC's hot, humid climate.

BIKE SECURITY

One of the reasons Adonia chose her apartment building is the bike room in the basement, where she locks her bike each night. Working for a bike organization means she can store her bike on a wall rack in the office kitchen during the workday, but she usually locks her bike to one of the many sufficiently safe staple bike racks in front of the building, as do many other commuters.

ROADSIDE REPAIR

Adonia carries some patch kits in her pannier, but if her tire busted, she would probably walk her bike to the nearest bike shop or take the Metro home.

BIKE EQUITY

Adonia has been involved in bike activism since 2008. Prior to her time on staff at the League of American Bicyclists (November 2013 through May 2015), she was a member of the organization's Equity Advisory Council, a group of ten people from around the country who have experience promoting bikes among women, youth, and communities of color. At the League she worked to develop resources that would help bike advocates integrate equity, diversity, and inclusion into their work. This meant getting unrepresented bike users involved in bike advocacy, as well as creating opportunities for new groups to use bikes without feeling like they had to fit a certain profile to do so.

"If you're interested in bike equity, spend some time getting a feel for the current diversity among bicycle users where you regularly bike," Adonia says. "Does your local bike organization do culturally appropriate outreach with all groups, or do they wait for bike enthusiasts to come to them? Many bike users face significant barriers to participation in bike advocacy, such as not knowing the jargon or even the language, not having flexible jobs where they can take time off to attend a meeting at city hall, or not having opportunities to evaluate from their own perspective the potential value of bike projects. You may not know how to overcome these barriers, but it's a great starting point to notice where they exist."

COMPARING CITIES

Since Adonia biked in Seattle, Portland, and Los Angeles before she moved to Washington, DC, I was curious to learn if confidently picking up bike commuting in a new—and oh so different—city is as easy as she makes it look. Here's what she had to say:

"Biking in DC has given me a lot of opportunities to think about different road cultures. When I lived in Portland and Seattle, most bike users *complied* with stop signs and red lights. In Los Angeles, it was a lot more flexible, but there weren't as many people on bikes. In DC, there's actually a lot of people riding, and most of them blow through intersections. This is how people do things on foot, too—and even in cars to a certain extent. Everyone's just pushing through as quickly as they can, whether that means rushing through after the light's turned red or starting into the intersection before the light turns green. And yet instead of embracing this flexibility of intersections here, it seems that the local bike planners want to control more tightly where bike users can go, with cycle tracks and a lot of signage and regulation. Fascinating to someone who studies street culture and infrastructure!"

ADONIA'S TIPS FOR NEW BIKE COMMUTERS

"The most important thing you can do is spend time getting to know what feels comfortable to you when you're traveling on a bike. *Ciclovías*, or Open Streets events, in which certain streets are temporarily closed to cars to allow free movement to people biking and walking, are good opportunities to get comfortable riding in the street if you haven't done so before. There's no 'right' way to bike commute. If it takes you a while to figure out the best route, that's fine. If you feel like getting off your bike and using crosswalks to get through a busy intersection, go for it."

BACKPACKS

A backpack, especially one with a chest strap, is an effective bag for city bicycling. However, even a light backpack can contribute to a sweaty back—and a heavy backpack can make for a miserable long ride. If you choose to wear a backpack, make sure it doesn't cause a blind spot: my bicycle-specific backpack holds a lot of stuff, but when I wear it on my road bike, it obstructs my view over my shoulder. I consider it a bit of a safety hazard.

MESSENGER BAGS

Messenger bags designed for bicycling feature a cross-body strap not always found on sling-type bags. On commuter bikes with even the slightest angle in body position, a messenger bag with just one main strap will slide around to the front, banging against your legs at worst, hanging annoyingly at least.

REAR RACKS

A rear rack is great for city bicycling, providing two areas for attaching stuff: on top and hanging down from the sides. The rear rack usually attaches to eyelets near the rear hub and bolts to the brakes or seat stays near the seat post. Depending on the rack, you may be able to transport up to 50 pounds on it.

If you don't have eyelets, fear not. There are racks designed for bikes that aren't made to accommodate traditional racks, such as mountain bikes and road bikes. These racks might clamp to the seat stays or telescope out from the seat post.

Many items can simply be strapped to the top of the rack, either with bungee cords—usually found in the automotive aisle of Target-type stores, hardware stores, or drugstores—or small bungee nets that form an enclosing square over your belongings—found in the motorcycle aisle or in bike shops. Take care that nothing, such as backpack straps, dangles down that might get caught in your spokes while the wheels are turning.

PANNIERS

Panniers (pronounced "pan-EARS" by most), which hook to the sides of a rear rack, are popular for city bicycling. Some come with backpack straps, a shoulder

MORE FOR MEN AND WOMEN, FROM ALDAN

I will concede that in a hilly town like Seattle, having the ability to "pull up" during the pedal stroke is nice. For this, I installed half-baskets onto my platform pedals, which give me some up-pull without requiring bike shoes. The half-baskets I use don't have a strap (which just gets in my way) and have a leather sheath, which keeps the metal edges from scratching my wingtips.

One more tip that could influence your bike wardrobe: The way you carry your cargo can affect both your look and your comfort. Many folks love their backpacks and messenger bags, but I find them uncomfortable, and they often lead to that conspicuous "sweat patch" on your back. I prefer to let the bike carry the load with a rear rack and panniers (or a wooden crate— my current setup). With my stuff off my back, I don't get as hot, which means it's easier to wear normal clothes on my ride. If you've never used a rack, I encourage you to give it a try, as it's been the biggest factor in my overall comfort for bike commutes.

strap, or a small handle for toting. You can buy them as two connected bags or as single bags. It's not necessary to use two panniers, though one heavily loaded pannier will take some getting used to; distributing heavy loads equally is more stable. Panniers are often designed specifically for one side of the bike: angled on the side closer to the pedal to avoid heel strike and straight on the rear to maximize storage space.

REAR BASKETS

Attaching a basket or two to your rack is a great way to make an easy-to-use cargo hold. You've probably seen milk crates atop rear racks. These are usually zip-tied on, but stretchable bungee cords can also do the trick, if pulled taut. In general, something that needs to be easily removable is good to secure with bungee cords, but something that should stay put is best attached with a more permanent method.

Other bike baskets hang off the sides of the rack. Bicycle-specific baskets will include mounting hardware and come in removable and fixed-on varieties. Removable bike baskets are often called "shopping baskets" and come with a handle, just like a small grocery store basket. Folding baskets fold down flat when not in use, keeping your bike as narrow as it is without baskets.

There's usually some horizontal wiggle room when attaching baskets to your rear rack, so before the final tightening or zip tie, take a full pedal stroke or two to ensure you've got heel clearance.

FRONT BASKET

I find a front basket very useful for storing shed clothing layers and gloves—it's easy to stuff things in at red lights, whereas it might take too long secure an item inside a pannier. Too much weight in a front basket will affect steering, though. Your bike may feel a bit wobbly and you'll need to work harder to control both riding straight and turning. Some smaller front baskets mount only to the handlebars—and some are even removable, with a built-in handle for carrying—but many have struts that reach down for connecting permanently to eyelets on the fork or the front axle to more sturdily connect bigger baskets that can accommodate bulkier items.

Check if a front basket will be compatible with bus travel. Some bus bike racks clamp over the front wheel, as close to the forks as possible, and a basket may interfere with stability.

SMALLER BAGS

A variety of smaller bags can be useful for city bicycling. Many are for bike touring, recreational mountain biking, or carrying

Tandem commute bike with front and rear baskets

minimal repair tools and a few personal belongings on long road bike rides.

Seat Bag

Seat bags, sized for a spare inner tube and a few small tools, attach under the bike saddle.

Top-Tube Bag

Popular with multiday endurance racers, top tube bags are well sized and well placed for holding snacks, but also for keys, phone, and wallet.

Frame Bag

Bikes with some space between top tube and down tube can accommodate a frame bag or frame pack. While they make great use of space and can hold quite a bit of stuff, they use the spot where many bikes

have one or two water-bottle cages, so your water will have to go elsewhere.

FENDERS

Fenders not only keep a line of muddy water from forming up your back in wet conditions; they also protect your bike. The rain that hits your bike from above doesn't do any harm, but the dirty water blanketing the road, mixing with mud and oil, gets kicked up into your drivetrain by your fenderless tires. Dirt that works its way into your chain will grind it down more quickly or require more frequent chain cleaning on your part. The more coverage, the better—your bike should have full-length fenders and mud flaps on front and back. The mud flaps protect your bike, your feet, and even the bicyclist behind you from the "rooster

Fenders and mud flaps

tail" of spray that comes from the rear wheel on wet roads.

Similar to the racks mentioned earlier, many fenders attach to the eyelets and specific points on your frame. If your bike doesn't have eyelets, there are other fender options. I like having fenders on all my bikes, year-round, although many people remove their fenders for the summer. Getting splashed just once with dirty water as I failed to notice a puddle was enough for me to want to err on the side of year-round coverage.

PUMPS

You could get away without owning a pump. It's easy enough to pop into a bike shop to top off low tires. You get free air (as opposed to the air at the gas station) and a nice, easy-to-use pump, and you're connecting with your local bike shop(s). Many other businesses with bike-enthusiast owners or themes now sport public bike pumps too. But if you want

to take matters into your own hands, it's nice to own a pump . . . or two . . . of your own.

There are a few different kinds of pump heads:

> *Presta only*: with a one-quarter-inch diameter opening to accept the valve in the pump head.
> *Schrader only*: with a three-eights-inch diameter opening in the pump head.
> *Dual valve*: two separate holes to accommodate either valve type.
> *Universal:* one opening accepts both Presta and Schrader.
> *Flip*: a two-sided piece labeled with an opening for Presta on one side and Schrader on the other screws to the end of the pump hose.

I like having a floor pump at home—this is a large, footed pump with built-in air pressure gauges. Easy to use, it adds air more quickly and with less effort than a smaller pump. While it's possible to travel with a floor pump sticking out of a backpack or pannier, it's big and awkward, so not exactly the best mobile choice.

My second pump is a small one that I keep on my bike at all times for using while out and about. Smaller pumps often have hardware for mounting them to your frame—which is great if you ride recreationally or have secure bike parking—but I like to keep my pump hidden inside a bag. The smaller the pump, the more pumping it will take to inflate a tire, so go for the pump that's as big as you can comfortably accommodate.

KICKSTANDS

Bikes don't always come with kickstands, but if they're not light-as-possible road bikes, they should. It's usually easy enough to find somewhere to lean your bike while loading your bags or putting on a sweater, but having a kickstand makes things like that even easier. Kickstands are easy to add after the fact and come in several styles.

Kickstands that mount to the chain stays behind the bottom bracket are right in the middle of the bike and very easy to use. Other kickstands attach toward the back of the bike—mounted to the chain stay and seat stay by the rear hub. This type is considered sturdier, particularly if you have a lot of weight at the back of the bike.

Center stands, or two-legged kickstands, hold the bike perfectly upright rather than leaned to one side; I'm partial to these, but they're quite a bit more expensive than regular kickstands. And if your bike doesn't hold small children who prefer being perfectly upright versus leaned to one side while loading, it doesn't make a big difference. As for nonhuman cargo, bikes carrying a lot of weight from panniers on the back and in the basket up front should stay upright with a regular kickstand, but a center stand makes things a bit more stable.

FRONT-WHEEL STABILIZERS

Unencumbered handlebars will usually track where you aim them even when you

Center stand

remove your hands. But park a bike with a front basket—even an empty one—and the handlebars might lunge to the side, gouging your basket into your frame and toppling the entire bike. If you find yourself catching your bike repeatedly or even just getting caught off guard when your handlebars sway when you're parking with a particularly heavy front load, a front-wheel stabilizer can help.

A front-wheel stabilizer is a spring that connects the fork to the down tube. It's loose enough that it doesn't restrict your steering into turns, but taut enough to hold your handlebars in place when your hands aren't holding them steady. They're especially helpful for loading and unloading the front of your bike, but the tautness may also help while you're riding, preventing the handlebars from swinging out of control if you hit a bump.

MIRRORS

Sadly, distracted driving is on the rise, and while rear-end collisions of bikers by cars were very rare for a long time,

Front-wheel stabilizer

they're becoming more and more common. When I rode with a friend who had a very large rearview mirror mounted on the handlebars of her upright bike, I was amazed at how far behind us she could see. I turned to check over my shoulder each time I thought I heard an approaching car, and before I had a chance to process the scene, she was already telling me, "That car is turning off to the right, but it's a whole block behind us."

After that experience, I'm partial to enormous mirrors that come straight up from the handlebars, but not all bikes— nor all body positions on various bikes— can accommodate that. Mirrors come in many sizes, from enormous rectangles that look like they belong on vintage automobiles to tiny stickers that affix to your glasses.

Mirrors allow you to see what's coming up behind you without turning your head at all, or at least as much, while at the same time still keeping a better view in front of you. Of course you'd still want to turn your head to check your blind spot if you were to change lanes—just like if you were in a car. (An added reason for doing so on a bike is that your turned head helps signal to those around you what your intentions are—more on this in Chapter 6: Riding Techniques.)

CHAIN GUARDS

A chain guard protects your clothing and skin from getting marred by bike grease. It is most easily attached to a bike without a front derailleur—having just one chainring in the front makes for consistent spacing around the cranks.

At the upper end of the spectrum, a fully enclosed chaincase is the best protection—both for your clothes and for your drivetrain. The chain and gears are completely protected from dirt entering the system. Chaincases are commonly

Cell-phone mount and kitty-cat bike bell

found on Dutch bikes, which is one reason Dutch bikes last forever and are considered maintenance free. These will only work on bikes without derailleurs, which means single-speed and internally geared hub bicycles.

At the other end of the spectrum, chain guards are common on upright city bikes with a single front chainring. The chainring and much of the top of the chain are covered, preventing grease stains, yet since the rear sprocket is exposed there is room for a rear derailleur and gears.

People who ride bicycles with front derailleurs aren't totally without options. There are a few chain guards designed to work with some front derailleurs. And some protection is possible with a mountain bike bash guard. These are made to protect the front chainrings from bashing against logs and rocks while riding over bumpy terrain, but are also fairly effective at keeping chain grease away from legs and clothes. A bash guard only works with two chainrings, but some riders opt to sacrifice their big ring if they find they don't use it often and prefer to have a bit of chain shielding.

BELLS

I love that bicycle bells are a requirement in the Netherlands and other countries with a high percentage of bicycle commuters. A ding of the bike bell serves as a warning to others when you're passing, be it a person walking on a multi-use trail, another person on a bicycle, or a car signaling to pull out of a parking spot. Some upright city bikes and commuter bikes come with bells, which is a nice acknowledgment of their practicality. Your voice isn't always loud enough (see more in the Sharing Multi-Use Trails section in Chapter 6) to alert others to your presence, so having a bell within easy reach on your handlebars is a good safety accessory.

I find some bell tones quite cheery, so don't be too shy to ring every bell in the bike shop to find the one you like the tone of best. Bells also come in novelty shapes and beautifully painted patterns, and some even light up.

MUSIC

I wouldn't say music is a necessary part of the bike commute, but given the number of people wearing earphones while walking and those listening to music in the car, adding music to biking may be necessary for some. People on bikes who listen to music do so using either small speakers or earbuds. There are no laws disallowing speakers, but a few states have rules about headphones. Rhode Island doesn't permit headphones at all; Florida allows them on bike paths and sidewalks, but not streets; and California, Delaware, and Maryland require one ear to be uncovered. Of course verify the information for your state.

SPEAKERS

There are many bicycle-specific speakers to be found. Some attach to your handlebars; others are sized to fit perfectly in a water-bottle cage. Most connect to your smartphone either by wire or wire-lessly. Most of these have some degree of waterproofness, but if you only ride in dry weather (and have somewhere to stow a speaker in case of sudden rain), cheaper speakers not designed for bicycling work fine. All of these little systems max out at a reasonable volume; be wise and keep music low enough that you are not dis-tracted from the activity around you.

I sometimes listen to low-volume music via a waterproof radio/MP3 player attached to my handlebars—I find it makes climbing hills just a little bit eas-ier. I've never had to strain my ears to hear something nor have I been surprised by the sudden appearance of a car or bike I didn't hear approaching. But if I find myself in a distracting situation, I'll turn off my music.

I loaded several MP3s of *Star Wars* music—both from the soundtrack and spoof songs—onto my bike sound system to lead a *Star Wars* Day (May the 4th be with you!) Kidical Mass family bike ride. I didn't play music while leading the group ride, but the kids enjoyed listening to it during the pre-ride Yoda-helmet-ears craft project. I still play the songs from time to time, and while I prefer the beat of "The Imperial March (Darth Vader's Theme)," the main title track seems to garner the most smiles and giggles from my fellow bicyclists.

EARBUDS

Earbuds—not to be confused with in-ear headphones, earphones, or in-ear moni-tors, which block outside noise—are not noise canceling and let in a lot of out-side sound, like traffic noise. Just as with speakers, don't let yourself get distracted if you bike while listening to music through earbuds.

DRINK CAGES AND CUP HOLDERS

It's good practice to have water along on your bike. Even the casual commuter can get dehydrated. Water can also come in handy for rinsing your hands after chang-ing a flat tire or replacing a dropped chain. I once watched a man—next to his upside-down bike, presumably with flat tire freshly repaired—wipe his greasy hands on a patch of grass and then on some stalks of lavender for the entire two minutes I was waiting at a red light. I would have pulled over to offer him my spare water bottle had I not been on the opposite side of a four-lane road. Hope-fully you only have cause to use your water for drinking.

Most bikes are equipped with a couple sets of water-bottle cage mounts, usually within the triangle of the frame—one pair on the down tube and one pair on the seat tube. If you have a step-through city bike, you may need a compact side-entry cage—mine has such a small triangle I wouldn't be able to fit a water bottle into the top of a standard cage. Cages come in many different styles, materials (usu-ally metal or plastic), shapes, and sizes, including rectangular for holding flasks.

I find the squeezable plastic water bot-tles easiest to use in bike drink cages—they're easy to squish in and tug out. But metal and glass containers work, too, although a metal bottle in a metal cage might rattle without a thin cover.

But there's more to drink than just water . . . and no, I'm not referring to the aforementioned flask and flask cage but to handlebar cup holders designed for the purpose of holding travel mugs. Pair one with a leak-proof travel mug and you're safe to caffeinate while riding. I tend to see more bike-riding coffee drinkers on Mondays than other days, but daily coffee drinking while biking is definitely a thing.

CELL-PHONE MOUNTS

Anything that distracts you while riding your bike is a bad idea, but I like having my phone at the ready for checking the time with the touch of a button, to pull over and take a picture of something interesting, or for navigational purposes.

Universal smartphone handlebar mounts will attach any type of phone to your handlebars—or stem, as the case may be—in or out of any smartphone case. Other mounts are designed to work with specific phones, or with specific phones in specific waterproof cases. My phone is in a fully waterproof case (inadvertently tested in a toilet with stellar results) that pairs with a same-brand handlebar mount I can easily switch from bike to bike and reliably use even in the heaviest rain.

CHAPTER 5

Urban Bicycle Infrastructure

I **WAS AN EAGER** Drivers Education student in high school, poring over the California Drivers Handbook before taking the test to enter the world of licensed motorists. I remember learning many particular things from that era, like the middle lane of a three-lane highway is only for passing in either direction, and the downhill-facing car on a steep narrow road must back out of the uphill car's way, but I can't remember a single instruction—in class or in the manual—about sharing the road with bicycles. Perhaps this reflected the times. Not that many bicycles were on the road back then, and certainly much of the modern-day bicycle infrastructure—like bike lanes, cycle tracks, and sharrows (definitions to follow)—didn't exist. While I find it unsafe and annoying, I'm not too surprised when I find the bike lane blocked by a double-parked car or when I have to share the green bike box with a car while waiting for a red light. Most people don't understand these new features, and there's no public outreach to educate them.

Some cycling infrastructure is self-explanatory—the narrow lane with an icon of a bike rider or the words "Bike Lane" suggest where on the road bikes are expected to ride. But more often than not, you may simply wonder what those funny chevrons mean, or when it is OK to cross a green box in your car. This chapter will help you decipher the street paint and the street signs. More in-depth coverage of using the facilities defined here will come in Chapter 6: Riding Techniques.

Of course, you don't need any sort of bicycle markings to legally ride on any given street. Unless you see a No Bicycles sign, you can bike on it. You won't experience the same uninterrupted flow as you would on a Neighborhood Greenway—where stop signs and speed humps hold cross-traffic at bay while you cruise by—or in a bike lane

BY DEFINITION

Cycling infrastructure/bicycle facilities
(n) The network of roads, streets, paths, and sometimes sidewalks used by bicycles. Also includes bike-specific traffic signs and signals.

Sharrow

on a high-traffic arterial, but many bikers choose unmarked arterials or quiet side streets since they are often the most direct routes across town.

SHARROWS

Sharrows are Shared Lane Markings painted on roads to indicate that people driving and people biking are sharing the space. They look a bit like arrows, as you probably guessed from the name, usually two chevrons above a bicycle icon, although there are some variations, such as a person on a bike enclosed within an arrow.

Sharrows are very common because it's a cheap way for a city to create a bicycle provision—just add paint! (And maybe a few Share the Road signs for good measure.) This is great on small, quiet streets where sharing space already feels natural since people drive at speeds not too much faster than their pedaling peers. But on

fast-moving arterials, sharing the lane with car-bound traffic is often uncomfortable for cautious bicyclists, whether or not there is a sharrow. In a shared lane, a driver will need to pull out to the left to pass a bicyclist—and it's the driver's discretion how close to get before moving to the left as well as how much room to

Bike lane crossing rails

give between the car and the person on the bike while passing.

For people in cars, sharrows offer a nice visual reminder that they should expect to see bicyclists on this road. For people on bikes, they serve quite a few purposes.

SHARROWS AS LANE POSITIONERS

The sharrow's placement in the bike lane indicates where to ride. Follow the line down the middle of each sharrow to stay a safe distance from the right edge of the road, a zone where a car door might swing open. This, however, only applies to well-placed sharrows. In Seattle, many of the older sharrows are painted on the right edge of the lane, which mistakenly encourages people to bike as far right as possible. Proper riding technique (coming up in Chapter 6) calls for keeping as far right as is *safe*, not as far right as *possible*. Use the sharrow to remind yourself of this riding technique, but if it seems poorly placed, use your better judgment.

SHARROWS AS SAFE ROUTING AIDS

A succession of sharrows can be used to guide bikers along the best path through a tricky spot in the road, such as a curving maneuver to cross train tracks at a perpendicular angle.

SHARROWS FOR WAYFINDING

Sharrows with chevrons oriented in a different direction than straight ahead are used to indicate turns when following a bike route.

Bike lane with bicyclist push button

BIKE LANES

Bike lanes are four- to six-feet-wide sections in the road marked by a solid white line and a bike icon. They're usually on the right side of the road, either next to the curb or a car parking lane, and are for use by bicycles only—not pedestrians, motorcycles, or cars.

Bike lanes separate bikes from cars, which makes for a more comfortable ride than sharrow biking. Lane positions are clearly defined, with room for a person driving to fit alongside a person riding a bike, without having to swing outside the lane to make room.

I most often appreciate my bike lane for allowing me to chug along at a comfortable pace while people in cars whiz by to my left. They're not swerving around me like they would be in a sharrow situation, and I'm not continuously glancing back over my shoulder as I hear an approaching car.

Separate spaces for travel means bikers can comfortably travel at different rates of speed than cars—and this goes both ways. Even better is when dozens of cars are backed up at a red light and it's clear sailing in the bike lane all the way to the intersection. Sometimes lanes with sharrows have enough shoulder for bikers to navigate past a line of stopped cars, but that's not a given. There's *always* room to do so in a bike lane. This, I feel, is what bike commuting is all about—being in constant motion even in a situation where cars are stopped in big backups, not to mention that moving to the front of the red light places you away from exhaust pipes, as discussed in Chapter 1.

Keep in mind, a line of paint to separate car space from bike space certainly doesn't keep everyone in his designated spot. Bike lanes are often placed right against the lane for parked cars, putting you in the "door zone" (see Chapter 6). This

Mixing zone

is the space in which a person will swing the door open to exit the car. Besides watching for doors, you'll have to watch for cars as they pull into a parking spot and pull out to re-enter traffic.

In bike lanes against the edge of the road, there are no doors to fear. However, gravel, glass, and other road debris collects here—and might poke at your tires. Drainage grates are another hazard found on the edge of the road.

The different kinds of bike lanes listed below all attempt, in varying degrees, to keep bikes and cars in their designated spaces on the road.

MIXING ZONES

Bike lanes are made up of long lengths of solid white paint lines encouraging separate areas for bikes and cars, but there are many situations that call for mixing zones, where bikes and cars share the space for a bit. This might happen when the road narrows for a bridge or similar reason, or near an intersection. Sometimes the bike lane turns into a sharrow to indicate mixing, and sometimes the bike lane simply disappears with no warning. Needless to say, finding that the bike lane has disappeared isn't the most comfortable approach to a mixing zone; the two treatments following make for a more predictable reaction.

Dashed Lines

Some areas of bike lanes that allow for the mixing of cars and bikes are indicated by a dashed line. This is common at the approach to an intersection to show where right-turning drivers should cross into the bike lane, either to get into a right-turn lane on the opposite side of the bike lane or to move into a bike lane that is doing double duty as the right-turn lane.

Dashed lines are also sometimes used as visual aids through an intersection, much like the way sharrows are used as safe routing aids. In fact, bike-lane-width dotted lines through intersections often have sharrows painted in the middle.

Green Paint

Green paint can also indicate a mixing zone, sometimes with dashed lines to really drive the point home. The bright paint acts as a visual reminder for people in cars changing lanes or crossing intersections to watch for people on bikes traveling along the green strip.

CONTRA-FLOW BIKE LANES

Most bike lanes flow in the same direction of traffic, but contra-flow bike lanes allow bikes to ride against the flow. Contra-flow

Contra-flow bike lane

bike lanes work nicely on one-way streets: one direction is for cars and bikes sharing the main lane; the other direction is just for bikes in the bike lane. Sometimes contra-flow bike lanes are installed temporarily to help bicyclists navigate around construction zones.

As you can probably guess, contra-flow bike lanes work nicely on streets with slow-moving traffic. The one pictured on the previous page routes bicyclists one block, from a multi-use trail to a bridge that connects to many points south. This contra-flow bike lane provides a direct route, not to mention it is the only option with a gentle slope. These are the sort of bicycle facilities that make city riding a true joy—a little gem of a block that makes me feel like a VIP.

BUFFERED BIKE LANES

A buffered bike lane is a standard bike lane with a separated section on one or both sides. The buffer is comprised of parallel white lines, often with hash marks or chevrons between them to create a visual separation between the bike lane and adjacent lane. Buffers vary in width but are usually two or three feet wide.

Left-Side Buffer

A buffered area to the left of the bike lane creates space between the car travel lane and the bike lane. It also serves as space for fast bike lane users to pass slower bike lane users without having to enter the car travel lane.

Right-Side Buffer

If the bike lane is alongside a parking lane, a buffered area to the right of the bike lane makes room for the car door zone. This is the most common reason for a right-side buffer.

PROTECTED BIKE LANES

Protected bike lanes are physically separated from motor vehicle traffic. The barriers may be made of any number of things:

> Raised curb
> Planters
> Bollards (short posts)
> Parked cars with the passenger side toward the protected bike lane

Protected bike lanes come in one-way and two-way varieties. Either type can be installed on a one-way or two-way street. They can be in the street, raised to sidewalk level, or somewhere in between.

Protected bike lanes feel like bike paths, as they are situated away from cars and take up little space. Intersections and driveways still penetrate the protected zone—especially dangerous since the protected portions inspire a sense of safety—but mixing zones are well marked with dashed lines and/or green paint, and intersections use signage and often even separate stoplights for the bike lane and the main travel lane.

Protected bike lanes are also called "cycle tracks," but for some that term connotes cycle-*racing* track, or velodrome.

Two-way protected bike lane with barriers   *Two-way protected bike lanes with plastic flexposts*

MULTI-USE TRAILS

Off-street trails make for great commute corridors. Multi-use trails (also called shared-use paths) are used by pedestrians, bicyclists, skaters, equestrians, and other nonmotorized users. This means bicyclists are often the fastest path users and must be careful and aware of slower company. Some trails have speed limits, often 15 mph, but there is no national standard, with "a safe speed" being the recommendation. In most cases, the trail still intersects with roadways here and there, but often far less frequently than on-street bike facilities. This makes for much less stop-and-go and less room for conflict with other vehicles.

Multi-use trails have to be at least ten feet wide—much wider than the average sidewalk—which makes them especially popular for walking with dogs or biking with children. When you cycle along multi-use trails, be prepared for encounters with these unpredictable trail users.

Still, many commuters prefer spending time on these people-powered highways, even if they have to slow down a bit, to spending time on the street.

NEIGHBORHOOD GREENWAYS

Neighborhood Greenways are quiet side streets optimized for people on bikes and on foot, thanks to a few changes. The names of these types of streets vary from city to city—they're called Bicycle Boulevards by NACTO (the National Association of City Transportation Officials) and Neighborways in Boston.

Neighborhood Greenways also vary in their execution. In Seattle, they started as a grassroots effort but were adopted by the Department of Transportation (see profile of Seattle Neighborhood Greenways in this chapter). So far each street has a slightly different implementation, ranging from simple signage and road paint to signs, paint, speed humps,

Seattle Neighborhood Greenways

Fear of unsafe streets can be a big obstacle blocking many people from happy bicycling—or bicycling at all. That's where Seattle Neighborhood Greenways comes in. Formed in 2011, it began with six neighbors who met in a church basement to talk about how they could bring low-traffic, bike- and pedestrian-friendly streets known as "neighborhood greenways" to Seattle. Since then it has grown into a vast coalition of volunteers who advocate for safe streets policies and infrastructure all across the city.

In more than twenty different neighborhood groups, volunteers scout their neighborhoods for the best places to put neighborhood greenways, and identify streets and intersections in need of safety improvements. Together, they lobbied to get nearly 250 miles of neighborhood greenways into Seattle's 2013 Bicycle Master Plan update, unanimously passed by the Seattle City Council in April, 2014.

When, all too frequently, people get seriously injured or killed while walking or biking, the Seattle Neighborhood Greenways organization holds Memorial Walks and Rides to honor these victims of traffic violence and look for practical solutions to remedy the problem. They also put pressure on the city to adopt "Vision Zero," for a future free from traffic violence.

By speaking up during budget hearings, the collective advocacy of Greenways volunteers has directed millions of dollars into safe, family-friendly street infrastructure. More importantly, volunteers and staff in Seattle Neighborhood Greenways have helped change the conversation in Seattle, getting their neighbors, elected officials, and transportation officials behind the idea that streets are for all people, not just for cars.

Seattle Neighborhood Greenways has a vision for Seattle, a vision of a vast linked network of streets where people feel happy biking, walking, and meeting their friends and neighbors. A vision of a city where not a single person is seriously injured or killed in a traffic collision. A place where top-notch infrastructure like protected bike lanes and greenways get people of all ages and abilities walking and biking from their homes to the places they need to go.

cross-traffic stop signs, and traffic diverters depending on its budget and the current recommendations. But they all have the same goal of slowing speeds while optimizing all travel along the greenway. Neighborhood Greenways don't look very different from other side streets, but the addition of traffic-calming measures makes a big difference when using them. Many Neighborhood Greenways feature:

› Reduced speed limits (20 mph or 15 mph)
› Traffic-calming devices, such as speed humps
› Sharrows
› Stop signs for cross traffic coming from other quiet streets
› Traffic lights for crossing busy streets
› Curb cuts/curb ramps for sidewalk users

Some Neighborhood Greenways wend their way through neighborhoods with turns marked by directional sharrows and street signs. Additional signs often point out directions to other neighborhoods or points of interests like schools and libraries. Between these markings, Neighborhood Greenways take on the feel of slow-moving bicycle thoroughfares.

Neighborhood Greenways are considered "Complete Streets," enabling safe access for all users, regardless of age, ability, or mode of transportation—appealing to inexperienced and risk-averse bicyclists. Compared to protected bike lanes and shared-used paths, they don't cost much to implement. My ideal commute from my quiet neighborhood to our bustling downtown would be taking a Neighborhood Greenway from my front door to a nearby multi-use trail that cuts through several bigger neighborhoods to protected bike lanes in the downtown core area. Those three elements exist on my commute, but there are less comfortable roads with sharrows and regular bike lanes in between.

///////////////

RAILS TO TRAILS

Rails-to-Trails Conservancy is a non-profit organization whose mission is to create a nationwide network of trails from former rail lines and connecting corridors to build healthier places for healthier people. Today, more than 20,000 miles of rail-trail form the backbone of a growing trail system that spans communities, regions, and states. More than 9,000 miles of potential rail-trails are waiting to be built.

///////////////

BIKE BOXES

A bike box is a designated area at an intersection with a traffic signal. Set at the front of a lane or multiple lanes, it provides an area for bicyclists to get in front of motor vehicle traffic during red lights. This makes you more visible to the people in cars behind you and puts you apart from exhaust pipes—always a good thing. Bike boxes are often painted

Bike box

green, contain bicycle icons, and are accompanied by signs showing the placement of cars behind the bike box.

HOW TO USE A BIKE BOX

If the light is red, enter the bike box via the bike lane and position yourself according to the direction you're going.

Left turn. Move to the left side of the bike box and signal a left turn. If the bike box is in front of two lanes, one of them being a left-turn lane, line up in front of that left-turn lane.

Proceeding straight. Move to the middle of the bike box.

Right turn. Stay in the bike lane on the right edge and signal a right turn. If a right-turning lane crosses over the bike lane, leave the bike lane to turn right, just as you would in the same situation without a bike box.

LEFT-TURN BOX

Have you heard of the *Copenhagen Left*? Left-turn boxes are placed to help you make two-stage turns, which most commonly go by the exotic-sounding moniker: the "Copenhagen Left."

Making a left turn can be easy if you find yourself on a narrow one-lane street

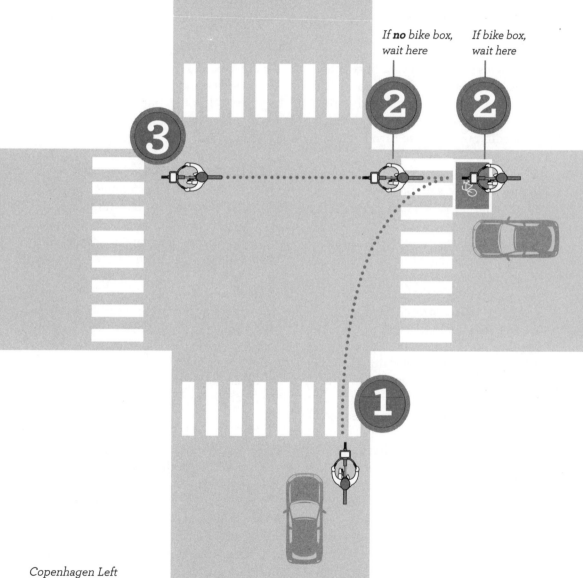

If **no** bike box, wait here

If bike box, wait here

Copenhagen Left

riding in the center. But added street width makes moving to the proper position to turn left a little trickier. Consider how you'd make a left turn in the following two-way traffic situations:

> You're in a bike lane on the right side of the main travel lane.
> You're using the right lane of a road with two lanes traveling in your direction.
> You're traveling in the one lane that flows in your direction, but there's a left turn lane into which cars are speeding up to use to turn left but also to overtake you.

In each of these situations you *can* move left to perform your left turn and many bicyclists do this as a rule, but if you are more cautious, or if there's simply not an opening in traffic, a two-stage turn is a lot easier.

To perform a Copenhagen Left, you proceed through the intersection as if you were going straight and stop near the corner on the far side of the street. Reorient yourself to face your desired direction so once the light changes you're ready to head straight (formerly left). However, it can be a bit confusing to stop near the corner, especially in congested areas, so the left-turn box provides a spot to stop that's visible to bicyclists performing Copenhagen Lefts and cars driving near the area. The box will probably be behind the crosswalk well clear of the intersection.

Making a Copenhagen Left involves waiting for an extra light cycle, but it's much faster than the three right turns my father would perform in the car rather than make a left, while my brother and I groaned from the back seat. He really didn't like making left turns! The Copenhagen Left is a similar concept, just with less groaning and gas guzzling.

BICYCLE-SPECIFIC TRAFFIC LIGHTS

Traffic lights and sensors specifically for bicyclists help direct traffic in a predictable way and allow people on bikes and people in cars to coexist on the road.

BICYCLE SIGNALS

Bicycle-specific traffic signals are red, yellow, and green just like standard traffic lights, except that the light shows a bicycle icon and is usually accompanied by a Bike Signal sign. These special lights are placed at intersections that have standard traffic lights. When the bike signal turns green first, bikes can safely proceed through an intersection before cars are allowed to make turns. If the car signal turns green first, people on bikes wait while turning cars clear the intersection.

BICYCLE SENSORS

Loop detectors are wires placed an inch and a half deep in the pavement to trigger the light to change in a bicyclist's favor. The metal in your bike trips the sensor by breaking the magnetic field. They're big—the width of a car—and designed to be triggered by cars, but many are adjusted to detect people on bikes too.

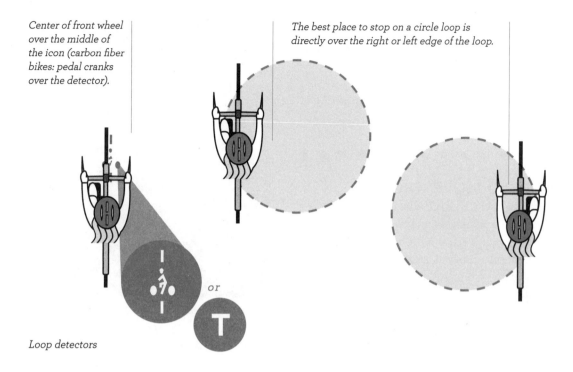

Center of front wheel over the middle of the icon (carbon fiber bikes: pedal cranks over the detector).

The best place to stop on a circle loop is directly over the right or left edge of the loop.

or

Loop detectors

Small bicycle icons are stenciled over the spot where you should place the rim of your bicycle to trigger the light. The standard marking is the "pole-dancing bike"—a small bicyclist icon with a line above and below—but you might also see a simple T (see illustration). I put the center of my front wheel over the middle of the icon, but riders of carbon fiber bikes are advised to move a bit forward and place their pedal cranks over the detector because there is more metal there to trip the sensor.

Even when there is no stencil, you can usually see the outline of a loop detector and place your bike in the proper spot to trigger the signal. Loops come in a variety of shapes, but circular loops are the most common—because they're the most economical. The best place to stop on a circle loop is directly over the right or left edge of the loop.

As stated above, *some* loop detectors aren't adjusted to work with bikes so if I find myself at an empty intersection—meaning no vehicle stopped at the oncoming light, triggering the light for both of us, and no expectation of a car pulling up behind me anytime soon, and if the pedestrian walk button is easily accessible (near the corner with curb cut well-placed for me to get to it)—I'll push the button and return to the street and wait for the light to change. Or when I have passengers, I will send one of my children on the fun errand of hopping off the bike to push the button! Or if I'm feeling conversational and someone crosses the street in front of me, I'll solicit her to push the walk button for me on her way by.

///////////////

READ MORE ABOUT BICYCLE FACILITIES

If you find bicycle treatments fascinating and want to learn more about their usage—perhaps to make suggestions for additions in your own city—see the National Association of City Transportation Officials (NACTO) publication. *Urban Bikeway Design Guide*, available free online at http://nacto.org/cities-for-cycling/design -guide or for purchase through Island Press.

///////////////

WAYFINDING SIGNS

I am a sucker for a well-marked bike route—no need to memorize the rights and lefts when a bike route jogs its way through neighborhood after neighborhood. Simply follow the arrows on the green signs or the painted route advice on the road.

PAVEMENT MARKINGS

Sharrows indicate the sharing of the road but also lead people down long and

Wayfinding sign on a Portland Bicycle Boulevard

convoluted bike routes. Regular, straight-pointing sharrows confirm you're heading the correct way, and directional sharrows advise turns along the route. You may also see words, like "Bike Route" with associated arrows or "bike dots"—12-inch circles with bikes in the middles, no arrow to indicate straight routing and small triangles to indicate upcoming turns.

DIRECTIONAL SIGNS

Directional signs mark or confirm bike routes and direct bicyclists to popular destinations. Directional signs use arrows, or arrows combined with mileage. Some even show arrows, mileage, and the minutes to your destination.

CHAPTER 6

Riding Techniques

A LOT OF US haven't biked regularly since adolescence. Seeing our familiar streets from behind the handlebars of our grown-up bike, after experiencing them through the windows of a cozy steel cage, can be a little daunting. My fears were increased when I first found myself responsible for keeping others safe: my two children each riding on his own separate bike (rather than on my bike where I'm in control) and friends to whom I was showing a new route. But being out there and experiencing the same predictable driving—and noting any unpredictable driving well in advance—was easier the second time, and then the third time, and now it's a joy to parade along with kids and/or friends in tow, calling out landmarks and hazards alike. The more you ride your bike, the more comfortable you'll be and for a lot of reasons: you'll get stronger, your repeat routes will become more familiar, you'll recognize traffic quirks (such as the rush of people just off the 8:55 bus that fills the street despite the red light), and you'll feel more at ease riding alongside cars.

Bicycling is safe. The National Highway Traffic Safety Administration annual statistics for traffic-crash fatalities show in 2013 there were 32,719 total fatalities; 21,132 were in passenger vehicles, 4,668 were motorcyclists, 4,735 were pedestrians, and just 743 were bicyclists. For most of us, though, reading statistics typically isn't encouragement enough to leave our comfort zone and participate in a new activity that might not look completely safe at first glance. For me, gaining familiarity with the rules of the road helped ease me out of my comfort zone and send me spinning on my way.

Following proper riding techniques will help you feel more confident on your bike in traffic as well as further increase your own safety and the safety of other road and bikeway users around you. To drive a car you must follow a set of rules and be trained and tested before receiving a license. While much of it is common sense, some of it really needs to be learned and memorized. The same goes for biking—you'll naturally perform many safe riding techniques thanks to your common sense, but there are a few counterintuitive things—like avoiding bike lanes painted in door zones—that all riders should learn before heading out on the road to avoid alarming near misses. There's a bit of etiquette to pick up too.

Mostly, you just ride. And ride and ride and ride. There's not too much to it: you go, you stop, and you turn. Don't delay getting out there and giving it a go. After all, it's just like riding a bike.

▰ ▰ ▰ ▰ ▰ ▰ ▰ ▰ ▰ ▰ ▰ ▰

BIKERS ED

Urban riding skills classes with classroom and on-bike components are available in many cities and are terrific, especially if you feel hesitant to start biking. The League of American Bicyclists offers many classes in their Smart Cycling program. Classes are offered across the country by certified League Cycling Instructors (LCIs). Their Traffic Skills 101, Traffic Skills 201, and Commuting classes are particularly suited to bicycling in urban areas; check out their website for more details.

Local organizations also offer classes. For example, Seattle's Cascade Bicycle Club offers Urban Cycling Techniques. The class consists of a three-hour, lecture-only evening session and a second five-hour, on-the-bike session on the weekend. Check out your city's bike clubs and organizations for similar classes.

▰ ▰ ▰ ▰ ▰ ▰ ▰ ▰ ▰ ▰ ▰ ▰

RIDING DEFENSIVELY

I am the person who looks the wrong way up every one-way street I pass. Usually twice. I've seen too many people driving the wrong direction on the streets in my neighborhood to take anything for granted. Nor do I expect people to stop at stop signs and red lights or drive on the correct side of a traffic circle as they approach me. Despite my overly cautious and completely untrusting approach, being out on my bike is still the best feeling in the world. And my good mood isn't usually ruined when I see traffic infractions, because I can spot them before they get too close for comfort. Only once in five years and over 10,000 miles have I had a close call.

My close call occurred while biking through an intersection, when a woman ignored her red light to speed across the limit line and through the entire crosswalk to jerk to a sudden stop at the corner, half in the travel lane, awaiting an opening to make a right turn on red. I don't think she saw me, and the couple inches of space between her car and my tire were pure luck. She zipped off before my heart stopped racing, and now I've added intersections near highway off-ramps to my list of road sections to be especially cautious around—and have switched my routing at that intersection in particular.

Riding defensively means being aware of what's going on around you:
> Constantly evaluate the road around you.
> Take the initiative to be safe, rather

than trusting others to always follow the rules of the road.

› Expect the unexpected.

A defensive rider will look both ways even when the light is green, take up the whole lane to avoid getting hooked by a car turning right, and be preemptive by signaling turns and using lights even during the day.

Riding defensively *doesn't* mean going out there scared. It's very hard to get hit when you're being defensive. There are countless times when I'm out riding that I see a driver who doesn't see me. I might not like that her car drifts into the bike lane in front of me, but I don't feel in any danger. Nor do I feel bad for her when she belatedly notices me and thinks she came close to hitting me. I wave and smile and hope she'll pay more attention in the future, and feel glad that I've become exceptionally good at intuiting bizarre traffic moves.

MAKE EYE CONTACT

Making eye contact isn't a guarantee that someone won't try to quickly make a left turn in front of you from across an intersection, but it does let you know you've been seen. Try to catch the eyes of people around you as much as possible, especially at intersections. You'll also notice people walking trying to catch your eye. The Law of Gross Tonnage is at work here (see below). People on foot might find you a bit intimidating and want verification that they've been seen by you.

PERCEIVED SAFETY

Some bicycle facilities simply look safer than others, like a raised curb separating the bike lane from the car lane versus a faded sharrow in the middle of the right lane of a four-lane 35-mph thoroughfare. That "safe" separated bike lane has lurking dangerous spots and the "unsafe" shared road is safer than one would think, but our perception makes one more appealing than the other. The perceived safety of the separated bike lane makes it welcoming for bicyclists, particularly those out-of-practice bike riders who will feel more confident about getting back on their bikes and riding with this infrastructure.

Of course, perceived safety doesn't mean that a protected bike lane is perfectly safe. Critics of protected bike lanes warn that their intersections are much less safe. It's important to be aware of spots like intersections and driveways, where it pays to be especially cautious.

Thankfully, perceived safety is being studied, and programs like PeopleForBikes' Green Lane Project, which is collaborating with US cities to install protected bike lanes, are seeing increased usage. The more bicycle facilities are perceived as safe and inviting, the more people will use them. The more drivers grow accustomed to seeing bikes and interacting with them in bike-and-car mixing zones, the safer it will be for everyone.

BE AWARE OF BLIND SPOTS

Being careful about staying out of blind spots is an easy way to keep diligent about being seen. These are the most common blind spots for people driving motor vehicles:

› Directly alongside the car
› Out of sight of mirrors—if you can't see a car's mirrors, the person driving that car can't see you.

OBEY THE LAW OF GROSS TONNAGE

The larger vessel has the right-of-way. Caveat, the Law of Gross Tonnage is not written for bicycling. In fact, it's not even a law; it's a nautical term. It's also referred to as "the law of common sense on the water," but the principle holds true on the road, too, and its message resonates with cautious or novice people on bikes.

In the water, the larger vessel is less maneuverable, might have trouble seeing smaller boats, and will do more damage in a collision. It's easy to see the correlation to cars and bikes on the street. We're taught in Drivers Education classes to never seize the right-of-way. Every day I witness a lot of people who have apparently forgotten this lesson, but thankfully I remember it and am even more inclined to abide by it when I'm on my small two-wheeled "vessel."

Some days it's frustrating to repeatedly be denied the right-of-way. I'll often arrive at an intersection first, only to have to wait for a person who would rather accelerate and beat me through rather than yield the right-of-way. I might be a bit of a cynic, but since I'm used to experiencing this, I often stop just before the intersection to let speeding cross traffic pass through, rather than wonder if I'll be spotted and given my right-of-way. As a car flies through the intersection, it's often obvious the other person hasn't even seen me waiting off to the side, further supporting the Law of Gross Tonnage.

The Law of Gross Tonnage also comes into play with perceived safety. While noodling around in a rowboat, I'm much more comfortable in the quiet shallow waters near small bird-inhabited islands than while crossing the ship canal between the boat dock and said islands. Following the same strategy on the road and taking the vessels with higher gross tonnage out of the equation (they'll still sail through the occasional intersection) makes for a more appealing bike commute.

RIDING PREDICTABLY

One of the safest things you can do—more than covering your body and bike with bright lights, reflectors, and ultrabright colors while dinging a loud bell repeatedly—is to ride predictably. Being predictable equals being visible. A big part of this is simply riding in a straight line.

Here's an example: When riding on streets without bike lanes, it's tempting to take up as little room as possible, ducking closer to the curb whenever you find yourself next to a string of open parking spots providing space for drivers to pass. I used to do this all the time and see others do it as well. But by doing this, you're swerving in and out of traffic, making yourself less visible and less safe. Instead, you should confidently ride in a straight line, always in the lane. This way you stay visible, even though it means feeling exposed. Remember, it is the duty of the vehicle passing you to curve around you, pulling out into the next lane of traffic, even if it's over a yellow line, when it's safe.

RIDE AS FAR TO THE RIGHT AS PRACTICAL

All fifty states have bike laws that say to ride "as far to the right as practicable." Don't misinterpret "as far right as *practical*" as "as far right as *possible*." While it's possible to ride an inch away from the right curb, it's not at all practical—there's no room to avoid debris and other hazards and it invites people driving to pass much too closely. It's counterintuitive to a lot of people who are new to riding in cities, but taking up adequate space in the lane makes you visible *and* makes you safe. Keep these three guidelines in mind:

1. Ride in the right third or middle of the lane.
2. Leave enough room to your right to maneuver away from hazards.
3. You get to decide what is practical—it's not defined.

Being predictable and sticking to that straight line also means not stopping alongside the curb at intersections to prop a foot up on the curb and stay seated in your saddle—although I hate to take away this enticing perch! Most of us keep our saddles high enough that while it's possible to reach our toes down to the ground at a stop, it's not the most comfortable position. I'll often do this, but it's usually easier to maintain my balance by sliding forward off my saddle and planting a foot flat on the ground. Heaving myself off and on the saddle at every red light is not appealing to me, but if I instead choose to move myself to the right edge of the road, I'm no longer as visible to everyone else. Now, this isn't an issue in protected bike lanes—which extend all the way to the intersection, unlike unprotected bike lanes—because the curb is mere inches from the spot in which you are riding, not multiple feet. Just one more reason to love protected bike lanes.

EVALUATE UNPREDICTABLE INFRASTRUCTURE

It's not always easy to tell what it means to be predictable. Most of the time, being predictable means riding in a straight line and making your intentions known if you're going to deviate from that straight line—but there are some streets and intersections out there that don't always allow for predictability. A not-so-predictable situation might be a right-turn lane containing forward-pointing sharrows, which indicate that people riding bikes can proceed straight. If you worry that using the right-turn lane as an OK-for-bikes-to-proceed-straight lane might confuse people in cars around you (and it might; I don't find it the most sensical marking), ignore these lane markings and follow in the predictable manner: use the right-turn lane if you're turning right and move to the right third or center of the lane to your left if you want to go straight.

Have you ever seen someone turn right from the center lane? I have. I wouldn't be surprised to find a car to my left executing a right turn, despite my presence to the right, whether or not I am placed in a right-turn lane with a forward-facing sharrow. Don't be intimidated if you encounter an unpredictable intersection—learn from it. This might mean pulling over to watch how other people treat a bike lane that suddenly ends in the middle of the block: signal early and leave the bike lane to ride in the middle of the traffic lane for the rest of the block.

I'll often stop at a five-way intersection and just wait for someone to impatiently wave me through rather than take what I think to be my turn only to have three cars barrel into the intersection at the same time. I wouldn't necessarily categorize this as my being *predictable*, but having failed to figure out the predictable way to act in this situation, I've found my safe-enough way through it. And at this point one blames the infrastructure and writes a letter to the city, meanwhile looking for an alternate route. Or keeps at it, recognizing it as a problem spot to treat with extra caution.

VEHICULAR CYCLING

Protected bike lanes are wonderful, but odds are your commute isn't entirely without some street riding, so it's critical to become proficient in what's called vehicular cycling.

Vehicular cycling, also called bicycle driving, is the practice of following the same rules that cars follow, sharing lanes as equal vehicles in traffic. Bicyclists have the same rights to the roadways, and must obey the same traffic laws as the drivers of other vehicles. These laws include stopping for stop signs and red lights, riding with the flow of traffic, signaling, using lights at night, yielding the right-of-way when entering a roadway, and yielding to pedestrians in crosswalks.

This all sounds perfectly reasonable, comfortable, and safe. And it is. On small streets. But imagine pretending to be a car on a four-lane highway, riding in the middle of the lane, trusting 45 mph traffic to pass around you, without feeling unsafe.

Vehicular cycling is actually a controversial topic. True vehicular bicyclists who identify by the term are supportive of riding in this manner *only* and feel that no bicycle facilities are needed—no sharrows, no bike lanes, and especially no protected bike lanes. The fact of the matter is that many of us simply will never feel comfortable "bicycle driving" on large streets. However, the lessons of vehicular cycling are indeed important for bicycling on regular streets . . . although for me and many others, this means regular streets that are low traffic, not fast multi-lane roads and arterials.

TAKING THE LANE

Taking the lane, also called claiming your space, means riding in the middle of the lane, taking up the entire lane, just like a

IDAHO STOP

Stopping at stop signs and waiting for red lights to change is an important part of vehicular cycling. In fact, it's an important part of any sort of bicycling, driving, and walking, but an interesting exception is the Idaho Stop.

The Idaho Stop Law makes it legal for bicyclists to treat stop signs as yield signs—they must slow down, yield to traffic in the intersection, check all directions, and stop if necessary, but can roll through if it's safe to do so. The idea is that because bicyclists move more slowly, have no blind spots, and are able to maneuver more quickly than cars, they are able to yield the right-of-way at an intersection without coming to a complete stop.

The Idaho Stop Law also allows bicyclists to treat red lights like stop signs. This is based on the same arguments as the stop-sign-as-yield-sign. It also means that, for traffic signals controlled by sensors, bicyclists don't have to worry about being unable to trigger the loop detector and cities don't have to invest in bicycle hot spots.

The Idaho Stop is currently only legal in Idaho (Idaho Code 49-720). New bicycling infrastructure—such as Neighborhood Greenways, which have stop signs only for cross traffic, and protected bike lanes, which have separate bike signals allowing bicycles to enter intersections ahead of cars—negate the need for an Idaho Stop, but its appeal is apparent for car-centric infrastructure.

In other states, the only time you are allowed to go through a red light is in the case of an unresponsive signal. From the League of American Bicyclists:

1. In most states, after three minutes, you can treat a red light as a stop sign.
2. Pass through a red light only as a last resort.

In either case, yield to other vehicles while crossing the roadway.

car does. When you ride along the right edge of a travel lane, it can appear to drivers behind you that there's room to fit alongside and pass. Most lanes don't provide enough space for a car to comfortably pass (at least three feet away, although five is better) without crossing over the lines into the neighboring lane. By riding in the middle of the lane when there is not sufficient space for side-by-side bike plus car, you demonstrate the space needed for *your* vehicle and deter dangerous overtaking. Again, this is easy to imagine doing on a 20-mph neighborhood street, but a little hard to consider on a fast multilane road or arterial.

LANE POSITION

When the lane is sufficiently wide that it's not necessary to ride in the center, position yourself on the right, one-third of the way into the lane to ensure you're visible to drivers around you. This should also keep you clear of the door zone (see Avoiding the Door Zone later in this chapter) for streets with parking on the right side.

Don't worry about performing mathematical lane division equations in your head while riding. If you think drivers behind you might think there's room to pass to your left when in fact there isn't, move out even farther into the lane. Many riders are hesitant to move left toward the middle of the lane. It's tempting to stay as far from hurtling cars as possible. However, passing motorists will usually give you the same amount of space on your left that you've left between yourself and the curb or parked car to your right. So take control of this visual cue, and experiment with what works best for you and your commute.

SIGNALING AND TURNING

So you've got riding in a straight line down pat. You'll probably want to stray from that straight line at some point, though—grocery store to the left, library to the right, money in the road at twelve o'clock! Hand signals for turning and slowing down are required by law. The signals are designed for use with the left hand and assume you're riding on the right side of the road, with your left hand most visible to traffic.

› *Left turn.* Raise your left arm straight out from your left side.
› *Right turn.* Raise left arm out to the side, elbow bent with your hand pointing straight up. Some states allow right turns signaled with right arm straight out to your right side.
› *Stop.* Raise left arm out to the side, elbow bent with your hand pointing straight down.

I learned to make my signals with a flat hand. This provides the biggest surface area, I guess, but nowadays I like to point with my forefinger to further get my message across. Of course with any hand gesture it's *very* important that no one mistake which finger is being shown. So I'm careful that I'm not accidentally glaring, and I sometimes give a little waggle to make it explicitly clear "I'm going thataway!" I'm not convinced everyone remembers the hand signals they learned way back in Drivers Ed, so I like to think my pointing is helpful in keeping my intention predictable and me safe.

Signal *before* turning or braking and for a *short* time: Signal 100 feet before your turn and hold it for a few seconds. Then place your hand back on your handlebars to turn. But if you like your signaling hand to lead you through your turn and you're confident in your one-handed turning ability, go for it! It's fun. Not to mention you're continuing to signal your intention to those around you who may not have been paying attention earlier.

CHANGING LANES

You will also use the left- and right-turn signals for changing lanes. And this is where the alternate version of the right turn signal may come in handy. Downtown cores tend to have a lot of one-way

Right turn

Alternate signal for right turn

Left turn

Stopping

streets and you might find yourself following a bike lane or line of sharrows on the left side of the road. Making your way right now seems much better served with a right-handed extended arm, doesn't it? You'll still signal left turns from the far left lane with your left hand pointing straight out.

SCANNING

Scanning—looking back over your shoulder before changing lanes—not only works for seeing what is going on around you, but also communicates to the people around you that you're planning to change your position.

To scan, touch your chin to your shoulder and look fully behind yourself. It's important you don't accidentally pull your handlebars to the side while doing this, so practice out of traffic first, like in an empty parking lot while riding along a painted line. You can also follow a suggestion from the League of American Bicyclists and take your turning-side hand off your handlebar if you have trouble keeping your bike pointed straight with it still in position. This sounds a bit unsafe to me—having both hands on your handlebars and learning to keep your bike pointed straight through practice is better. But try the hand-off-the-handlebar technique in that empty parking lot if you think it's the answer for you.

After you scan and see the coast is clear, perform your hand signal and move over one lane. If you need to cross multiple lanes of traffic, do it one lane at a time, scanning and signaling each time.

SIGNALING, SCANNING, AND HANDLEBAR TYPE

I much prefer signaling on my upright commuter bike to my road bike with lower handlebars. In fact, I hate signaling turns while traveling downhill, squeezing my brake with all my might in what feels like an awkward position. Scanning is also marginally more difficult on my road bike. I have to crane my neck more to see behind me due to the forward cant of my body. For these reasons, I tend to recommend that novice urban riders not consider riding with drop bars. There are many people who aren't bothered by this the way I am, and don't get me wrong, I love riding my road bike. However, if you find yourself reluctant to signal or feel a little antsy while changing lanes, take a look at your handlebars. Any change in angle, whether it's accomplished by a completely new set of handlebars in a different style or a different stem that moves your handlebars higher or closer to you, might change your position enough that your scanning and signaling abilities become more carefree.

LEFT TURNS, INCLUDING THE COPENHAGEN LEFT

Does crossing multiple lanes of traffic to get to a left-turn lane sound a little intimidating? I don't always care for it. Sometimes traffic just feels too busy to assert myself, and sometimes I don't have time to reposition myself—it can take a block to make my way over multiple lanes, after all.

Here are all four ways you can turn left:

> *Like a car.* Turn left from the left lane.
> *Like a pedestrian.* Dismount your bike and walk across the street, first straight across and then to the left, over two green lights.
> *Turn right and make a U-turn.* If you're leaving a major street for a quiet one, you can probably easily keep to the right and make a right turn, and then perform a U-turn on the quiet street to get set up to cross with the next green light.
> *Use the Copenhagen Left.* Proceed through the intersection as if you were going straight and stop near the corner on the far side of the street. Reorient yourself to face your desired direction so once the light changes, you're ready to head straight (formerly left). If there is room between the limit line where cars stop and the crosswalk, position yourself between the two to wait for the light. Alternatively, there may be room for you in front of the crosswalk that still doesn't have you sticking into the cross-traffic lane (often there's a setback here providing room for this maneuver). See Chapter 5 for how to use a left-turn box when performing a Copenhagen Left.

BEYOND HAND TURN SIGNALS

There are other signals and gestures beyond the basics that can be helpful too. At confusing intersections, like all-way stops or five-way intersections, I like to point to the street I'm crossing to if a simple right- or left-turn signal might not do the trick. I also like to wave while passing stopped cross traffic. It's not just a nice gesture; it's an attention grabber to ensure I'm seen, especially if I'm unable to grab eye contact. And my smile and wave are usually met with a smile back. I don't think the average driver is smiled at—or smiles herself—very often, so besides increasing my safety, I feel I'm raising the overall happiness quotient of the city.

TRAVERSING INTERSECTIONS

Just an extra word of caution about intersections. You know your signals and you know to make eye contact if possible, but there are a couple more things to be aware of as you traverse these crossings.

Bike lanes often end before intersections, which can be a bit confusing. While bikes are allowed to ride in traffic (car) lanes, cars are not allowed to drive in bike lanes, so the cessation of the bike lane provides a legal way for a car to move over and perform a right turn. It's a bad idea to stay in the space where the bike lane used to be since there may be right-turning cars. The disappearance of the bike lane hopefully makes you think that the predictable thing to do is move left, into the lane. And it is!

This is an even bigger issue when there is a right-turn lane. Do not ride to the right of a right-turn lane unless you are turning right.

The League of American Bicyclists

Cycling around town might seem like the newest thing in green and healthy living, but Americans have been bicycling—and advocating for bicycling—for over a hundred years. Founded in 1880, the nonprofit League of American Bicyclists (originally the League of American Wheelmen) leads the movement to create a bicycle-friendly America for everyone through education and advocacy. The league believes bicycling brings people together and that when more people ride bikes: *life is better for everyone; communities are safer, stronger, and better connected; our nation is healthier, economically stronger, environmentally cleaner, and more energy independent.*

The league's education program, a core activity since the late 1970s, is the basis for virtually every bicycling education program in the country. Classes are offered for brand-new bicyclists as well as experienced riders who want to refine their skills or learn to teach others. The league also offers the only nationwide cycle instructor certification program for league Cycling Instructors (LCIs), an intense three-day seminar that certifies students to teach Smart Cycling classes to adults and children.

On the advocacy side of things, the league's National Bike Summit—the premier bike advocacy event of the year—includes keynote addresses from top government officials, members of Congress, and leaders from advocacy and industry; workshops that highlight innovative advocacy ideas and trends from around the country; and a lobby day.

League-sponsored National Bike Month encourages anyone and everyone to try pedaling to work for just one day in May on Bike-to-Work Day. The most action-packed bike-commuting day of the year, Bike-to-Work Day has free breakfasts, group rides with mayors, and energizer stations with free bike-related supplies. The league's National Bike Challenge takes this to the next level, challenging people to ride as much as possible from May through September. In 2014, over 45,000 people logged close to 23 million miles in the three-month National Bike Challenge. Whether you're signed up as an individual or with a team of friends or coworkers, it's a lot of fun to watch one's spot on the leaderboard, which can be filtered for national or local results, workplaces, gender, and more.

The league's newest programs are Women Bike and Equity Initiative. Women Bike envisions creating pathways for women of diverse backgrounds to embrace biking as an everyday activity that not only improves lives, but also changes perspectives on how we move through our communities, our world, and our lives. The National Bike Summit has included a National Forum on Women & Bicycling since 2012. Through the Equity Initiative, the league works directly with local leaders of demographics underrepresented in bicycle advocacy— youth, women, and people of color—to develop bike advocacy skills and create on-going relationships. And an internal equity assessment and transformation will create a more diverse leadership within the league.

For free resources, including instructional videos and a list of state laws, visit the league's website: www.bikeleague.org.

AVOIDING THE DOOR ZONE

The door zone is the area that extends four to five feet to the left of the parking lane. Since bike lanes are four to six feet wide and the door zone is four to five feet wide, when placed next to the parking lane with no buffer, only the outer left edge of the widest bike lanes is safe. It's a frustrating and unsafe situation. Here's a bicycle facility, clearly marked where one is supposed to ride, but it's simply not safe. You should *never* ride in the door zone. A suddenly opened car door can do damage in a number of ways:

› You might crash into the open door and fall into the bike lane.
› You might crash into the open door and get thrown into traffic.
› You might swerve into traffic to avoid the open door.

The door zone is an invisible hazard. Unless you've experienced a car door opened in your path, it's easy to imagine each car as a predictable immobile structure. That's how I thought until I was biking with a friend in a paint-separated bike lane and she observed, "You like to ride in the door zone." A painted buffer separated us from moving traffic, yet the bike lane was still built into the door zone of the parked cars to our right. She was very aware of the door zone because she had been *doored* herself on this same street and only recently recuperated from the broken collarbone that resulted. So now I know to avoid the door zone.

Some bike lanes have a safe area in which to ride. They might be alongside the curb or have a buffer, either in the form of a painted street or just extra space, between bike lane and parked cars. But some are completely built within the dangerous door zone, which is confusing for people biking as well as people driving. While it doesn't threaten your predictability to ride in a straight line next to a bike lane rather than in a bike lane while avoiding the door zone, it certainly might confuse the people driving on that street.

TIP FOR DRIVERS

In the car, open the driver's side door with your right hand. This forces you to swivel your body to the left, reminding you to check for bicyclists.

I make my choices about unsafe bike lanes based on the street. If I can completely avoid a street that has a bike lane built entirely in the door zone (and there are a lot of these), I use a different street. If there's no better street, I'll ride on the outer edge of the door zone, but I don't feel very comfortable doing so. People tend to pass very closely, which I imagine is to demonstrate their displeasure at my not riding in my marked area.

There is *one* instance in which I'll ride in the door zone—if I'm riding uphill and therefore traveling slowly enough that I can see into each and every car I pass. But

even this isn't foolproof; people might bend over to retrieve items from the floorboard while simultaneously popping open the car door.

PASSING

Announce your intentions before overtaking another bicyclist or walker. Do not pass someone who is concurrently passing someone else. This puts you three abreast and takes up a lot of room. If you want to pass a pair of riders riding two abreast, one should pull in front of the other, single file, so you can more safely pass by. Wait for this to happen before you proceed.

SCAN BEFORE PASSING

Don't forget to scan over your shoulder before passing. What you are looking for: Cars if you're leaving a bike lane to pass another person biking and bikes passing you who haven't announced their intent.

WHAT TO DO WHEN PASSING

Bicyclists in New York are required to have a bell, but elsewhere it's optional. Again, I like to follow the Dutch custom that all bikes be outfitted with lights and bells, so I put bells on all my bikes. (I ride at a slow pace, so I don't do too much passing, but there's not a day that goes by that my bell doesn't come in handy.)

I know a lot of people who refuse to call out a warning before passing. My theory is that these are the people who ride fast enough that they probably don't like having to say it repeatedly as they pass so many people. They're fast and confident, but that doesn't mean the rest of us are. Doing one of the following will keep the rest of us from getting spooked:

› Say nothing but ring your bell (one ding is fine).
› Say "On your left."
› Say "Passing."

PASS ON THE LEFT

Pass on the left only. People are not expecting to be passed on the right, and it's not safe to ride somewhere you're not expected. Only pass when it's safe to do so and give plenty of warning to the person you are passing so they have time to respond.

There might be times when your only option is to pass on the right, say, if someone is riding (or walking in the case of a multi-use trail) on the left. In these cases, it's safest to slow down, given the departure from the norm, and indicate your intentions. If changing your script from "On your left" to "On your right" is confusing—I get mixed up on crowded trails with slower foot and bike traffic covering all sides of the path and worry about calling out the wrong directive and causing a dog walker to step into my path—stick to "Passing" or "Bike coming by" when navigating your way past people on the "wrong" side.

YOU DON'T HAVE TO PASS

Maybe this goes without saying, but you're not required to pass someone. If you're riding in the bike lane alongside a busy street, you're welcome to simply slow down and wait as long as necessary for a spot in which you feel completely safe to pass—or not. This doesn't mean to follow closely behind someone rather than pass—never, under any circumstance should you be less than a bike length behind another person so you have room to see hazards, such as potholes, and time to react to a sudden stop. As I say to my children (what feels like several hundred times a day as we ride our bikes together), "It's not a race." Just like the driver who's "stuck" behind a bike in traffic, you're not losing very much time by slowing down. You're still moving, after all, just marginally slower than before.

DON'T SPLIT LANES

Splitting lanes means traveling between two lanes moving in the same direction. Bicycles and motorcycles fit in this space and it's a tempting way to evade traffic slowdowns. Lane splitting is legal in California and Nebraska currently (and in Nebraska only because the law prohibits motorcycles specifically, implying that bicycles are free to do what they want).

CROSSING RAILS AND AVOIDING OBSTACLES

Ideally, bike routes don't include crossings over train, light rail, or streetcar rails, but in many cities it's unavoidable. The most important thing is to always cross at a 90-degree angle. I cringe when I watch people bolder than myself cross at 45-degree angles or less, yet their success hasn't influenced me: I always slow and hit rails at a perfect perpendicular. If you have a healthy fear around rails, dismount and walk your bike over them.

Metal rails will be slippery when wet. Crossing at a 90-degree angle still works well in wet conditions, but riskier angles are more slippery. And if you're walking across wet rails with your bike, don't step on the metal. In fact, it's best to avoid any metal object in the road, wet or dry. Grates, construction plates, and sewer covers should be avoided religiously in wet conditions, but skirting around them in dry conditions is a good idea too. Avoiding any changes in surface material will keep your wheels rolling consistently.

RIDING ON SIDEWALKS

In an ideal world, all of our streets would feel welcoming to all people on bikes, but as it is, there are a lot of people who ride on the sidewalks for part or all of their journeys. I don't blame them—cars are fast and powerful and can do a lot of damage.

It's illegal to ride on the sidewalk in many cities, and if that's the case in your city, don't. Walk your bike for unrideable portions if you can't find an alternate route to avoid breaking the law. But for a lot of commuters in cities with legal sidewalk riding, a short jog along the sidewalk makes a route work.

Riding on the sidewalk feels safer to a lot of bicyclists, especially along fast-moving roads with no bicycle facilities—and sometimes even for fast-moving roads *with* bike lanes—but there are many hidden dangers. If you're just getting started, and know what to look for and how to ride, a few blocks along the sidewalk next to a busy arterial can be a good option to turn a harried commute into a less stressful experience. Riding on the sidewalk, however, should never be a sustained approach.

If you do ride on the sidewalk, follow these guidelines:

Go slow, no faster than a jogger. This will allow you to safely move among pedestrians and to be more readily spotted by cars at intersections.

Yield to all pedestrians. Don't pass walkers unless it is safe, and politely ask or warn with your voice—your bell is for the street or trail only, and not appropriate on the sidewalk.

Be extra cautious at every intersection. Drivers don't expect bikes to enter the intersection from the sidewalk and the faster you're moving, the less time you both have to react.

Slow down and check every driveway and doorway. Motorists entering driveways and people exiting passenger-side doorways are big underestimated dangers on the sidewalk.

Watch for obstructions. In addition to pedestrians, be prepared to navigate around recycling bins, bus stops, poles, and other sidewalk furniture.

Ride on the sidewalk on the right side of the road. Drivers pulling out of alleys, parking lots, and driveways are looking for an opening in traffic onto this busy

Painfully accurate "Beware of rails" sign

road and will look left first (or only). Approaching from the other side lessens your chances of being seen.

Be prepared to walk if it's too crowded. Rather than remaining glued to your saddle, be prepared to become a pedestrian-pushing-a-bike if the sidewalk is too congested to allow you to ride safely. Don't worry, it will probably be for only a block or two.

Sometimes sidewalks provide the benefit of an avoidance route. If traffic is backed up behind a stopped garbage truck, and it's legal to take to the sidewalk, catch the next driveway up and turn off the backed-up street. I figure we bike commuters are due these concessions. And I hope that while watching me easily skirt around traffic, a driver might be moved to think about bicycling as a means of getting around.

SALMONING

Salmoning on a bike is riding the wrong way—akin to swimming upstream. Salmoning is usually riding the wrong way on a one-way street, but can also be using the bike lane or shared lane on the wrong side of a two-way street.

People might choose to salmon to save time—it's quicker to take the closest street the wrong direction rather than ride an extra block to the street in the right direction. Or rather than wait for a light to change, taking the bike lane on the wrong side of the street to save a precious minute.

No matter the reason, it's extremely unsafe and accounts for 25 percent of bicycle-car collisions. Situations where you are tempted to salmon are perfect for walking your bike along the sidewalk if there's no better route.

I like to repeat the mantra, "This would be a great place for a protected two-way bike lane," and perhaps someday it will be added.

■■■■■■■■■■■■■

TALK, DON'T DING

Ringing your bike bell on the sidewalk is not the appropriate way to announce your presence. You should be traveling at or near walking pace, but you'll inevitably need to pass a few people—*slowly*—and must do so courteously.

I have three bells and don't even ding the quietest of them, nor do I bark "On your left." I like to keep it a bit more conversational. I'm moving slowly enough that there's time to call out a whole sentence. "Hi, I'm going to pass by on your left. Thanks!" And even with that, I sometimes receive a glare or—even worse because it makes me ache for a better infrastructure that would make me feel safe on the road—an "Oh, sorry!" as if the pedestrian were at fault.

■■■■■■■■■■■■■

SHARING MULTI-USE TRAILS

Many of my destinations involve some riding on a multi-use trail and it's the best part of the ride. It's safe to admire the view of the lake even while moving along at a good clip because any hazard looming up ahead is easy to spot well ahead of time. At the right time of day, I can go entire blocks without passing anyone. Multi-use trails aren't without their share of hazards, though. There are usually people walking two or three abreast, dogs on long leashes, and intersections with streets.

On multi-use trails, pedestrians have the right-of-way, so pass carefully. Most multi-use trails have signs requiring "Use Voice or Bell to Pass." There's always going to be someone who thinks "On your left!" means "You're in my way, move right!" and someone who thinks it means "Look over your left shoulder and veer left into my path," so always say it from far enough away—and therefore loud enough—that you have room to maneuver or slow down. That said, I also get many thank-yous.

Pedestrians (and bicyclists) on multi-use trails might use headphones so your voice might not be loud enough. If you see headphones, use your bell. A friend of mine whose daily commute takes her along a multi-use trail has two bells: her regular bell for initial warning and her louder bell if the first one isn't heard. You should always pass cautiously, but especially so if you think you haven't been heard.

Observe any posted speed limits; otherwise, move at a pace that allows you to adjust your course or stop easily. If you're riding in a group, ride single file. Above all, remember that the trail isn't your highway—be courteous and share.

LEARN MORE

The Ride Smart program from The League of American Bicyclists provides tips, rules, videos, and classes. The videos are especially helpful if a class is not offered in your city, or for immediate visual explanation of riding techniques.

DEALING WITH AGGRESSIVE OR UNSAFE MOTORISTS

Hopefully all of your disagreements with drivers will be of the "You go first; No, you go first" variety, but some drivers get unduly angry with bicyclists. Maybe it's jealousy of our ability to avoid most traffic, or oddly displayed fear at being near a vulnerable road user. Some people are just incredibly angry drivers and feel safe within their tank-like cars to overreact to any perceived slight.

The best medicine for dealing with aggressive motorists is: Don't start it. It is all too tempting to shout at drivers to stop texting, and I sometimes daydream about thumping the trunks of cars stopped in the bike lane . . . but I don't. I have yelled when scared by a texting driver a couple times and it doesn't leave me feeling satisfied. Let it go, but for truly dangerous situations, call 911. Take a photo of the driver, license plate, and car, showing color and make if possible.

My method for coping with unsafe drivers is to skew my behavior far in the other direction. Every driver who screeches to a stop across the limit line, coming closer to me than would have been the case had he noticed me earlier, gets a wave. I've discovered I'm not the only bicyclist to have adopted this behavior. The wave is essentially a "Thanks for not needlessly injuring me with your inattention!" While it might not match the severity of the situation, it allows me to go about my day with my good mood intact. And while to the motorist it may appear that she almost struck me, I probably saw her coming, as I sadly always assume drivers won't obey traffic laws and am always subconsciously prepared to move my bike out of the line of attack. I don't think it's a bad thing for the driver to not realize all the effort I've put into the situation, and I hope she will be inspired to drive more cautiously in the future.

The wave works for dealing with aggressive behavior too. In this case, it's more of an "I didn't hear you, but you're probably shouting hello!" wave or an "OK, I hear that you're angry, but let's try to get along!" Either way, the "Let it go" wave shouldn't escalate the situation the way returning the sentiment would.

Taking obvious photographs of aggressive motorists will sometimes cause the yelling to stop. Bicyclists who commute with helmet cams (video cameras affixed to the tops of their helmets) tell me they have experienced less in the way of road rage since adding the camera to their safety gear. So, armed with the knowledge of what to do *just in case* someone unpleasant crosses your path, rest assured you'll have an overly positive experience out there on the road. It's not unreasonable to expect to never be yelled at or passed too closely, and only enjoy the exchange of smiles and waves with your fellow road users.

CHAPTER 7
The Route

HAVING A GOOD ROUTE for your grocery store run or daily commute to work can make all the difference between a carefree endorphin boost that sets the tone for a great day versus a stress-inducing battle with two-ton metal boxes that makes you want to stow your bike at the back of the garage.

My routes evolve over time, and yours probably will too. I usually do some research before heading somewhere by bike the first time with the expectation of finding a good-enough (i.e., perceptibly safe-enough) route. Odds are the best bike route won't mirror a familiar car or bus route. And just as there are often a variety of car routes from point A to point B, there are multiple good bike routes. One, for days with pleasant weather and time to spare, might be a longer but more scenic route with less hill climbing and fewer intersections. The others might be shorter but with different tricky spots (like a left turn onto a busy street or a five-way intersection notorious for impatient drivers). I'll decide which route to take depending on the time of day or my mood.

EVALUATING A GOOD BIKE ROUTE

We won't all have the same criteria—I know people who actually seek out hills! I tend to choose comfort over speed, but I do like to know the faster routes just in case I'm running late, although it may mean busier streets. Consider the following elements when planning your bike route:

› Type of bicycle facility (like me, you may find multi-use trails, protected bike lanes, and greenways preferable to regular bike lanes and busy roads with sharrows)
› Speed of traffic
› Volume of traffic at your time of travel
› Road conditions (potholes, metal construction patches, or current blockages)
› Presence of streetcar or train rails
› Hills (in terms of both ascent and descent)
› Scenery
› Street lights if used in the dark

Here are some things I consider when I'm thinking about a ride:

Length. It's OK for your bike route to be much longer. Divorce yourself from the idea that your bike commute must be as quick as possible. You might feel trapped in your car during a driving commute, but your bike is hardly a jail. You'll enjoy your ride whether it's 20 minutes or 30. There's nothing wrong with a route twice as long as the direct route if it makes for a more comfortable ride. When new to biking on Seattle's hills, I would travel forty blocks out of the way (twenty north to the hill I could manage and then twenty back south to my destination) to make my way around an intimidatingly steep hill. I no longer have to go quite so far out of the way, but I still don't choose to go as the crow flies.

Major obstacles. Do you need to cross or bypass a river or freeway? Some bridges or overpasses might be better candidates than others, dictating a big part of your route. For example, to cross the freeway a few blocks east of my house, I can head directly east and use the sidewalk of the arterial overpass, or I can travel a half mile in either direction to go under the freeway to the south on a multi-use trail, or go to the north in a paint-separated bike lane. My destination will usually dictate which route I choose, but the multi-use trail is by far the safest.

Avoid the bus (or don't). Sharing lanes with buses is scary and uncomfortable, but this doesn't mean bus routes must be avoided. Some buses may come by only every 20 or 30 minutes; seeing one bus on a given ride isn't quite the same as leap-frogging down a crowded downtown street that serves a dozen bus lines. I've found several nice routes by following the path of a bus. A lot of them tend to wind slowly up hills, carving out the perfect line for a person on a bike not insistent on taking the direct, steep route.

Move over one street. In a grid-based area, move one street off the main drag you use for driving or busing to discover a much more pleasant route. When you find yourself on a street that feels uncomfortably busy due to high speeds or a high volume of traffic, try making a quick right to the next street over; it might be a lot quieter.

Different routes for different times. Your great route from point A to point B might not work so well in reverse if your reverse trip happens to coincide with a busy time that your initial trip misses, like rush hour or school-release time.

FINDING YOUR ROUTE

Nowadays you might turn immediately to your smartphone whether walking, biking, or driving, plug your destination into your map app, and have your phone bark directions at you, trusting its choice. This might yield fantastic results, but there are many other ways to find a bike route: utilizing online bike maps, paper bike maps, and mentors, to name a few. Don't let the worry of not having the perfect route discourage you from hopping on your bike. There are numerous ways to pedal from point A to point B, a lot of them great, some of them good, and just a couple of them not to your liking. You may be able to determine if your route is a great one through a little bit of research, and if you end up in a spot you don't like, bikes make it easy to pull off the road to regroup . . . maybe to let your smartphone bark out an alternate way around the shopping mall in the middle of your path.

BIKE MAPS

Bike-specific maps are great because bike-friendly routes are marked clearly. Many indicate hills and offer a variety of bike route options, based on bicycle facility type—such as multi-use trail, bike lane, or sharrow.

Keep a local bike map with you. If your start and end points are the same day after day, it's not a crucial piece of your gear, but it's a good resource to have if you want to add a side trip after work and your smartphone is out of juice. I like to keep extra bike maps tucked away to dole out if I encounter someone in need, or even as an incentive for would-be city bikers—who doesn't love a big map that folds into a tiny tidy square?

Bike shops carry bike maps—usually free, provided by the city or local advocacy group. Grab a few so you can mark one up and still have a pristine spare. Here's where to find them in some of the larger metropolitan areas:

› In Seattle, the Department of Transportation provides a free bike map that can be ordered online in paper version or downloaded in digital form. There's also a free online interactive map.

› In San Francisco, the San Francisco Bicycle Coalition (a long-standing advocacy group) provides a free online bike and walking map to all and printed maps to members.

› New York City's Department of Transportation provides free maps you can pick up at bike shops and libraries, or they'll send a free copy if you call 311. They also offer a downloadable version.

› The City of Minneapolis produces a free Minneapolis Bicycle Map, available in most bike shops and libraries. Plus, there are online interactive and printable versions, as well as a smartphone app version.

› The City of Austin sells the City of Austin Bicycle Map in many bike shops and at its office. It also offers a free downloadable version.

› The Tucson Metro Area Bike Map is produced by Pima County and is free at bike shops, libraries, local ward offices, and the County-City Public Works Building. It can also be downloaded or mailed to out-of-town requesters.

ONLINE TOOLS

I typically use online tools along with bike maps to plan my routes. My personal system is a bit convoluted, so I can't in good conscience recommend it to others. But since I have a horrible sense of direction, can't remember multiple turns, and seem to go somewhere new every week or two, it's the only thing that really works for me. Hopefully it will inspire you to try something, anything, and ultimately create your own much less labor-intense solution.

I start with the default bike directions Google Maps chooses and then compare it to the crowd-sourced bike-friendly street recommendations of a local neighborhood greenways group. The latter routes are quiet side streets—with special consideration for bicycles if they've been formally converted into greenways, but with no traffic-calming measures or signage typical of greenways otherwise. Even the not-yet-formalized greenways are pleasant streets to ride upon and usually my street of choice. Then, since proposed greenways—and even some existing greenways—don't necessarily have traffic signals for crossing busy arterials, I check Google Street View and weigh the pros and cons of a busy street with a stoplight versus a quiet street with the annoyance of having to wait for a clear crossing. If there are long stretches between busy streets, I might decide to travel along the greenway until one block before the busy crossing and then jog one block over to the sharrow or bike lane on the parallel arterial to cross with the light.

Google Maps

Google Maps is my first map of choice since I'm familiar with using it for all my mapping needs, whether it's biking, transit, walking, or driving. A good starting point, it usually gives several route options with a time estimate for each.

I like to drag the route around in neighborhoods I'm a bit familiar with, where I know hills and intersections I would rather avoid. For intersections I'm unfamiliar with, but suspect might not be to my liking, I switch to street view to check for traffic signals and to get a feel for street speed—I know a four-lane street with no bike lane probably won't be part of my route of choice if I can find an alternative. Google Maps defaults to a busy street with bike lane over a neighboring quiet street with no bicycle facilities, so depending on your comfort level, you might choose to make some changes to this default route, which is where the next online tool comes in.

REPORT A PROBLEM TO GOOGLE MAPS

Notice something wrong about your bike directions from Google Maps? You can give feedback that the Google techs will use to better their map directions. Once, Google's first choice of bike directions between a local multi-use trail and bridge told me to "Carry your bike up the stairs" for two flights. I suggested an alternate route as the first choice and they agreed and changed the map results. I've also submitted pictures to suggest proper routing.

In Google Maps, find "Report a data problem" by clicking the question mark icon.

Ride the City

Ride the City, a website dedicated to helping bicyclists find safe routes, doesn't have maps for every city yet, but it hits all the biggies, with over twenty US cities and many worldwide. It's incredibly robust.

> The main screen allows you to select one of three different route types: safer route, safe route, and direct route.

> Results display with each turn-by-turn direction accompanied by an icon to show what sort of bike facility to expect, such as path (multi-use trail), lane (bike lane), or shared (sharrow).

> You can save your route preferences by rating street segments.

> As with Google Maps, you can submit route suggestions if something looks off. Or if you're so inclined, you can make your own edits to Open Street Map (www.openstreetmap.org), such as marking a street as having a bike lane so it will more readily come up in route results.

Ride the City also displays bikes shops on its maps.

City-Specific Online Tools

Check if your city has a city-specific website and/or smartphone apps for bicycling directions. When in Portland, I skip Google Maps and use the PortlandBike app on my phone for any and all directions. It better mirrors the directions I receive from local friends, avoiding unnecessary hill climbing and utilizing sneaky cut-throughs, and allows me to manipulate the map if I want to make changes.

Many bike clubs include an online forum that can provide the perfect platform for soliciting route advice, whether or not there's a dedicated area for doing so. If yours doesn't offer this option, suggest it!

FITNESS SITES

Fitness sites such as Bikely, Ride with GPS, and MapMyRide (see Resources) won't necessarily yield the most direct or bike-friendly route, but taking a look at local bicyclists' saved routes might reveal a cut-through or other useful route trick. They're also great for saving your own routes for future reference.

GUIDEBOOKS

A guidebook including a portion of your city is another often uptapped resource for route finding. A good guidebook writer can make you feel like you have your own private tour guide. For example, *Biking Portland* by Owen Wozniak provides turn-by-turn riding directions for fifty-five rides in the area, many of which depart from downtown Portland, offering pleasant routes along the river, including comfortable crossings and quiet streets—perfect for bike touring and bike commuting alike. Guidebooks are terrific sources for finding hidden trails in a city.

COWORKERS

Real-live people are wonderful sources of advice. If you're commuting to an office, check in with any coworkers who bike commute. Even if they come from a different side of town, they probably have ventured various places after work and have some tips that will apply to your own commute. And even "fast and fearless" experienced bike commuters will have applicable advice. You might not care for each turn of their route, but don't be shy to point out you prefer quiet, slow streets and multi-use trails. Most "serious" commuters should be able to put themselves in your shoes and make some route adjustments to account for your tastes.

If a coworker comes from a similar area as you, ask to ride with them for your test run! Having a mentor alleviates a lot of worry. Don't hesitate to ask questions and identify parts of the route you'd like help reworking as you encounter them.

BIKE COMMUTE MENTOR PROGRAMS

Many cities or workplaces have mentor programs that take all of the guesswork out of bike commuting!

In Washington State, Tacoma's non-profit Downtown On the Go offers the Bike Buddy program for downtown employees. Bike Buddies assist with route planning, give information about putting bikes on local buses, provide resources for bike maintenance and gear, and accompany you on a practice ride.

Some large offices offer in-house mentor programs like the National Institutes of Health's Ride Mentors list. Volunteer mentors are listed by route for ease in connecting with an appropriate ride buddy. They, too, offer information on route finding, putting bikes on the bus, gear, and safety.

You might not find a year-round program, but keep an eye out for new information in the months or weeks leading up to National Bike Month (May).

GROUP RIDES

Recreational group rides are a good way to get out on the street and practice your urban riding skills while in the safety of a group. You're likely to pick up some route tips while you're out enjoying the ride. I prefer slower-paced social rides for this purpose since I tend to pay better attention to the route, and most bike clubs offer rides of all paces (more on bike clubs in Chapter 13). Of course a group ride from near your house to near your destination of choice is ideal, but any ride you think might traverse an area you'll frequent should yield helpful tips. And engaging with people on the group ride will yield even more information.

Bike Trains

You may have heard of bike trains for school-age kids, but now they exist for adults headed to work too. A bike train is a free, community-based bike commute service that runs on a regular schedule, designed for newer bicyclists who would like to gain skills and confidence. Each bike train is led by a friendly volunteer "conductor" who organizes the group, helps newcomers, and models legal and safe bicycling. In addition to providing skills practice, bike trains create a fun

Cascade Bicycle Club

Seattle, Washington

Bicycles are more than a mode of transportation—they improve lives. Nonprofit Cascade Bicycle Club, the largest bicycling club in the United States with over 15,000 members, does just that through education programs, advocacy, events, and rides.

Fueled by the belief that healthy habits begin early in life, Cascade's Education Department offers in-school bicycle safety in four school districts, after-school riding clubs, bike-to-school encouragement, as well as summer camps. Focused on fostering livable and connected communities, Cascade also provides adult riding and maintenance classes, commute workshops to organizations, and resources to promote healthy transportation.

Cascade's Bike Month program in May introduces thousands of people to transportation bicycling. It is a monthlong effort dedicated to removing the hurdles that keep people from bicycling and to getting more people on bikes more often. The event includes free bike tune-ups and classes, the Bike Month Challenge, and Bike-to-Work Day promotions.

With a goal to make bicycling safe and convenient for people of all ages and abilities, Cascade's advocacy team works to make sure that all who ride a bicycle in the Puget Sound region have safe, comfortable, and convenient places to ride. To reach this goal, Cascade focuses on three key areas: (1) educating and empowering community leaders; (2) training city staff and transportation engineers around bicycle infrastructure design, planning, and policy; and (3) informing and electing leaders who will work to fund bicycle infrastructure and create safer streets regardless of political affiliation. Cascade's advocacy work is nationally recognized and includes programs like the Advocacy Leadership Institute and Connect Puget Sound.

Meanwhile, Cascade's events-and-rides staff organize several major rides throughout the year. Perhaps the most well-known ride is the annual Seattle to Portland Classic (STP). The quintessential Northwest ride—and a bucket-list item for many—the STP is the largest bicycle event in the region and Cascade's biggest fundraiser: 10,000 riders tackle the 200-plus-mile ride from Seattle to Portland every year. The STP and other major rides make Cascade's education, advocacy, and rides programming possible.

In addition to organized rides, hundreds of Cascade volunteers lead more than 2,000 free group rides a year.

Ranging from five-mile Sunday brunch jaunts to strenuous endurance rides, there's a free group ride for everyone.

The "Chilly Hilly" is a popular annual group ride in the Pacific Northwest.

community and offer safety in numbers. Most bike trains contain five to eight riders—enough to make a visible group, yet small enough to be manageable by a sole conductor. Riding with a prearranged group of others can make an otherwise impossible bike commute not only possible, but easy and fun.

Where Are the Bike Trains?

Bike trains can happen anywhere there is a volunteer conductor and a few interested riders, so look for one in your city. As of this writing, bike trains exist in Los Angeles, New York City, San Diego, San Jose, and Seattle (see Resources), all with plans for expanded routes and additional resources for local commuters.

ANYONE

Don't be shy—ask anyone and everyone for route advice! Trial and error is a good way to find a favorite route, but experienced peers are a resource not to be squandered. Even the Lycra-clad road-bike rider wearing earbuds shouldn't mind unplugging an ear at a red light to let you know how he got there from the other side of the hill. While it's not common practice in a car to ask your neighbor for his favorite route to the farmers market across town, when you're on a bike it makes perfect sense. If you're lost, don't hesitate to flag someone down for help, but otherwise stick to route questions when you're both safely stopped. Most bike riders, whether they're out for a training ride or commuting to the office, share a sense of camaraderie and are happy to help a newbie.

As I've cycled more and more, I have progressed from only helping lost bicyclists who flag me down to pulling over alongside bicyclists looking at maps to offer help, to engaging just about anyone on a bike who might have a tip to share.

Less invasive than asking for advice out on the road is soliciting guidance while seated at your computer. Email friends who get around by bike or who know people who bike; broadcast on social media; and search out local biking resources through recreational clubs, advocacy groups, or Meetup.

TAKING YOUR ROUTE TO GO

Once you've put together your initial route to test out, you need to bring it along on the ride. Kudos to you if you can memorize it, but if you're not sure you can retain each turn, you'll need to bring your directions with you: a printout or written list, or something in electronic form on your smartphone or cycling-specific GPS device.

My personal method for bringing a new route on the road is just about as convoluted as my initial route making. After all the street-view peeking and dragging around of the route, I turn my finished product from Google Maps into an easy-to-follow version for out and about. I take a screen shot of the map, paste it into my image-editing software, and then key in the names of each street I turn on in very large type so I can easily see them on my little smartphone screen. I then save the image to my phone's lock screen. I can easily access this at stops with the jab of a button on my phone, which is mounted to my handlebars. I guarantee you can find a quicker way to create and save your own set of route directions.

CUE SHEET

A cue sheet is a turn-by-turn list of directions, easy to print out or write down and secure to your handlebars with a bike-touring-specific device or a $1, 2-inch spring clamp from the hardware store. Some websites, like Ride with GPS, have cue-sheet printing capabilities, sometimes as a paid service. There are also smartphone apps that create cue sheets for both printing or viewing on the screen. Peek at your cue sheet at red lights or pull over at safe spots to memorize the next turn or two.

MAP APP

Applications designed to run on smartphones are extremely helpful tools for route displaying and finding. Even with my cue sheet, I often refer to a map app. Sometimes it's to make a side trip or to navigate around an unanticipated tricky spot . . . and sometimes I get lost despite my twenty-step route-creating-and-saving process. Ride the City, mentioned earlier in this chapter, also has an app version with safer, safe, and direct options, as well as bike shop locations.

GPS DEVICES

I tend to think of bike-based GPS devices, also called bike computers, as tools for

Josh Fassbind

Nona Varnado

Los Angeles, California

Social entrepreneur Nona Varnado has been biking for transportation since 2001. She started with recreational weekend rides on a borrowed bike when living in Greenpoint, Brooklyn, and then accidentally won a bike race and discovered she could get around the city faster and more enjoyably by bike.

Now in Los Angeles, her regular commute is seven miles, almost always by bike, but she also utilizes public transportation, rideshare, and (very rarely) rental vehicles.

BIKES

One of Nona's greatest loves is her trusty Cannondale cyclocross bike from 2003. Originally her racing bike, it's now her daily ride with a rear rack and pannier.

CLOTHING

While she appreciates the perspective that bike commuters should wear normal clothes while riding, Nona points out that some American streets, particularly in LA, dictate dressing in a way that supports longer distances, faster riding, and the "dance moves" bicyclists use while navigating cities with less bike-friendly infrastructure. Wanting practical and comfortable clothing that works well for bike commuting, she started her Nona Varnado apparel brand in 2009 and still regularly wears a pair of NV Riding Pants from the first sample run.

Nona tends to wear pants, shorts, dresses, and some longer, more flowing skirts. She has a formula for bringing new apparel into her wardrobe: "Once I find something I like, I look to see if it's cut appropriately for both my figure and for riding a bike," she says. "I own fifteen pairs of pants, but only one wide-leg pair. It might be in fashion this season, but my commuter bike says otherwise. After that I look at the material: is it too delicate to last? Can I sweat in it? If I get a little grease on it, does that mean it's ruined?"

Even with these clothing constraints, Nona dresses to look situation appropriate, whether she's headed to work or a party. She's found a big middle ground that is stylish, but not so fashion oriented that she can't ride as skillfully for fear of destroying something too delicate or flowing.

BIKE SECURITY

Nona's workplaces allow and encourage indoor bike parking, but around town she always locks her frame and both wheels with a very sturdy, yet light ABUS Bordo folding lock, handily kept in its holster on her bike frame.

ROADSIDE REPAIR

Nona keeps a tool bag with her and even varies the tools it contains based on which bike she's riding or how far she's going. When she's on a long ride or leading a ride, she's prepared to change flats, but since most of her riding is within dense city limits, she usually takes the one- to two-mile walk or bus ride to a shop if anything happens.

BICYCLE CULTURE INSTITUTE

Nona is the executive director of nonprofit Bicycle Culture Institute, an organization that works with large companies, brands, other nonprofits, and community organizers to develop high-quality education, workshops, program materials, and training. Their three ongoing projects are L.A. Bike Trains (small groups of people commuting by bike together to work, one of which Nona "conducts" or leads), the Los Angeles Bicycle Festival, and Red#5Yellow#7 (R5Y7), an educational project space and art gallery that connects people to new bike ideas.

training competitive bicyclists, but the ones with map displays and turn-by-turn navigation are perfect routing tools for any sort of bicyclist. At a few hundred dollars, they aren't cheap, but they're weatherproof, work well, and don't drain your smartphone battery. And the accompanying data-saving software isn't only useful for training purposes—it's a good way to review routes.

HAVING A BACKUP PLAN

You might not have a preconceived backup plan for your commute if you usually take the bus or drive to work. If you miss the bus or it's too full and skips your stop, you catch the next one. If your car won't start, work takes a backseat while you accompany your car to the mechanic. Now, it's not expressly necessary to prepare a backup plan for bike commuting either, but being ready for the unexpected is always a good idea. Hopefully you're equipped to change a flat tire or put back a dropped chain (see Chapter 9 to learn about both), but sometimes your spare inner tube is faulty or your backup plan is so tempting, you'd rather abort the ride and fix things later.

For the sake of example, let's assume something on your bike has broken, but a backup plan can be useful for any number of reasons—a broken messenger bag, a surprise box of doughnuts to transport, or a lost puppy you want to bring to the office.

WALK YOUR BIKE

If you're close to your destination and you don't want to deal with a repair on your way in, walk your bike on the sidewalk. You don't want to ride your bike with a flat tire—you might bend the rim and break spokes—but the weight of your everyday cargo is fine to keep intact on the bike for any distance while walking.

GETTING A RIDE WITH YOUR BIKE

Your city probably has buses equipped with bike racks. Knowing the bus stops along or near your route is a smart backup plan. I consider the bus an easy Plan B— it's already coming, my bus card is always

HILLS

Some people say, "The hills flatten out." I wish it were true! But they do become more familiar. I'd much rather scale a hill I know than explore a new hill. Even if it's steeper or longer, at least I know what I'm getting into with my familiar, old, miserable hills. And you'll get stronger the more you ride, which I guess is the same observation made by American cycling great and three-time Tour de France winner Greg LeMond, "It never gets easier, you just go faster."

Mostly there are two types of uphill routes: short and steep or long and gradual. I used to exclusively favor long and gradual routing—I would double a two-mile trip (which sounds much more impressive—or ridiculous—when stated, "I used to go forty blocks out of my way . . . "?) to find a scalable hill and couldn't understand why anyone would want to punish herself with a harder climb. But I got stronger and now I'd rather crawl my way up the steeper route. It's easier now that I'm used to it—it's much quicker, even if I have to work harder. The long, drawn-out exertion from the more gradual route now requires resting along the way, whereas the steep, short climb doesn't.

Of course, it's also OK to walk up those dreaded hills! Those words won't mean anything if you need to prove something to yourself, but let me assure you, it's not a rule that you must always pedal to move your bike. It might sometimes be faster to walk your bike, and in those instances it will probably also be a lot easier. If you're reluctant to embrace the idea of walking your bike, yet are stuck with a particularly punishing hill, figure out the number of times you need to ride it to prove to yourself you *can* tackle it. Unless you're very stubborn, that number should be one: ride up that hill one time so you can assure anyone who asks that you are able to ascend said hill. Then you're off the hook and can walk it. I guarantee it will make for a more pleasant commute, especially if you've decided to walk that hill ahead of time.

Another option is to slalom up the hill. If the street is very quiet—so quiet you can pop over to the wrong side of it—you can make your climb easier by zigzagging up. I've never done this myself, preferring to rest momentarily on the way up if need be, but it can ease a difficult climb. Only slalom if you know it's safe to take up the whole road.

in my wallet, and I don't have to do anything special to my bike—such as remove a wheel—to fit it on the rack.

Bikes fit inside most cars, if you opt to use a personal vehicle as your backup plan.

Maybe you can use your partner, a friend, or a coworker as a regular forewarned emergency rescuer. Check ahead of time to see how the person feels about transporting your bike in their car. If you have quick-release wheels, removing both will allow your whole bike to fit in most trunks. (For more information on quick-release wheels, see Chapter 9.) Put the bike in the trunk first—greasy chain side up!—and lay the wheels on top of it. Most people won't be as keen on transporting a bike inside the passenger area of their car, but with the front wheel removed, a bike can slide into the back of a car, behind the front seats. This loading also goes for taxis, car share, and rideshare. Even in a very small two-seater car, with the front passenger seat folded forward, you can squeeze in a bike, which is only useful in a car-share situation when you and your bike are the only big things squeezing into said small car. A two-seater carrying two people can accommodate a bike hanging out the open hatchback. More expensive, but simpler, is to call for a van taxi that can easily accommodate a bike.

Some car insurance companies now provide transportation service for disabled bikes and their owners. You might already have this service or be able to augment your plan with your current insurer to make it bike inclusive.

LEAVE YOUR BIKE

Does dragging your bike along sound like too much trouble? Leaving your bike behind is an option too. Out of sight, out of mind! If you're at a spot you'd feel safe leaving your bike for the day or until lunchtime when you can better attend to its untimely needs, securely lock it up and you're free to walk or catch the ride of your choice.

LEAVE YOUR BIKE AT A BIKE SHOP

Even safer than locking up your bike is leaving it at a bike shop—that is, if you want them to repair it. Unless the shop is very short on storage room, they shouldn't object to your leaving the bike for the day while you're at work and retrieving it on your way home. You might have a favorite local bike shop (LBS), but it's good to know all the bike shops along your route, even just for the sake of sharing their locations with would-be commuters at work or fellow bike riders with roadside problems. Not all bike shops open early enough for preworkday issues, so as you make your list of nearby shops, note their hours of operation.

TAKING A PRACTICE RUN

Before your first ride to work or any time-sensitive new location, do a test ride on the weekend both to get a feel for the route and to get a basic idea of how long it will take. You might decide to make or think about some street changes when you imagine the weekday volumes of cars and/or bikes. If the weekend won't work, try nonpeak hours if possible, either for a test run or for your first few rides in. And remember, if you can recruit a mentor or buddy for this practice run, do so! It's likely to be beneficial for both of you. Escorting someone from home to work or school for the first time often shows me a couple nice streets I was previously unaware of and will likely use in the future. And there's that sense of accomplishment I feel at helping to establish one more bike commuter.

A practice run can also be driven by car. I prefer to route-test by bike to see things from the appropriate vantage point, but sometimes you're pressed for time and it's more convenient to tack your route test onto an errand in your car. You'll still get a feel for the trip and identify the big, glaring errors.

GO FOR IT!

So you've got your route figured out, you've put it in portable form, you have a backup plan, and you've taken a practice run. Time to put all that preparation in action—you're as ready as you'll ever be! You didn't bother to formulate a backup plan and totally forgot about taking a practice run? No worries and no excuses; it just adds to the adventurous element of this first ride.

Give yourself a bit of extra time your first time out. For my inaugural rides, I've randomly selected ten minutes as my buffer time, which I add to the Google Maps time estimate—mostly to counteract hitting every red light and bumping into a friend along the way. A more thought-out figure might be the amount of time it takes you to change a flat tire, which is five minutes if you're a pro and twenty to thirty if you're out of practice. I tend to need and use my buffer time, but be prepared for turning up earlier than your office building or other destination opens. It's never happened to me, but it can happen and you don't want to be taken by surprise. Most importantly, remember to have fun!

GO FOR HALF OF IT!

If you want to start slowly, look into setting up a temporary carpool in one direction for you and your bike. Biking in the homeward direction might take away the stress of arriving on time in the morning, although biking in the outbound direction and knowing you've got a ride home at the end of a long day can be a pleasant relief. Either way is a great first step toward two-way commuting. Notice this plan lends itself to a future emergency backup plan too.

YOUR EVOLVING ROUTE

Your primary routes will probably change a bit over time. New bike facilities get added (and sometimes taken away), you stumble upon better options, or as your riding skills increase you might transition toward a more direct route on faster streets.

CHAPTER 8

Less Than Ideal Conditions

MY PERFECT BIKING DAY is between 68 and 72 degrees Fahrenheit, with the sun shining, a slight breeze, and a perfectly flat trail or street. I've enjoyed many rides in just those conditions, but I've also experienced my share of rain, cold, heat, and hills, in sickness and in health, and routinely with a stiff neck. Some cities support dry and temperate bike riding year-round. Some cities have *real weather*—if you live in one of those, you might opt to only go out when conditions are fair. That's great! Any trip replaced by bike is a good one. And fair-weather-only riders have been known to change over time—as the saying goes, "You're not made out of sugar, you won't melt."

It's really not that bad to be out in less-than-ideal conditions, whether that's intense sun or intense cold, as long as you're prepared. I can't be the only person who dislikes driving in the rain more than I dislike riding my bike in the rain.

Of course, if the rain gets too wet or the cold too intense—or the heat unbearable—partway through your ride, there's no shame in bailing out at the closest bus stop or even turning around and heading back home for a do-over by bus or car.

RAIN

While I'm tossing around old sayings: *There's no bad weather, just bad clothing.* Unless you don't mind getting drenched while riding and then changing when you arrive at your destination (which is a valid option), you need only a few special items to keep yourself dry. Most of my own bicycling-specific gear is rain related, but I might be a bit biased.

FOR YOUR BIKE

Before addressing your own wardrobe, examine your bike's. Clad your steed in fenders and mud flaps and you'll keep away dirty ground water kicked up by your wheels.

Fenders

If you don't have fenders on your bike and you get caught in the rain or ride through a puddle, you'll get a wet streak up the middle of your backside. You'll also make the person behind you angry as you spray them with a rooster tail of water. And (I think this is most important, though we tend to think only of ourselves in the heat of the moment) your bike will undergo extra wear and tear. For rainy conditions, you will want full coverage fenders. See "Fenders" in Chapter 4 for more information.

Mud Flaps

Adding little mud flaps to the back of each fender gives you even more protection from the rain. Full fenders cover a lot of each tire but can't extend all the way down to the road or they'd get banged up when they encountered bumps, potholes, and curbs. Mud flaps are flexible—a lot of them are rubber or leather, although the do-it-yourself cut-up plastic water bottle seems quite popular, just not as flexible—and reach much closer to the surface of the road. The front mud flap will protect your feet and chain, and the rear mud flap will keep any water from kicking up behind you—nice for riders behind you and important for your cargo if you pull a trailer.

WHAT TO WEAR

When rain is accompanied by cold, your raingear can do double duty by keeping you warm on top of increased layers underneath. If it's cold enough, and your ride is short enough that you won't get sweaty, using your current waterproof raincoat and any rain pants or snow pants should do the trick.

Remember that rain is accompanied by reduced visibility—and more cars with their lights on—so extra reflective bits on your raingear will show up well. Most raingear comes in regular or high-visibility color options and often includes reflective touches.

Helmet Covers

You might find that your head gets uncomfortably wet in the rain, especially when wearing a vented helmet meant for air circulation but that also lets the rain in. Waterproof helmet covers will keep your head and hair dry. Some include flaps on the back to prevent rain dripping down inside your collar plus visors on the front to help shield your face.

While most helmet covers with silly designs are not waterproof, they do block quite a bit of rain. They also work well for warmth and visibility to others and make many people more likely to regularly don their helmets. The waterproof ones make up for their lack of novelty patterns by coming in high-visibility colors with reflective details.

Rain Jackets

Bicycling-specific apparel, which is designed for movement and breathability, can make a big difference for longer rides in the rain. A bicycling rain jacket will have small vents under the arms that you can unzip for ventilation, as well as a shape that accounts for your body's

Rain cape

Handlebar gloves

hunched-over position—wider across your shoulders and longer in the back. Some rain jackets have a flap at the lower back that can be unsnapped to cover you better when riding in the rain or cold, but tucked up for better ventilation in drier weather—and a more traditional look when walking around.

Rain Capes

The rain cape is great for those of us who run hot while biking in the rain, and it provides amazing coverage for just one piece of gear. Similar to a regular poncho, it is sized to fit well on a bike—not too long to risk getting tangled in spokes nor too short to provide adequate coverage. Hidden thumb loops or handholds keep the front of the cape in place over your handlebars, effectively covering your hands and legs. However, this also covers handlebar-mounted lights, so riding with

a rain cape might necessitate a front light that is instead mounted to your helmet, front rack, or fork. For more movement, you can put your arms through slits, but this exposes your arms to the rain and allows the cape to shift back, uncovering your legs. The hood can go under or over the helmet or lay flat on your back if your helmet doesn't let in too much rain.

Gloves

For cold rain I like to wear my waterproof cycling gloves, but on warmer days, they make me sweat. I'll keep them on just until I'm no longer cold and then go barehanded the rest of the way. Nonwaterproof gloves and mittens work just as well for this purpose. If you notice your wet hands slip around on your handlebars, keep your gloves on or experiment with a bit of handlebar tape or different grips to make riding in wet conditions safe.

Handlebar Gloves

Handlebar gloves are waterproof oversized mittens, also called pogies, that attach directly to the handlebars, wrapping around the brakes and shifters. They stay put on the handlebars and are roomy enough for a thin-glove-clad hand to fit inside if it's too cold to go bare-handed.

Glove and Boot Dryer

There's not much I like less than pulling on a pair of wet gloves. For this reason I used to leave the house with three sets of gloves. The first set was waterproof, but ended up wet from sweat during the two-mile ride to our preschool. The second set was a cheaper, nonwaterproof set that got wet during the two miles to the elementary school. And the third set was for the post-drop-off trip back home or to another destination. That works for one whirlwind hour of drop-off flurry, but what to do with three sets of wet gloves that I was going to need again in a few hours? Enter the glove and boot dryer. The glove-specific dryer is quick and works just as well for shoes—much quieter than listening to shoes thump around in a clothes dryer. If I biked to the same office every day, I'd probably own two of these! It could be handy to keep one at the office if you find yourself spending time rotating your wet gloves on the radiator. Not to mention that wowing your coworkers with such a handy tool could encourage a new round of bike commuters. Of course, biking for transportation needn't be about cool toys, but the right gizmo can make a big difference.

Rain Pants

Pair a rain jacket with bicycling rain pants and waterproof gloves and you're pretty well covered. Bicycling rain pants are roomy at the knee to accommodate pedaling and usually have zippers at the bottom so you don't have to remove your shoes to get them on and off. If your pants don't stay completely dry in your raingear (who wants to spend the day with damp pant cuffs?), bring an extra pair for the workday.

Rain Chaps

I get overheated in regular rain pants, and since only the tops of my legs get wet, I prefer to wear rain chaps. The waterproof fabric drapes over the tops of my legs down to my knees, with a few buckles to hold them in place. In addition to keeping my pants dry without making me sweaty, they can easily be donned and removed with shoes on. Being able to quickly take off my rain chaps during each brief indoor stop on my normal commute, without the need to balance on one foot, is terrific. My chaps even work over my usual cycling "uniform" of a knee-length skirt over leggings if I leave the middle set of buckles undone.

Saddle Cover

Since the seat of my pants isn't covered when I wear rain chaps, I need to keep my saddle dry when I leave my parked bike uncovered in the rain. That way I don't have to sit on a squishy, wet seat when I ride away. It's also important to keep your saddle dry if it's made of leather to avoid the premature aging of your saddle, not to mention that a wet leather saddle tends to transfer its color to your clothing. Even synthetic saddles are hard to wipe completely dry and so it's worth covering one if parked exposed to the rain.

I like a saddle cover with an attached loop that secures the cover to the seat post. This prevents theft and keeps it from falling off when rolled up and wedged in the rails under my saddle. The advertisement-covered free saddle covers I've received also work well, but they don't stay wedged securely in my saddle rails for long. Plus I'm not good about remembering to keep one in my bag, since I want to leave it out to dry when possible. Plastic bags and shower caps also make fine seat covers for the do-it-yourself crowd.

You can ride with your seat cover in place over your saddle—they're easy to wipe dry—and some people keep their saddle covered at all times to disguise the pedigree of said saddle.

Shoe Covers and Booties
I generally wear leather boots in the winter and they stay dry enough for a half-hour ride in all but the heaviest rain. I find pedaling in regular rain boots a bit uncomfortable, but it can be a workable solution. If you cycle in tennis shoes or cycling shoes, cycling shoe covers, also

called "booties"—the kind worn by competitive cyclists, with holes in the bottom to leave room for a cleat to attach to a pedal—can keep your feet warm and dry. They work for regular shoes too. Make sure you get waterproof ones because some are just for warmth. Shoe covers are ankle-high and should reach to the bottom of your rain pants, but they can be paired with hiking gaiters if there's an exposed gap. Or cover your boots with motorcycle boot covers.

Spare Shoes . . . or Two
My trio-of-gloves solution works for other clothing items too. Bringing a spare pair of shoes (and socks!) to change into is one of the easiest wardrobe swaps to make—easily done at any dry bench, so no need to find a changing room. If you have the room, bring two sets of spare shoes if the thought of stepping back into damp shoes at the end of the day sounds repellent.

Another reason to bring spare shoes is slippage: My favorite shoes work fine on my pedals in dry weather but slip on occasion in wet conditions. So in the rain, I pedal in thicker-soled shoes that grip my pedals well and change into more comfortable shoes once I've parked my bike.

Retaining Waterproofness
Your raingear should last for a long time, but it might need a bit of help to retain its waterproofness. Time, overwashing, or a backpack or messenger bag rubbing against your rain jacket can compromise its ability to keep water out over time.

Check with the manufacturer of your raingear for tips on caring for your garment. Waterproofing sprays and washes will replace a washed-off or worn-off water-resistant outer layer for many fabrics, but certain materials simply require a tumble in a warm dryer to reactivate.

SAFE RIDING IN RAIN: IT'S SLIPPERY

In addition to donning your raingear, you'll want to gear up with a few of these rain-riding tips:

Dress to counteract limited visibility. You are more visible in reflective gear than in bright colors, but both are a good idea. Cycling-specific raingear is usually accented with reflective tape, but if your gear isn't made for active wear, you will want to add something reflective—leg band, arm band, or iron-on. The movement of reflective accents on your ankle is particularly good for visibility.

Avoid riding through puddles. Puddles can conceal potholes. Hitting a pothole will cause a pinch flat in an underinflated tire, not to mention that the unexpected bump can cause you to crash.

Avoid riding over metal grates and plates. They are very slippery when wet.

Watch out for slippery road paint. I notice this most when stopped at a light in certain painted bike lanes—my bike is fine, but when I set my foot down on the green paint, I start to slip.

Give yourself extra stopping distance. Brake slowly and lightly.

Take corners slowly.

COLD, SNOW, AND ICE

If you have skiing or snowboarding apparel, you're set for cold winter bike commuting. I don't like driving a car in the snow, but biking in the snow is relatively easy. There's more room with fewer people out and about, and everyone who is driving or walking or bicycling is moving slowly and cautiously.

FOR YOUR BIKE

Just as you have to keep your body comfortable and functioning in the winter cold, you need to give that same attention to your bike. Some people even have a bike that's specifically for winter—maybe a slow, heavy fat bike with tires 4 to 4½ inches wide that can handle any terrain, or just a sturdy bike with knobby mountain bike or special snow tires.

Traction Tires

On my one snow day a year, I use my old mountain bike. Its knobby tires are perfect for gaining traction as I climb the hill by my house—and they keep me from skidding out as I come back down. It's also great in slush, although my regular smooth city tires are fine in slush as well.

Many people are most comfortable riding their regular bikes with the usual tires—even smooth, skinny road-bike tires—in snow and slush because those conditions don't make for a slippery ride. If this describes you, try lowering your air pressure to the bottom of the range printed on the side of your tire to provide more traction. (If there's no lower limit printed, reduce the pressure by about 20 percent.) This is all fine and good unless there is ice on the road.

Ice is a "special tire" situation. If you live somewhere blanketed with ice in the winter, get a set of studded tires. The metal studs dig into the ice and help prevent slipping. Studded tires work in snow and on plowed roads but are heavy and slow, not to mention an added expenditure, so they're generally favored only by people who regularly encounter icy situations. Studded tires are available in widths to fit most bikes.

Samantha Arnold, who commutes by bike in Chicago, has a *real* winter commute and owns studded tires (see Samantha's full profile in Chapter 2). She doesn't need to use them every winter, but she made good use of them during a recent polar vortex, installing them as soon as the worst hit and leaving them on until things thawed and she was relatively sure it wouldn't freeze up again. She finds them more useful on ice than in snow: "They slow your sliding down and allow you more time to gain control. On my big heavy bike, it gives me lots of time. I leave them on until it's apparent there won't be much more snow/ice . . . they are really loud on pavement, so I'm motivated to swap them out."

Fenders

Just as in the rain, fenders in the snow will protect you from getting splashed (and splashing others) with icy-cold slush. They will also keep much of the snow and slush from sticking to your bike as well as protect your bike from the wear and tear this can cause. For a full discussion about fenders, see Rain, above, and Chapter 4.

Keep Snow and Slush Off Your Bike

Remove any snow and slush that sneaks past your fenders. Use your gloved hand, a towel, or a brush to wipe off the snow—especially from your chain. If you have a single-speed bike or internally geared hub, you're better set for freezing temperatures because exposed gears can freeze up and essentially turn your bike into a single speed until it's indoors long enough to thaw out.

To help prevent freeze-ups, keep your chain clean and lubricated throughout the winter—check it every few days (see Chapter 9 for chain maintenance).

If you feel like your bike collects too much snow while you ride, don't house your bike in a heated space. Your cold garage-stored bike will be less "sticky" for the snow to accumulate upon.

WHAT TO WEAR

On the coldest days, I suit up in full snowboarding gear: snowboarding jacket and pants, three pairs of socks (overkill, but my boots are a little too big), snowboarding boots, snowboarding gloves, balaclava, snowboarding helmet, and goggles. For quick out-and-back runs (such as the library or grocery store) I'll opt for thermal underwear, but longer trips work best when I need only shed outer layers upon arrival.

In less extreme cold temperatures, regular raingear works fine—even breathable raingear will block the wind and chill. For raingear tips, see Rain, above.

Cycling-Specific Cold-Weather Wear

Samantha says, "Cold-weather commuting is all about layers. And keeping your fingers and toes warm—that's the hardest part. I'm partial to 'lobster-claw' gloves with gloves underneath . . . it's the only way I can keep my hands warm. Tights plus leggings or jeans/pants are great for women in cold weather. Running or bike tights under pants work great for men too . . . also rain pants over pants or leggings work well. And those little toe- or hand-warmer packets are key for cold weather."

Consider specialty items to address your particular chilly areas, such as ear pads or ear warmers designed to attach to bike helmet straps (see Helmet Accessories in Chapter 4). Handlebar gloves will protect your hands better than regular gloves (see Rain, above). Whether or not you opt for handlebar gloves, doubling up two pairs of gloves is a good bet. Lightweight gloves will make it easy to manipulate your bike lock or deal with any mechanical problems, and waterproof and/or wind-resistant gloves or mittens on top will keep you warm while riding.

You'll want to protect your eyes from tearing up in the cold. Try ski goggles, although they might not fit over a bike helmet as well as they do a ski helmet with its built-in clasp. Wraparound clear or tinted bike glasses will better block out wind than regular glasses or sunglasses.

Underdress

The general rule is to underdress slightly, to match how you'll feel ten minutes into your ride. I like this rule in theory, but since I usually start out with two steep downhill blocks, I would rather start out adequately warm and shed a layer once I've warmed up. However, when I head out in the uphill direction, I do heed this rule. Experiment to see what works for you and your specific routes.

Bring Extra Extremity and Base Layers

Damp hands, feet, and head are uncomfortable in rainy weather but can be dangerous in cold weather. Consider packing extra lightweight gloves, balaclava or cap, and socks. These can come in handy both for the return trip if you've gotten wet and don't have time for things to dry out, or if you have to deal with a flat tire or unexpected stop on the way somewhere.

SAFE RIDING IN SNOW AND ICE: GO SLOW

Snow is pretty fun to ride in. It's slowgoing whether you want it or not, but everything is sparkly and muted, with only the sound of the snow crunching under your tires. And your coworkers will incredulously ask, "Did you really ride to work today?" several times each day.

› Give yourself a lot of extra time in snow and ice. You'll move more slowly through snow and you might want to create an alternate route to avoid ice. Some of my winter routes are twice as long to avoid blocks of shaded streets that are notorious for accumulating black ice. Take your time and don't set yourself up for a slippery situation.

> When there is snow on the ground, reduce your air pressure. Lowering the pressure to the minimum suggested on the side of your tire will improve your traction. Less air pressure in your tire creates a bigger surface area to make contact with the ground.

> Avoid all patches of ice! I speak from experience. Slips on ice are incredibly quick—one second you're fine, the next thing you know, you're lying on your back alongside your kid-containing trailer with twelve eyes (two human, ten of the stuffed-animal variety) staring at you. Be especially careful of shady spots that might hide melted and refrozen snow.

HEAT AND HUMIDITY

Not getting sweaty in the first place is my favorite way to deal with hot days. And no matter the length of your commute, you should almost always be able to wear normal clothing in the heat without getting so sweaty you want to change after riding—as long as you're willing to travel at a reasonable pace. If you can head out early to beat the heat and give yourself extra time to pedal slowly, do that. But if you can't, there are plenty of creative solutions.

FOR YOUR BIKE

Wearing a backpack or messenger bag in the heat will quickly make your back sweaty. A front basket or rear rack with basket or pannier to carry your bag will make a huge difference (see Chapter 4). Equipping your bike to carry enough water bottles within easy reach is also key. If my water is tucked away in my bag, I'm probably not going to bother stopping to fish it out. But if I have two full water bottles in the drink cages on my frame and one easily reachable in my front basket, I'll not ignore my thirst.

WHAT TO WEAR

Wear your regular clothes, of course, but add a couple things to make the ride more pleasant.

Helmet

A lot of warm-weather hotheadedness is dependent upon hair thickness, but if you find your head feeling too hot, consider switching to a helmet with a lot of big vents. The attractive commuter-style helmets generally don't have a lot of vents and with my thick hair, I'm only able to wear mine in the cooler climes of winter. You will have to be careful to not get sunburnt through your helmet vents, possible even with thick hair, so consider adding a cap, mentioned below.

Sweatband

Even if you plan to sweat profusely and shower after your ride to work, don't jeopardize your vision by allowing sweat to stream into your eyes. A rolled-up handkerchief tied across your forehead can absorb any sweat created by your helmet or hair, but bicycling-specific caps, headbands, and visors might be more comfortable and will fit better inside a helmet. Thin caps designed for hot-weather riding are more comfortable than regular cycling caps in the heat.

Fabrics to Wear and to Avoid

Thin merino wool wicks sweat, dries quickly, and doesn't get stinky. You can find merino wool undershirts, shirts, and even underwear. Loose clothing is also particularly comfortable, such as a long-sleeved loose cotton shirt over a merino wool undershirt. Polyester gets, and stays, stinkier than cotton and other natural fabrics.

Light colors reflect heat while dark colors absorb, although while you're moving, you're generating enough of a breeze to counteract any heat absorption. So if your commute keeps you moving along enough that you don't feel the heat settle on you, you're good to go in any color.

A Change or Partial Change of Clothes

You've arrived sweaty, toweled off, but don't want to put your sweaty outfit back on. What about just part of it? Changing is easy enough, but if it's just your shirt or just your underlayers that feel uncomfortable, selectively replace them. One bicyclist I know swears by changing her bra several times a day in summertime.

Storing Sweaty Riding Clothes

Hang up your sweaty riding clothes if possible. If space is limited, an empty desk drawer can do the trick. Lay your items as flat as possible and leave the drawer open an inch so they dry out and are ready to wear or transport home at the end of the day.

Bring a Washcloth

I keep a washcloth in my messenger bag to mop my brow at the end of a hot ride—and that's it for me. But I know there are many masters of the bathroom stall washcloth bath out there. Some people swear by disposable baby wipes, but in the interest of not adding to the landfill, I recommend bringing a washcloth and laundering it after one use. A dry washcloth, or one wetted with witch hazel (antimicrobial, astringent, even pain-relieving for sore muscles), is perfect for wiping away sweat.

No Shower Necessary . . .

Shower if you want to. If you have the time and inclination—and the facilities—to shower and change at work, go for it. If you have the time and inclination, but no shower facilities, see if a nearby gym will give you a lower rate for using the locker room to shower and change.

However, if you shower at home before leaving on your bike, you'll get sweaty but not stinky. If you don't mind drying out at work, you can arrive damp and spend ten minutes cooling off.

BONKING

Sometimes it's fun to borrow terminology from the bicycle racing world. "Bonking" is what bicyclists and other endurance athletes call hypoglycemia . . . although it's sometimes misused for mere dehydration. Either way, it's bad and should be avoided. It's not something that normally affects the everyday transportation bicyclist, but there are those days you've skipped lunch to run a faraway errand by bike and then you forgot about your half-finished breakfast pastry that was meant to be an afternoon snack.

Bonking comes on suddenly and causes you to feel extraordinarily weak and dizzy. Moving becomes difficult and you might feel confused or hostile and have difficulty speaking. Catch it early and you can reverse the effects on the go by taking in simple carbohydrates to get your blood glucose levels back up. Sports drinks are ideal for this, but even straight sugar or candy—with water—will do the trick. Keeping an energy gel packet tucked away somewhere on your bike is a good idea, just in case.

Safe Riding in Heat: Water

Water is probably the most important thing when riding in the heat, for both hydration and cooling. While sticking your sweaty helmet in the freezer for half an hour between hot rides might sound like the best idea ever (or maybe that's just me?), it's pretty painful! But there are plenty of useful tips to keep you cool:

› Hydrate ahead of time. Water takes five minutes to two hours to be absorbed into your system depending on conditions, so drink a glass or two of water before you set out.
› Drink frequently while riding.
› Freeze your water bottles so you'll have cool water on your bike.
› Squirt water on your head, through your helmet vents for extra cooling—but only if you still have enough left over to drink.
› Tie a wet bandana around your neck.
› Slow down. Any movement generates a breeze that will keep you cool, especially if you have a nice layer of sweat worked up.

Watch for dehydration. Some common signs of dehydration are thirst, dry mouth or lips, headache, dizziness, and yellow urine. Most of us don't stop for restroom breaks while riding, but assuming you ride often throughout the summer, notice if your urine isn't as clear as usual. And drink more water before and during your next ride accordingly. The other signs you'll monitor while on your bike, and hopefully stave off by drinking a sufficient amount of water in advance of those symptoms. Headache and especially dizziness are signs you should stop riding to rest and hydrate until you feel well again.

Anthony Ongaro

Patrick Stephenson

Minneapolis, Minnesota

Patrick Stephenson lives in downtown Minneapolis, listed #1 in *Bicycling* magazine's "America's Top 50 Bike-Friendly Cities" in 2013 for its thriving bike community, 120 miles of on- and off-street bicycle facilities, indoor bike parking, and other cycling-friendly facilities. Even before he started bike commuting in 2009, Patrick was well aware of the good bicycling infrastructure in Minneapolis and impressed by the secure indoor bike parking and showers at his Minnesota Public Radio (MPR) office, but knowing and doing are two very different things. Having a friend who bike commuted was what put him over the edge. Although Patrick thought his friend was "superheroic" for bike commuting on a daily basis, he was inspired to give it a try.

Patrick remembers getting lost three times when he first started bike commuting. With some route advice from a bike mechanic at Freewheel Midtown Bike Center, he slowly, gradually, and nervously found his way around. Patrick now bike commutes twenty-six miles round-trip three to four times a week (and rides the bus on nonbike days), his tentativeness long gone. Now he revels in the beauty of riding across the Mississippi River, experiencing the transition from steel and pavement in downtown Minneapolis to the green side streets of St. Paul, and inspires others to try bike commuting.

BIKES
Patrick admits his Trek Madone 4.5 road bike is a little "high-falutin" for a commuter bike, but figures his route is long enough to deserve it. Plus he likes its speedy feel after a winter commute riding his slow, heavy Surly Krampus—a rigid (no suspension) mountain bike with fat 3-inch-wide tires. For icy winter riding, Patrick puts studded tires on a single-speed bike.

CLOTHING
Patrick wears functional clothing for bicycling: skinny jeans, bike-themed t-shirts, and cycling caps when his hair is of sufficient length that his helmet leaves its mark. Bicycling has also taught him to love wool in all its forms, especially merino.

BIKE SECURITY
At home, Patrick locks his bikes together in a shared building garage and hasn't experienced any problems. At work, he doesn't generally lock up thanks to MPR's keycard-access garage and security cameras. While out around town, he relies on a U-lock.

ROADSIDE REPAIR
Patrick's repair kit includes a spare tube, multitool, and tire lever, but he usually heads to bike shops during those rare times of bike trouble.

30 DAYS OF BIKING
Patrick's passion for biking prompted him to start the annual 30 Days of Biking challenge in 2010 with his friend and bike commute mentor, Zachariah Schaap. The challenge is simple: ride your bike every day in April and share your adventures online (Twitter, Facebook, and/or a personal blog). What started as a mostly local phenomenon has blossomed into a worldwide movement with close to 7,000 participants in 2014 and generous sponsors, including Free Bikes 4 Kidz, who donated a bike to a kid in need for every thirty pledged participants.

PATRICK'S TIPS FOR NEW BIKE COMMUTERS
"Just do it. Even if you only ride one mile and take the bus the rest of the way. Trust me, you'll persuade yourself into riding more and more. Don't worry about people judging you. Get out there on your bike and just pedal. Your life will be better. Your mood will improve. It's a good thing and you deserve good things."

ILLNESS

It always hits me when the seasons change—a runny nose that eventually turns into a lingering cough. While I'd rather hide in bed all day, life goes on, and the fresh air perks me up a bit. But even better than sunlight and fresh air is seeing the bike commuter across the street blowing his nose in sync with me. Misery loves company, and I never suffer my sniffly bike commute alone, although I've only once had someone wave his tissue back at my pitiful greeting.

Per Commute by Bike and all reasonable parties, "If I'm too sick to ride, I'm too sick to work." But it's not bad for your body to bike when you're mildly sick. Use "the collarbone rule": if the problem/infection is below the collarbone, stay home, if it's above your collarbone you're fine to ride. Basically: chest cold bad, head cold fine. But wherever the cold, if biking makes you feel worse, you should stay home.

SADDLE SORES

I want to point out one horrible bike-borne ailment even though, thankfully, it isn't that common for bike commuters: saddle sores. When I got one, I assumed it was a cancerous cyst, since I'd only heard of the term but had never read a description. The feeling is akin to stepping on a Lego, but in a much more sensitive spot.

I like riding in regular clothing and sometimes what the recreational bicyclists say is true: seams from normal clothing can rub and chafe! Saddle sores form where your inner thigh meets the perineum, first just as a mild skin irritation, then as inflamed hair follicles. Sometimes they can get even worse, requiring surgery if left untreated. If you catch it early (hopefully even before it's inflamed), you can keep riding. It's a shame to let something so small ruin your commute ... although it certainly qualifies as below the collarbone.

If you notice any irritation in this area, one effective solution is to switch to wearing cycling shorts (without underwear, by the way)—the friction of the seam of your underwear probably caused the irritation in the first place. Adding a thick chamois cream inside your cycling shorts is recommended to prevent any painful friction. And wash the cycling shorts after every use! Some saddle sores are caused by poor hygiene. A simpler change that doesn't require a special purchase is switching to underwear with a different seam pattern—this will be my first change if I'm ever so plagued again.

Treat a saddle sore with an over-the-counter pain reliever and anti-inflammatory. Popular treatments are witch hazel, tea tree oil, diaper cream, and hemorrhoid cream. To avoid direct pressure on the sore, some riders apply those doughnut-shaped foam stickers made for corns and blisters (found in the footcare aisle of the drug store).

If you are suddenly experiencing saddle sores regularly, it's probably a sign you are in need of a new saddle—no euphemism here, the one on your bike.

Heart Opener yoga pose

Saddles can wear and start rubbing you in the wrong place, creating repeat saddle sores. Of course if you have any concerns, see your doctor.

INJURIES

I've seen people riding bikes with arms in slings and feet in casts, but something that major should keep you off your bike lest you further injure yourself or others! Just like with mild sickness, minor aches and pains fare OK on the bike. If your neck is sore, but not too sore to prevent or slow you from checking over your shoulder when necessary, grimace and bear it. Something more serious than a stiff neck, like a pulled muscle, should be rested. Of course, consult your doctor, but resting and icing will probably be the prescription, sidelining you from bicycling for a few days.

If you suspect that your sore neck, tingly hands, or painful knees are a result of your bike, invest in a bike fit, as

Turnaround Twist yoga pose

discussed in Chapter 2. I was lucky and my tingly ring and pinky fingers that caused me to repeatedly drop things went away once I got ergonomic grips—most likely providing the cushioning I need to combat the vibrations from the road. And my very occasionally sore left knee has stayed away since I raised my seat to the proper height. My recurring neck pain (which is from old car crashes and lessened, if anything, by biking) happens much less since the seat-height change too.

PREVENTION

Bicycling itself is great preventative medicine, but tacking on a little extra prevention is even better. Kelli Refer's book, *Pedal, Stretch, Breathe: The Yoga of Bicycling,* offers both lovely essays on bicycling and yoga poses particularly great for people who ride bikes. Two of my favorites are easily done with your bike as a prop! The second one even works well when stopped at a long red light!

Heart Opener

1. Standing over your bike, grab the saddle behind you.
2. Keep your low belly engaged, muscles clenched.
3. Lift your sternum to the sky.
4. Slide your shoulders down your back to support your heart.
5. Breathe into the front of your body and into your arms.
6. Gaze up to the sky and assess the accuracy of the weather forecast!

Turnaround Twist

1. Stand over your bike, feet forward.
2. Inhale, reach the crown of your head up to the sky.
3. Exhale, twist from the center of your ribs.
4. Use your saddle and handlebars for leverage in your twist.
5. Twist to the other side for balance.
6. Smile at everyone sharing the road with you!

CHAPTER 9

Basic Maintenance

JUST AS OUR BODIES do better with a bit of preventative care and quick action when something needs medical attention, your bicycle can benefit from the same. Yeah, you can choose to run it into the ground. Your simple, amazing, and reliable bike will keep grinding along, even with dry chain and nearly flat tires. But things will work more smoothly—and for longer—with just a little bit of TLC. You'll probably ride happier too.

The bicycle is a simple and reliable machine. Learning how to keep your bike in good working condition prevents parts from breaking or needing more intense maintenance, and it's empowering, cheaper, and easier than letting things go.

It's not imperative that you know how to fix things on your bike. Assuming you're in an urban setting, you're surrounded by bike shops. However, knowing how to make basic repairs in a pinch, like fixing a flat or putting a dropped chain back on, can contribute to your sense of being a confident bicyclist. Being able to rush home for a spare tube of the right size and change my friend's flat left me feeling like I could conquer the world. Never mind that I shoved the tube in with a twist and that a real mechanic coached her through fixing it herself later—perfectly installed tires and tubes are important long-term, but bikes are forgiving in the short term.

Nevertheless, it's helpful to be able to recognize when something instead needs your bike shop's attention. And knowing a few basic things about your bike will give you the confidence to investigate other problems on your own. The California Highway Patrol suggests what you can check while riding:

ANNUAL TUNE-UPS AND BIGGER STUFF

Get your bike tuned up once a year. And keep a maintenance log. This will help you keep up-to-date on tune-ups and assist you in keeping track of flat tires and the like. It's also handy for tracking expenses, a la "I've only spent $30 on upkeep this year—how about you and your car??"

"Listen for sounds of rubbing, squeaks, and rattles and immediately investigate their sources." I've successfully wiggled fenders and brake calipers to stop them from rubbing with no long-term ill effects. And if I can identify where the weird sound is coming from yet can't wrestle it into submission myself, I know where to point once I arrive at the bike shop.

BASIC BIKE CHECK

Prevention is the best medicine. The most cursory ABC check (Air, Brakes, Chain) is easy enough to get in the habit of doing fairly frequently.

> *Air.* Squeeze your tires to check that they're not flat.
> *Brakes.* Try to push your bike forward while squeezing the brakes to check that they work as expected.
> *Chain.* Take a quick peek at your chain to make sure that it isn't completely dry or horribly dirty.

Start by deciding on a routine. Some people do this just once a month—the first of the month or the first Saturday of the month is easy to remember—and some check everything each and every time they ride. Let your results guide you—if you notice your tires are always low on air, get in the habit of checking more often (high-pressure road-bike tires should be inspected every week, but wider tires with lower pressure retain air much longer). In rainy weather, you might want to keep a weekly eye on the state of your chain.

Some bicyclists rely on the kindness of well-meaning strangers who zoom by and call out, "Your tire's low!" or "Lube that squeaky chain!" You might bristle if you receive unsolicited advice, but don't ignore it. For some mysterious reason, it's easier to hear the sound of someone else's chain squeaking than your own.

TIRES AND TUBES

Some "tire" problems are really tube problems. During the basic bike check, you squeeze your tires, but you're actually checking the inflation of the tubes inside those tires. Both tires and tubes require upkeep and periodic replacement. Often something that goes wrong with one is completely independent of the injury to the other—a flat tire in the form of a popped inner tube often isn't on account of an injury to your tire. And worn out tires certainly can cause more popped tubes, but a worn out tire is easy to catch early enough that you'll use the same old tube in a new tire.

▰▰▰▰▰▰▰▰▰▰▰▰

YOUR BASIC MAINTENANCE TOOLKIT

1. Pump
2. Spare tube
3. Patch kit
4. Chalk
5. Tire levers
6. Multitool
7. Cleaning rags
8. Chain lube

▰▰▰▰▰▰▰▰▰▰▰▰

INFLATION

Flat tires are the most common bicyclist woe but they will happen less often if your tubes are kept adequately inflated. Proper inflation also prevents your tires from wearing prematurely. Low tire pressure not only puts you at risk of pinch flats (see below), but also causes your sidewalls to bulge out and weaken. Need more incentive to check your tire pressure? Fully inflated tires require less effort to spin in circles. If you've been riding with very low tires—as some of us obliviously do at times—and put them back up to the recommended air pressure, you'll notice an amazing difference. To learn about proper tire inflation and pumps, see Chapters 3 and 4.

How to inflate your tires:

1. *Find the valve.* For a floor pump, spin your wheel to place the valve at the bottom (6 o'clock). For a very small pump, unless it has a foldout foot rest, spin your wheel to get the valve to the top (12 o'clock) so you don't have to bend over so far.

2. *Remove the valve cap.* Both valve types might have screw-on plastic caps that you'll need to remove before inflating. It's OK if you don't have caps or if you lose the caps (they're very easy to lose!), but they do protect your valve stems if you've got them. If your bike has Presta valves (see Tires and Inner Tubes in Chapter 3), you must untwist a small locknut to open the valve—don't try to pull it all the

way off, just untwist to the top of the pin—that will allow the pin to depress once the pump is in place. Tap the top of the pin; you should hear air hiss out. This tapping of the pin also ensures that it's not stuck in place before you secure the pump.

3. *Attach the pump head.* For pump heads with levers: flip the lever into the down position, push the head onto the valve as deep as it easily goes, and then flip the lever into the up position to lock it in place. For pumps that screw into place: twist the piece at the end of the pump several times so the pump is well sealed to your valve.

4. *Pump.* When pumping, pull the pump all the way up and push all the way down. You shouldn't hear air escaping out the side of the head. If you do hear air escaping, you probably haven't attached the pump well enough, although it also might be a sign of a faulty pump head. Reattach and try again.

5. *Check the tire pressure.* The tire pressure is the number the pump settles at once you've stopped pushing down on the pump, not the highest number the pin hits while you're in the action of pumping.

6. *Carefully remove the pump head.* Unscrew your pump head (or close down the lever and remove) at a nice straight angle so you don't bend the valve or pull off the Presta valve's pin with the locknut. Note: the hiss of air you hear when you remove the pump

is coming from the pump, not the tire; your tire pressure is still right where you left it.

7. *With a Presta valve*, you'll need to retighten the locknut.
8. *Replace the valve cap.* Feel around on the ground or dig around in your pocket for where you left your valve cap and screw it back onto your valve.

▰▰▰▰▰▰▰▰▰▰▰▰

PUBLIC BIKE PUMPS

Many bike shops have floor pumps for the public to use easily located near the front door or service area. Some fancier bike racks have attached tools and pumps, as do bike-friendly businesses. My favorite coffee shops have stickers affixed to their bike racks to alert bicycling customers that they keep a bike pump inside for our convenience.

▰▰▰▰▰▰▰▰▰▰▰▰

WEAR AND DEBRIS

Periodically check your tires for wear and embedded road debris. Your tires are designed to repel debris, but burrs and glass can get lodged in the rubber. If this debris doesn't immediately puncture your tube, it will eventually make its way through the wall of your tire. Starting at the valve (so you can tell when you've run the circumference of your tire) slowly check for any cracks, cuts, bulges, or foreign objects. Promptly remove anything stuck in your tire, such as asphalt, glass, and plant matter.

If you ever ride through a patch of glass or something similarly pokey, stop as soon as it's safe and brush off or pick out anything stuck to your tires. Even the most flat-resistant tires will eventually be defeated by an ignored sliver of glass. I swat at my tires with a bare hand, but if the condition of your roads often leaves you stopping to clean off your tires, you might want to wear (or at least keep at the ready) full-coverage bicycling gloves.

This wear-and-debris check can be part of your basic bike check after your air pressure squeeze—it's quick. Or it can be a separate weekly or monthly task.

Small cuts from previously embedded small debris and cracks in the tread don't mandate tire replacing. Big cuts, big cracks, threads visible through the rubber, and any bulges are signs that your tire is no longer safe. Worn tread is *not* a sign of tire weakness or neglect; it just means your tire has come to the end of its natural life. You can track a tire's condition over time in several ways: Some tires have wear indicators hidden within their tread. For some, these are dimples that when smoothed out indicate it's time to replace the tire. For others, a layer of different-colored rubber or embedded threads make it clear you're about to start getting a lot of flats. An increased number of flats on older tires without wear indicators, for which you don't have another explanation (such as faulty inner tube valve or low tire pressure), is also a sign that your tires have worn out.

Replace your tires when they're worn out. You'll use the same skills as covered

Quick release lever

in the Fix a Flat section below, except you'll need to deflate your tube first to more easily get the tire off. To deflate a tube with a Presta valve, untwist the lock-nut and press the pin down until the air has hissed out; to deflate a tube with a Schrader valve, use a key (or something similarly pokey) to depress the pin if your finger won't fit. Or, of course, you can enlist your local bike shop to do the work.

QUICK RELEASES

While you're down in the wheel area, learn how to use and check your quick-release levers. Many wheels have levers that make it easy to take the wheels off—useful for changing flats, storing bikes, or getting more parts of the bike into a bike lock. I used to remove my front wheel several times a day for locking up, but

nowadays I only remove a wheel if I'm shoving my bike into someone's car.

Checking your quick releases can be part of your basic bike check, or just as needed. The first thing to check is that your quick-release lever is in the closed position. Quick-release levers are usually curved, cupping toward the wheel when closed, so it's easy to see if they're open or closed. Some even say "open" on one side and "closed" on the other. If you're unsure by looking if it's open or closed, flip it to the opposite position and feel if it loosens or tightens—hopefully that loosens it, signifying it was closed and you can replace it to its former position. Once you've determined that it's closed, give a little tug to ensure it doesn't pop open easily. And there's your basic check. You should feel comfortable learning how to open, adjust, and close your quick release even if you don't think you'll be changing your own flats or converting your bike to trunk-of-car size.

Note: Unless your bike is very old, your forks have safety tabs (also called "lawyer tabs" and "lawyer lips") so the front wheel will not fall out if the quick release is not closed. Quick releases don't pop open on their own.

Using Your Quick-Release Lever

Open the lever. Your lever should be hard to open if it was closed tightly enough in the first place. Pull it all the way down, 180 degrees.

Adjust. Make adjustments to the nut on the nonlever side: righty tighty, lefty loosey. For practice, loosen it a lot and then tighten it back up.

Undo the brakes. If you have rim brakes, you will have to unclip them before you can remove the wheel. Cantilever brakes are loosened by pushing the brake arm toward the rim while pulling the nipple end of the brake wire away to unhook it. Direct-pull cantilever brakes are loosened by unhooking the noodle from the arm. Caliper brakes have a convenient lever you flip up to release the brake shoes. Don't forgot to do the reverse to replace your brake once you've reinserted your wheel.

Close the lever. You'll know it's tight enough when you hit resistance when the lever is halfway closed, or parallel to the ground. If you don't start feeling resistance right at this point, open the lever back up all the way and tighten the nut a little more. Or loosen the nut a little if you feel resistance before the halfway point.

Again, remember to check that you've reattached your rim brakes at this point.

Lever Angle

Any angle will keep your wheel on, but closing the lever toward the back of the bike means you don't have to worry about it catching on anything, like an errant branch. Closing the levers parallel to the forks in the front and seat stay in the back will make it easier to pull the lever closed—with the heel of your hand on the lever while your fingers grip the bike, but that perfect alignment will make it harder to get your fingers in to get it back open. So I like closing my lever about a finger's width behind the fork and seat stay.

Spring Alignment

If you happen to loosen the nut too much and it falls off, you'll discover a cool conical spring on the skewer. There's actually one spring on each side of the shaft of the skewer that connects the side with the nut to the side with the quick-release lever, through the hub in the center of the wheel. The narrow side of each spring points toward the middle of the wheel. Shove the spring into the nut so it's outside of the fork when you put the pieces back together.

When You Don't Have a Quick Release

Quick-release wheels are very common, but not universal. If your wheel has nuts on both sides of the axle, you'll need a wrench to remove it—either an adjustable or most likely a 15-millimeter wrench. You don't need to fully remove either nut; just trade off loosening each side a couple degrees until you can pull the wheel free. If there are washers on the axle, memorize their placement just in case you do remove one of the nuts and they fall off.

FLAT TIRES (ALL TYPES)

A very proficient flat changer can do the job in 5 minutes; I am woefully out of practice since my flat-tire-riddled college days, so it takes me 30 minutes to change my own (or others') flats nowadays.

Fixing a flat has over a dozen steps, but learn the steps and, the more often you practice, the easier and quicker your flat fixing will get. That said, if you keep your tires properly inflated and check periodically for damage and wear, there's a very good chance you'll spend years flat-free.

Pinch Flats

Pinch flats happen when your inner tubes are underinflated and you hit a pothole, bump, or similar patch that compresses the tire hard enough to pinch the tube against the rim. When repairing your tube, look for two holes to patch. The double holes are close to one another and are why pinch flats are also called "snake bites."

Punctures

Riding through broken glass, nails, or thorns can result in a flat when the sharp object punctures your inner tube through the tire. The small hole in your tire won't lead to future flats because the odds of

something like a sharpish rock hitting this specific spot *just so* are very slim. However, it's important you find the hole and remove the offending object. If you don't immediately see what caused the flat, find the hole in the inner tube and match it to the spot on the tire: remove the tube and fully inflate it to easily find the hole. Your tire will still be in place, just with one side hanging off the rim, so you can align your tube's valve with the rim's valve hole and find the spot on the tire. If you may have flipped the tube around, you'll get to do this twice, once in each orientation.

Slow Leaks

While all tubes slowly lose air, a noticeable change should only happen over a matter of weeks, not a matter of hours. A tube that slowly deflates over the course of an hour or two is a slow leak and is usually best dealt with by reinflating until you are home, where you can more easily change the inner tube. Slow leaks can be hard to find so don't despair if you can't save the tube.

I've also used this approach with not-so-slow leaks. In a pinch, you can reinflate your somewhat-slow leak every few blocks to get home or to a bike shop. As long as you're careful not to ride on a flat tire that might dent your rim, chronic reinflating is pesky, but not dangerous.

Blowouts

Usually a result of overinflation, a blowout is exactly what it sounds like—a loud bang as your inner tube pops like a balloon.

Unfortunately, a blowout leaves a tear too big to patch.

Fix a Flat

You've probably noticed a theme among the various profiled riders throughout this book; although they're all capable of changing flat tires, they opt to accept professional help. Having the knowledge is great, but you don't need to get your hands dirty if you don't want to. I used to jokingly say that I set a wonderful example of a harried mom who could bike all over town successfully with two small children despite not knowing how to maintain a single thing on my bike. We visited a lot of bike shops—but mostly to use the restrooms, because I could wheel the bike inside. (There's often no time for locking up when you ride with children who have small, impatient bladders.) Once in the shop I'd sometimes ask to have air added to my tires if I needed it (I always needed it) or have my chain oiled if I needed it (unsurprisingly I always needed this too). But really, back then I wouldn't have dreamed of changing a flat by myself on the side of a busy trail or street with the "help" of two toddlers. Getting out the door was hard, but once our biking momentum was going, all was good. If that momentum was stopped by a flat tire, I'd keep that momentum going with a walk to the closest bike shop—after a stop at a park if need be. And fortunately, the weight of a kid passenger is not enough to bend the rim of a wheel with a flat tire—but *you* should not ride your bike when it has a flat.

To fix a flat:

1. *Remove your wheel.* If you have rim brakes, loosen your brakes first. (See Quick Releases, above.) If it's the rear wheel, first shift your gears to the smallest, outer cog.

2. *Removing your rear wheel.* You can shift your gears to the outer cog by first pressing the lever as many times as necessary, then lifting your rear wheel a bit off the ground, and using your other hand to spin the pedals. Alternately, you can flip your bike upside down, balanced on saddle and handlebars so you can shift and pedal simultaneously. (This method might prove troublesome, as you could scuff your saddle and may need to remove lights and other handlebar attachments—like bicycle computer or smartphone mount.) You will need to guide your rear wheel out to the left side a bit to clear the chain, but otherwise it's very much like removing a front wheel.

3. *Remove the tube.* Release any remaining air by depressing the pin in the middle of the valve. If you can't get your finger onto the pin of a Schrader valve, a key works well. If you have tire levers, wedge one between the tire and the rim, a few inches away from the valve, and hook it in place to a spoke. Insert a second tire lever and travel the circumference of the tire to loosen the whole side of the tire. You only need to unseat one side of the tire to remove your tube. Pull the tube completely out of the tire.

4. *Check the tire for damage.* There might not be any change to your tire, but look for embedded objects to remove—or holes. A small hole isn't really a problem, unless something sharp happens to wedge itself into that exact spot the next day. A hole large enough that your inner tube is visible through it means you need a new tire. If you're on the go with a large hole, placing a dollar bill between tube and hole is a popular way to create a makeshift tire patch.

5. *Get out your spare tube or find the hole in the old tube.* If you want to reuse your tube, inflate it so you can find the hole. When you find it, mark the spot with a pen or some chalk. Finding the hole will also give you a clue as to where to more closely examine your tire for damage. At home, finding the hole is most easily done in a sink or bucket of water, where the bubbles will quickly reveal its location. On the road you can run a moistened finger over the tube if you're having trouble hearing the telltale hiss.

6. *Patch the old tube.* Patch kits come with little tubes of glue, sandpaper, and patches, or one-piece peel-and-stick patches. Use the sandpaper to roughen the surface of the tube near the hole. This will help the glue adhere. Apply the glue to the tube and then cover with the patch. The vulcanizing glue will meld the patch and tube together. Be sure to press any tiny air bubbles out before holding it in place for the amount of time speci-

fied on your patch kit (probably one or two minutes). Peel-and-stick patches are even quicker. Both are prone to drying out, but your tube of glue can be softened up if you can find someone with a lighter to heat it up.

7. *Install the new or patched tube.* Partially inflate your tube so it's easier to manipulate and to reinstall without kinks. Insert the valve through the tire rim first and shove the rest of the tube up into the tire so it won't get pinched between the tire and the rim as you muscle the tire back into place—the next step.

8. *Reseat the tire.* This is the hardest part for me. Working in both directions at once, tuck the bead of the tire into the rim. It will get harder as you get to the end. If you're having a lot of trouble getting the last bit of tire in, you may have partially inflated your tube too much—try removing some air and see if that helps. You can also try to stretch the tire a bit from your initial insertion point. My bike mechanic friend Edward learned this method from his grandfather and swears by it, but he makes everything look easy. Replacing the tire is usually most easily done by hand, but you might use your tire levers to pop the last little bit in.

9. *Inflate your tube.* Prevent a second flat by pinching the tire beads toward the center of the rim, which will free the tube from the edges. This way the tube gets situated in the middle and doesn't get pinched between the rim

and the tire. You'll squeeze or kind of rock the tire back and forth all around the perimeter. Inflate as normal now.

10. *Replace the wheel.* The front wheel pops right back in; for the back wheel, set the chain on the small cog. Tighten the quick release. Reattach the rim brakes. You're on your way!

BRAKES

Obviously, moving forward is an extremely important part of riding a bike, but stopping quickly is just as important. I might be a bit biased, as I live in a hilly city and carry extra bodies on my bike—and have had the experience of squeezing the brakes with all my might at the top of a steep hill as 100 pounds of trailer bike and trailer (not recommended by manufacturers, mind you) hurtled forward toward a busy arterial.

Fortunately, brakes wear down slowly, so you can tell when they are getting close to needing replacement. The two most common types of bicycle brakes (rim brakes and disc brakes) have brake pads that periodically need to be adjusted or replaced. Depending on the conditions, how often you use your brakes, and how often you clean them, you might need to adjust or replace your pads after a month or after several years. Your particular usage will likely cause one brake to wear more quickly than the other, which is perfectly normal. Since there are many different kinds of brake systems, I'll focus on recognizing when there is a problem to bring to your local bike shop.

STOPPING POWER

You can see which tire each brake stops by looking at the cables running from each brake, but an easy way to remember is to think *R* is for *right* hand and *rear* brake. Check each brake separately. When you squeeze your left/front brake and shove your bike forward, your tire shouldn't roll at all. Same for the right/rear brake combination. It's also important that you can fit a finger between your squeezed brake lever and the handlebars: if you're pulling all the way against the handlebar when you squeeze the brakes, you won't have enough stopping power, which means your brakes need some attention—now.

RUBBING PADS

Look closely to make sure your pads aren't rubbing when the brakes aren't engaged: pads shouldn't rub against your tire rims for rim brakes or against your rotors for disc brakes. A fairly common cause of rubbing pads is that your wheel is not perfectly straight. Happily, it's easily fixed: open your quick release, make sure your bike is perpendicular to the ground—not leaning against anything—and retighten it.

PAD THICKNESS

Most *rim* brakes have grooves in the surface; when the pads have worn to the bottom of the grooves, it's time to replace them. If your pads don't have grooves, replace them when there's less than a quarter inch of pad left.

For *disc* brakes, you must remove your wheel to inspect them for wear. From the front and bottom you can see your brake pads inside the calipers. Pads thinner than 1 millimeter (a bit thinner than a dime) are due for replacing. For me, it's easier simply to notice when my brakes start squealing more than usual and stop braking as powerfully.

▰▰▰▰▰▰▰▰▰▰▰▰

CHANGING DISC BRAKE PADS

I haven't included disc brake pad changing instructions here as I personally consider it a job for my LBS. But many people consider this a home mechanic job. See the Learn Bike Maintenance section in this chapter for good places to learn about replacing disc brakes. You'll need to add a couple tools to your kit: needle-nose pliers to remove the old pads, and a pad pusher tool (or something similar) for inserting the new pads. And be very careful to line everything up perfectly.

▰▰▰▰▰▰▰▰▰▰▰▰

CLEANING YOUR BRAKES

For rim brakes, keeping your brake tracks—the part of the rim the brake pads make contact with—clean will drastically increase the life span of your brake pads *and* your rims. Wiping away dust and road grit with a dry cloth will do the trick. Wipe the pads to keep them clean too. Any particulate matter stuck between your brake pads and rim will abrasively eat away at both and decrease your brak-

ing power. Perform a cleaning any time your ABC check reveals noticeable grime.

Disc brake rotors generally don't need cleaning but can be wiped down with isopropyl alcohol if they get dirty. It is important not to get the oil from your skin on them—it will contaminate the pads—so allowing the alcohol to dry on its own is quick and sufficient.

CHANGING RIM BRAKES

When you've run your brake pads down to the bottom of their grooves, it's time to replace them. For brakes using cartridge brake pads, you need only change the brake pad cartridge. (You've got cartridge brake pads if the metal piece holding the pad is open at the back, allowing you to slip the spent pad out and a new one in.) Regardless of the type of brake pad, however, start by releasing the brake cable:

1. Release your brake cable, also covered earlier in this chapter in Using Your Quick Release Lever.

› Cantilever brakes are loosened by pushing the brake arm toward the rim while pulling the nipple end of the brake wire away to unhook it.

› Direct-pull cantilever brakes are loosened by unhooking the noodle from the arm.

› Caliper brakes have a convenient lever you flip up to release the brake shoes.

Cartridge brake pads:

2. Remove the pin or bolt. There will either be a pin you must remove before you can slide out the pad, or

a bolt to remove before releasing the cartridge.

3. Slide out the old pad.
4. Slide in the new pad. It should have an arrow indicating the front.
5. Replace the pin or bolt, if there was one.
6. Reattach the brakes.

Bolt-on brake pads:

2. Use a 5-millimeter Allen wrench to loosen the nut, and remove the brake pad. Note: There are five washers along the bolt. Your new brake pad comes with a new set of washers so don't worry if these fall off or you don't keep them in the right order.
3. Insert the new brake pad:
   (3a) Leave the innermost two washers on the bolt: the thickest one has the flat side against the pad and the concave side faces the end of the bolt, and one of the two convex washers is nested into it.
   (3b) Insert your new brake pad into the hole in the caliper. The longer end faces toward the back of the bike. There is probably also an arrow on the pad to indicate orientation.
4. Push the caliper arm up to hold the brake shoe against the rim, which will help keep it in place.
5. Place the rest of the washers on the bolt: the flat side of the remaining convex washer against the caliper, the concave side of the thinner concave washer against it, and finally the thin washer. Note: The thick and thin concave spacers can be swapped if

there is not enough room for the pad to fit between caliper and rim. If your old brake pad had the spacers in this order, you'll probably need to make this swap.

6. Hand-tighten the nut or loosely tighten it with your Allen wrench.
7. Twist the brake pad, if necessary, so it sits straight against the rim.
8. Hold the caliper arm and brake pad in place with one hand while tightening the nut all the way with your Allen wrench.
9. Repeat on the other side.
10. Reattach the brakes.

Both:

If your new brake pads don't fit between the caliper and rim, you can either swap the two concave washers (for bolt-on brake pads) or loosen the brake cable:

1. Loosen the nut holding the brake cable to the calipers a little bit, with your 5-millimeter Allen wrench.
2. Push a bit of excess brake cable past the loosened nut and retighten.
3. Check to see that your brakes are correctly positioned, first by spinning the wheel and making sure it spins freely. Then squeeze your brake lever to verify the pads hit the rims and stop your wheel. If not, fine-tune your adjustment of the brake cable.

CHAIN

Even a well-cared-for chain will stretch over time, but with proper maintenance, it can last for thousands of miles, as will the associated parts of your drivetrain. Chain links are held together by a pin, and the hole housing this pin elongates over time. Poor chain conditions such as dryness, rust, or grit will cause it to stretch prematurely, which in turn grinds down the teeth of the sprockets of your cassette on the back of your bike, the teeth of your rear derailleur, and the teeth of your front chainrings.

Lube your chain every 100 miles in good weather, and more often in wet weather. Here's an extreme example of how a bit of prevention saves a lot of hassle and pricey repairs:

I ride 200 to 300 miles a month on my cargo bike, carrying over 100 pounds of stuff. When I'm not careful about keeping my chain clean and lubed, it wears quickly, stretching out and in so doing chews up the teeth of the sprockets of my rear cassette. It can all happen fairly quickly, necessitating the purchase of new cassette and chain within six months. A clean chain can preserve the cassette indefinitely, although with my heavy hauling I still need to replace the chain a couple times a year. A regular bike won't need this level of maintenance, but similar destruction will happen over a longer period of time. As your chain wears out, you'll find yourself skipping over gears and dropping your chain more often.

Only use a product designed for lubing bicycle chains. People often refer to it as "chain grease," but you don't want to put grease on your chain. Nor oil. I opt for the brand my local bike shop recommends, but there are many options.

LUBING YOUR CHAIN

1. If you have a bike stand or a double kickstand, elevate your bike; otherwise set it upside down so you can spin the wheels and move the chain freely.

2. With the first of two rags in your palm, wrap your hand around your chain, loose enough that it can move through your closed fist while brushing against the rag. Pedal your bike with your other hand. Use your pedaling hand to shift through all the gears. This will remove dirt and any extra lube from your chain. Keep pedaling and wiping the chain until nothing comes off on your rag.

3. Sparingly apply new lube while you continue to pedal the chain. On most lube bottles, you don't even need to squeeze—hold the nozzle close enough that each roller hits the nozzle and picks up a drop of lube. You're getting the lube *inside* the chain—between the round rollers in the middle and the flat plates on the outside—so your aim isn't to create a drippy mess.

4. Use your second rag to wipe the sides and top of the chain to get excess lube off while you cycle through the gears a couple more times. By running through your gears, you'll lubricate your sprockets and chainrings while removing the excess.

5. A wet-looking chain after cleaning is bad—that means there's too much lube on it. Too much lube is worse than too little since the lube will

attract dirt and grime. You can wipe your chain dry using the technique in step 4 if you suspect you haven't wiped the lube off well enough.

IF YOUR CHAIN FALLS OFF

Sometimes chains slide off the front chainrings as you're biking, called "dropping your chain." Often this just *happens*—maybe you hit a bump while you were shifting or you tried to shift more than one gear at a time while pedaling forcefully up a hill—and is not a sign of a problem with your chain or gears.

Signal that you're stopping and walk your bike to a safe spot. If you have latex gloves in your repair kit, this is a good time to use them. The simplest thing to do is grab your chain and wrap it around the closest chainring (the big one, if it slid off the outside; the small one if it slide off to the inside). Lift the back wheel off the ground by lifting the back of your frame with your left hand and work the right pedal forward with your right hand to get the chain fully engaged. You might have to adjust your front derailleur by shifting up or down if it's not lined up with the chainring upon which you've placed the chain.

Try Without Touching the Chain

You might be able to get your chain back on without getting your hands dirty. Lift your rear wheel and *slowly* pedal forward with one hand. See if your derailleur will guide the chain back on. If it doesn't work, shift a bit (if you don't fully click the derailleur a full step, you can hold your

shifter down in an intermediate spot to get the derailleur to move just slightly) in the opposite direction from which the chain has fallen off to encourage it in the right direction.

Try It While Moving

If you can get a feel for getting your chain back on without touching the chain, you might be able to do the same thing while still on your bike. If your chain drops, stop pedaling and glance down to see which way it has fallen off. Very slowly pedal forward after shifting your front derailleur in the appropriate direction.

BUILD YOUR REPAIR KIT

Your repair kit will be small—a frame-mounted pump can attach to your frame or tuck into a pannier, and the rest will fit in a small saddlebag. The following list has redundant repair supplies, but they're small and redundancy isn't a bad thing when it comes to being prepared.

Spare inner tube. Quicker than finding the hole in your deflated tube and patching it on the spot is installing a new tube. Patch the old one later, at home, to be returned to your repair kit as your spare.

Pump. Get the biggest small pump you want to carry around. Tiny pumps are light and easy to stash in a small bag, but they take a lot more muscle to fill a completely flat tube. Bigger frame pumps also have pressure gauges, which is very helpful if you aren't comfortable going by feel.

Tire levers. When fixing flats, tires are hard to pry off by hand. You'll want

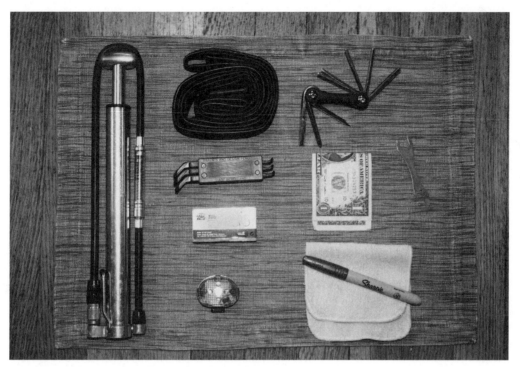

Repair kit contents

at least two tire levers, but three makes it even easier. You can cut down to just two as you get more proficient. I have used the handle end of spoons and forks in a pinch, but real tire levers with hooks for attaching to spokes are easiest.

Wrench. For non-quick-release wheels, carry a wrench that fits the nuts that hold your wheels on.

Multitool. You really only need Allen wrenches in the size for the bolts on your bike, but a bicycle multitool that has 4-, 5-, and 6-millimeter Allen wrenches and screwdrivers should fit everything. If your bike is vintage or exotic, make sure your Allen wrenches fit your bolts. I only use screwdrivers for attaching bike bells, but parts of your brakes and derailleurs will probably require screwdrivers if you get into more advanced repairs.

Patch kit. Even with a spare tube in your repair kit, it's good to have a small patch kit too. The patch kit contains several tube patches, glue, and a small sandpaper swatch. This will come in handy if you get two flats in the same outing (or forget to restock your spare tube). Preglued patch kits are even smaller, but the glue doesn't last as long as the tube in a regular patch kit. A preglued patch that's not sticky won't help at all. Still, I collect these free at events and keep them on hand for someone else's flat-tire emergency.

Pen or chalk. A pen or chalk is helpful to mark the hole on your inner tube if you intend to patch your tube on-site.

Latex gloves. Many people carry latex gloves in their repair kits to keep their hands from getting dirty. I don't, but when my chain falls off the chainrings, I get very dirty and end up wiping my hands on the closest patch of grass or risk transferring dirty grease to my handlebar grips for an endless cycle of dirtiness. Gloves can also come in handy in the event of helping out after a crash.

Rag. A small rag can be useful for wiping off your bike and/or hands.

Extra light. A small front bike light can help with repairs in low light as well as serve as a backup bike light.

Dollar bill. If your flat is the result of a hole in your tire, inserting a folded dollar between your tire and tube will protect the tube from repeat puncture short-term.

ROADSIDE SERVICE

Handling your own bike repairs on the go is terrific, but there might be a way to get help delivered. Some auto clubs offer roadside assistance for bicyclists. Services vary but may include the delivery of tools or the towing of broken bicycles. If you own a car, see if your insurer also covers your bike. Bike-only plans are available from some clubs.

KEEP YOUR BIKE CLEAN

Keeping your bike clean is a good way to keep an eye out for problems, like rust spots or loose pieces, and helps to keep all the moveable parts in good working order. A soft, dry cloth is the only tool you really need: wipe away dust when the bike is dry and wipe away water when it's wet.

Bikes can also be bathed. Although my bike charges through the rain without complaining nearly as much as I do (just a bit of extra squeaking on occasion), being rained on leaves it fairly dirty. The dry cloth technique gets a lot of the grime off, but not all of it. For some bike-bathing tips, I checked in with Sean McGraw, a former bike mechanic who races cyclocross (which can be extremely muddy) and seems to take pride in getting his bike extremely dirty and washing it *all the time.* Really, I'm convinced he spends more time cleaning his bike than riding it. Happily. I listened to him wax poetic about oxygen bleach and how clean it made his bright yellow shoe covers before I could get any bike-washing questions answered, but here is the jist:

› Use old t-shirts cut into rags for cleaning your bike.
› A daily postride wipe down is the best and easiest cleaning you can do.
› If you have rim brakes, the biggest thing is to dry the brake tracks. Your rims will last much, much longer. It only takes 15 to 30 seconds to wipe down your rims and brake pads.
› Always dry your chain so it doesn't rust.
› Spray down your bike with a hose to

knock off most gunk, especially after riding in the rain.

› Yes, your bike is waterproof, but don't aim water directly at anything containing bearings—your bottom bracket (where the pedal cranks connect) or the hubs (at the centers of your wheels). The best degreaser is dishwasher detergent in water. Mix in a 5-gallon bucket, apply to your whole bike with a sponge, and then rinse.

› Old toothbrushes are great for getting into hard-to-reach spots, like behind chainrings and behind your bottom bracket.

› After you rinse, drip dry for 15 minutes, but then wipe your bike dry and relube the chain so it won't rust.

LEARN BIKE MAINTENANCE

You can acquire bike maintenance skills through hands-on training, books, videos, and even smartphone apps.

CLASSES

I learn best with hands-on training and have taken three classes on bike maintenance, two quick and free seminars, and one four-hour-long session. As a general rule, the smaller the class size, the more attention you'll get and the more you'll learn. However, just as "no hour of life is wasted that is spent in the saddle" (although Winston Churchill was speaking about horses), any time spent learning about bike maintenance is time well spent.

Free fix-a-flat workshops are fairly common. You'll watch a skilled bike mechanic quickly fix a flat while explaining the steps. A reserved spot in a class will have *you* working through the steps, as well as picking up additional skills.

▰▰▰▰▰▰▰▰▰▰

HELP THEM HELP YOU

If you're not finding many class options, plant the seed in the ear of your local bike shop, library, or workplace—many would be happy to do the legwork of finding resources that provide the service—or see if you can facilitate it by reaching out to your local bicycle club.

▰▰▰▰▰▰▰▰▰▰

Bike Shops

Many bike shops teach repair classes, but it's not always listed on their websites or bulletin boards. Often this is because they're offered on demand for small groups or one-on-one. Prices vary, but the three-hour basic roadside repair class I took at a local bike shop was $50 each for four students and would have been $100 as a private lesson. Taking a class at your LBS or other shop close to home helps you build a stronger relationship with that shop. Close proximity also makes it easy to go back for follow-up advice or help. Bike shops may also offer free fix-a-flat clinics and multisession in-depth bike repair training. My particular class covered how to:

› Check your bike preride

› Fix a flat tire

> Fix a broken chain
> Deal with broken spokes
> Make a minor adjustment to your shifting and brakes
> Pack tools and parts appropriate to your bike, your skill, and your specific ride

Local Bike Clubs

Bicycle clubs and organizations often run a variety of courses on a regular basis. In the case of nonprofit bicycle clubs, your paid class fee supports their programming. Some provide training for free (with donations accepted) or allow payment in the form of volunteer time. A class conducted by a large club with many different arms might end up having additional programs you'd like to explore that you become aware of during the course of your class. Some examples:

> Bikes Not Bombs, Boston
> Bike Works, Seattle
> Cascade Bicycle Club, Seattle
> Cycles for Change, Saint Paul
> The Recyclery Collective, Chicago
> San Francisco Bike Coalition, San Francisco
> Time's Up, New York City

Outdoor Recreation Store

Classes taught by your local outdoor recreation store are a relatively cheap option with multiple dates to choose from. They also tend to have a large participant-to-instructor ratio and will not be quite the same as an intimate in-shop setting. This might prove most convenient and desirable for you. While you won't get as much personal attention in a very large class, you will experience some anonymity—maybe you don't want many sets of eyes on you while you struggle to change a flat tire for the first time.

Local Library and Bike-Oriented Businesses

Does your city have a bike-themed brewery or coffee shop? These places, as well as libraries and similar venues, often provide free seminars on bike repair. Bikes plus books, beer, barista-brewed coffee! You'll be in a fun setting, although that fun setting may become a bit of a distraction. But a free seminar might entice you to try a more serious class, and you'll have met a possible teacher and maybe discovered a new bike-friendly business you'll want to frequent.

Videos

Whether you want to undertake a basic repair or something very convoluted, someone has probably uploaded a video explaining how to fix it. This is especially useful for anything that strays from the ordinary—you may be able to search out a person with a similar bike build to yours and who has seen fit to upload a video with step-by-step instructions for an unusual task, such as fitting standard fenders to your no-frills road bike.

Books

Class tutorials and internet videos are great, but a book that can accompany you downstairs to the damp basement and sit near your greasy chain-cleaning supplies is a wonderful resource too.

Bikes Not Bombs

Boston, Massachusetts

For most bicyclists, a bicycle is a way to get to work, go to the grocery store, or to exercise. But in the hands of the people at Bikes Not Bombs (BNB), those two (or three) wheels become powerful vehicles and tools for social change. Using bicycles for social change specifically means training people to become bicycle mechanics as a viable career path, giving communities with limited transportation access to bikes and working to make Boston and beyond a better and safer place to ride.

Bikes Not Bombs, a thirty-year-old nonprofit, collects around 6,000 used bicycles a year, most of which are shipped overseas to economic development projects in Africa, Latin America, and the Caribbean. Other bikes roll into Boston-based youth programs like Earn-A-Bike, a six-week program during which teens completely overhaul a bike while learning how to safely ride and navigate the city of Boston. Bikes Not Bombs also offers girls-only programs as well as vocational education for teens and adults.

Bikes Not Bombs' retail shop refurbishes some of the collected bicycles and employs many graduates from the youth programs. Profits from sales and repairs go toward funding the youth programs and international work.

Through all of its programs, the Bikes Not Bombs community does the following:

› Addresses the root causes of inequality, violence, and oppression
› Supports the self-empowerment of individuals and communities as a means to achieve sustainable, effective social change
› Includes all people in the social change process in order to challenge the forces and effects of systemic oppression
› Acts in solidarity with local and international partners because this leads to collective understanding and strength
› Commits to sustainable, equitable consumption of resources as critical to the health of our communities and our planet
› Is courageous and bold in the face of injustice
› Uses the bicycle as a powerful vehicle and tool for social change
› Celebrates and builds upon the existing strengths of BNB's partners and participants—over 3,000 Boston youth have participated in BNB youth programs since 1990.

If you're in Boston, donate a bike, use BNB's bike shop, or volunteer in a variety of ways—process donated bikes, work in the office, photograph programs, or even help teach in the youth programs.

See Resources for details on some great repair and maintenance titles that you'll want to add to your library, including *The Big Blue Book of Bicycle Repair*, the Zinn & the Art Of series, and inevitably, *Bike Repair and Maintenance for Dummies*.

Smartphone Apps

While I don't normally concern myself with the weight of my bike components, since I'm more interested in comfort than speed, I draw the line at toting around a 1½-pound book of bike repair instructions. Enter the bike repair smartphone app. I'm not sure I'd personally be patient enough to learn something completely new from the small screen of my phone while sitting next to my broken bike, but I like it as an emergency backup plan. And I can imagine myself reading instructions to a friend with a broken bike on a sunny day. I'm not usually one to pay for apps, either, but I decided that having the robust Bike Repair app was worth a few dollars. It even retrieves cycling-related articles and gives outfit advice based on local weather.

The six-step "How to use a chain tool" has clear pictures and needs little supporting text, making it look easy to repair a broken chain, provided you have a chain tool. And the seven steps for wrapping handlebar tape (used on drop bars) make it look easy enough for any novice to quickly do a professional-looking job.

I also like the Bike Doctor app, also a few dollars. It's more verbose than the Bike Repair app, with "Fitting a new chain" divided into fifteen steps and "Wrapping handlebar tape" as thirteen, but also contains useful pictures for most steps. Bike Doctor is produced by the blog *London Cyclist* so some of the words differ from our American terminology, but the most notable is just the spelling of "tyre."

CHAPTER 10

Multimodal Bike Commuting and Bike Share

NOT ALL BIKE COMMUTES are door-to-door bike rides. When a route is otherwise too far or partially unbikeable, pairing bus, train, or car with biking can be an excellent way to reap the benefits of bike commuting. If your commute is complicated by a major barrier, such as a tunnel or a bridge with no bicycle access, using other means to cross should be on your radar. And if you must navigate a particularly difficult stretch of road, it's nice to be able to catch a ride to bypass it.

While I love the ease of hopping on my bike without having to worry about arriving at a bus stop at a specific time, I find certain destinations much more easily reached by a multimodal combination. On one occasion I had two free hours (before and after) to bike the entire twenty miles to my dentist, but in general, it's easiest to bike-plus-bus it. Door-to-door driving might be quicker when there isn't traffic—30 minutes—but more realistically the drive will end up being between 60 and 90 minutes, making the 70-minute multimodal ride an easy choice.

Combining your bike commute with a ride of some sort greatly increases your range. The majority of bike commuters go about five miles, but if your commute is longer and you don't want to bike twenty miles each way, day after day, imagine a commute that's a couple miles to a bike-rack-equipped bus, a 15-minute bus trip along the freeway, and a couple more miles biked on the other end.

CAR

It can be quite simple to transport yourself and your bike by car. There are several possible combinations for adding driving to your bike commute:

Drive your own car part of the way to your destination—with your bike along. Take a carpool from home part of the way to your destination—with your bike along.

Bike to the starting spot of a carpool that takes you to your destination—with or without your bike along.

Bike to the starting spot of a carpool, ride to the driver's destination—with your bike along—and then bike to your destination.

PROS:

› Choose exactly which part of the biking portion to cut out of the trip.
› In the case of using your own car, you stay on your own schedule (rather than a transit or carpool schedule).

CONS:

› Not as green as public transit.
› You will most likely need a car rack, and so will the driver of the carpool if you choose to bring your bike along.

CAR BIKE RACKS

You might be able to fit your bike inside your car or the carpool driver's car. Car racks, however, are often a simpler solution. Most don't require removing a wheel (to learn how to remove quick-release wheels, see Chapter 9) and all have the bonus of keeping the dirty bike away from the interior of your car or trunk. Remember, if your bike will be left unattended on a car rack, at least lock the frame to the wheel so it can't be ridden away, and if possible, lock your bike to the rack. The three main types of car racks are trunk racks, hitch-mount racks, and roof racks.

Trunk Racks

A trunk rack is the cheapest and simplest type of car rack. It attaches to the back of the car with three to six adjustable straps that hook to the trunk or the hatchback, anchoring it firmly in place. Bikes are placed upright on two prongs and held in place by two rubber straps. I got mine used for $60 and it holds three bikes. Smaller ones that hold one or two bikes are even more inexpensive.

For bikes with step-through frames (which can be hard to make fit on the rack since they lack a convenient top tube parallel, or near parallel, to the ground), you will want to get a top-tube insert so that the rack can carry the bike safely. In addition to making the bike *much* easier to hang, it also makes for a more evenly balanced load than a bike hanging at an angle made to fit.

Pros:

› Inexpensive
› Attaches easily and fits many different vehicles
› Folds for easy storage, such as in the trunk of a car

Cons:

› May put strain on the car
› Straps can break or get loose
› Straps must be carefully tightened each time
› Hard to lock the rack to the car
› Prevents the trunk from opening while bikes are on it

> May partially block rear visibility
> Adds length to the car

Hitch-Mount Racks

If your car has a hitch, you can spend a bit more money for a sturdy hitch-mount rack . . . and if it doesn't have one, an aftermarket hitch can be installed at rack stores and some moving/storage stores. Match your rack to your hitch-opening size: 1¼ inches or 2 inches. Adapters are available to make a 1¼-inch rack fit a 2-inch opening. Bikes either hang from a bar or sit on a platform.

Pros:
> Easy to install and remove
> Won't damage the car
> Locks to the vehicle
> Some versions can hold up to five bikes.

Cons:
> Expensive, especially for versions that hold more bikes, or have features like swing-away arms
> Heavy
> May partially block rear visibility
> Adds length to the car

Roof Racks

Roof racks are a good choice for people who wish to transport sporting equipment like skis, snowboards, and kayaks. They're also a good option for carrying tandem bikes and cargo bikes, since they won't stick out to the side as they would on other rack styles. Just don't forget that the rack and your bike are up there and that they add height to your car! Bicycle mechanic Kent Peterson says that every year he sees a customer who has destroyed a bike because they forgot it

Top tube insert

Trunk rack

was on the roof rack and slammed it into their garage or the drive-thru at a bank or a fast food establishment.

Pros:
› Allows for trunk access
› Doesn't block visibility out the back
› Can easily carry nonbike items too

Cons:
› Costs more than trunk racks (comparably priced to a hitch-mount rack)
› Requires installation
› Requires lifting your bike above your head
› Adds height to car, which can be more dangerous than added length—think garage clearance and tree branches
› Adds wind resistance and wind noise
› For fork-mount style, front wheel must be removed and stored in the car.

PARK AND RIDE

Park and Ride is generally thought of as a parking service for those who use public transportation or meet a carpool, but it works well with biking too. As Park and Ride lots offer free (usually) car parking outside the city center, they're good spots for switching from your car to your bike. (And don't forget that you don't need to drive a car to a Park and Ride. Park and Ride lots usually have bike racks so you could bike to a Park and Ride, then continue your trip with public transit or a carpool.)

PROS:
› Secure (usually) parking
› Easy way to shorten a trip from the suburbs

CONS:
› Some lots have limited space.
› Not as green as using public transportation (if you're driving a car to the lot)
› Adds the hassle of finding an available parking spot

BUS

Taking your bike on the bus can be a green, hassle-free way to avoid a certain road, a long distance, or bad weather. Most city buses have bike racks that accommodate two or three bikes. They're all similar, but there are several different makes and models, so check with your local transit company for loading, unloading, and other procedure instructions. You should be able to find instructions with photos and videos on your bus company's website and additional tips and locations of practice racks, if any.

PROS:

› Multiple bus lines make this a system that works for many destinations.
› Regular, recurring buses make for repeat options if you miss a bus or if the bike rack is full.
› It's green! Traveling by bus produces much fewer emissions per passenger than a single-occupant car.

CONS:

› Limited number of bike spots
› Must remove and replace gear
› Must remember to bring bus fare or pass
› Must follow the bus schedule

BUS AND BIKE TIPS

When you ride the bus with your bike, you'll have to think about a few more things than when you hop aboard with nothing more cumbersome than your bus pass and a paperback.

My very first bike-on-bus trip felt like a bit of a disaster. Keep in mind that I was traveling with 50 pounds of bike, a baby and a toddler, a bulky bag containing our three bike helmets, and countless baby accoutrements. Although I had watched the online tutorial many times and lifted my bike onto a practice rack, when the bus barreled to a stop thirty feet past the spot I had chosen to station my pile of stuff, I forgot everything I knew and ran with my bike toward the bus, baby strapped to my back, toddler wailing because he thought he was being left behind. I didn't smoothly squeeze the bike rack lever like a calm person would do and had trouble lowering the rack. I think someone offered to help me, but I was too frazzled to accept any offers and may have chirped something about having "watched the video and practiced, don't worry!" Lifting the bike in a real-life situation proved ten times harder and heavier than at the practice rack for some strange reason, but with a lot of huffing and puffing and wrestling with the tire clamp (also quite easy to use if squeezed smoothly and calmly, go figure) the bike was on and I raced up the steps with both kids in tow, sweat dripping from my brow.

It took me only a few adventures to feel like a seasoned pro. For specific rules, visit your city's transit website.

Preparing for Your First Bike-and-Bus Trip

› Read the instructions and watch the video provided by your local transit system.
› Can't find a video? Watch a video from a different city's bus system.
› Practice removing all loose and valuable items. This safety rule is part of most bus programs. It's to prevent you from losing items that might fall

off your bike and to avoid blocking the driver's field of vision. It will also make your bike significantly lighter to lift. Items to remove might include water bottles, air pump, lock, panniers, and lights.

> Practice lifting your bike several feet off the ground at home. Your unladen bike probably weighs between 20 and 30 pounds—and a heavy-duty city bike can weigh 50 pounds. If you're not already in the habit of lifting it, you'll want to find good handholds so you aren't stressed when it comes time to use the bike rack for the first time. Start with your left hand on your left handlebar and your right hand on the frame, near your saddle. Practice lifting with the bike facing the other way, too, taking care to not brush against the chain.

> If your system requires you to balance the weight of your bike in the air with one hand while manipulating the rack with the other, practice that too. For example, some Chicago Transit Authority buses require you to support the bicycle with one hand while swinging the red bicycle support arm outward and down to clear the wheel well.

> Find a practice rack.

> Find an agreeable bus driver on a scheduled twenty-minute break at the end of a run and ask if you can practice.

> Bring an experienced friend along to show you the ropes.

Waiting to Board

Wait near the bus stop sign with your bike so you and your bike are visible, and remove all removable and valuable items before the bus arrives.

Always approach the bus from the curb side, and tell the bus driver that you are loading a bike, either by voice through the door or by making eye contact through the window and gesturing.

If the rack is full, you'll have to wait for the next bus. With the exception of folding bikes, most cities will not allow a bike inside the bus, although Metro Transit in Minneapolis and St. Paul leaves this to the bus driver's discretion. Check your city's rules before asking. When traveling at times or on days when there might be many bikes on the bus, you should consider giving yourself extra time in case you have to wait for a second bus.

Loading Your Bike

Follow the local rules for your specific bus, but here's the gist:

If the rack is empty and folded in the storage position, squeeze the handle at the top of the rack to release it and pull the rack down until it latches or clicks.

Lift your bike into the empty tray. Some cities want you to put your bike in the outermost slot (so the bus driver can most easily see the length of the rack) while many others require that the first bike go on the innermost empty slot (making it easier for subsequent bikes to be loaded). See what other cyclists do or ask the driver if you're not sure of the local policy.

Release the support arm by pulling outward and upward or depressing the button if there is one, and then clamp the support arm to the top of your wheel, close to the frame. Check your local rules, but most will suggest putting the arm on top of your front fender. Some people with a lot of fender clearance will slide the arm between tire and fender. After mounting your bike on the bus, you can give your bike a quick shake to make sure it's fully in place.

Avoid kneeling or squatting in front of the bus. Never move past the bus into the traffic lane—it's impossible for other drivers to see you when you are in front of the bus. After you board, sit close to the front of the bus so you can see your bike.

Unloading Your Bike

As you get ready to disembark, let the driver know you're going to remove your bike. Pull the support arm up and off your bike tire and return it to the down position, then lift your bike off the rack and either keep it in front of your body or quickly set it on the sidewalk. If there are no other bikes in the rack and no one is waiting to load a bike, return the rack to its upright position until it locks into place. Remain on the sidewalk until the bus leaves the stop.

Other Bike-on-Bus Tips

› Bikes are sometimes stolen off the front of buses. However, you are *not* allowed to lock your bike to the rack. If you're worried about security, you can lock your bike's front wheel to its frame before the bus arrives. This doesn't prevent someone from lifting your bike from the rack, but it will prevent them from riding off with it.

▰▰▰▰▰▰▰▰▰▰▰▰

CARRYING YOUR BIKE

Carry your bike up a couple of stairs the same way that you walk it up a curb—keep your hands on the handlebars or on the stem to lift the front wheel and allow the rear wheel to bump along behind.

A longer flight of stairs is best tackled with both wheels off the ground, left hand on the left handlebar, near the stem, and right hand on the top tube, in front of the bottom bracket (where the pedals attach). Lift the bike a few inches off the ground, angled with the rise of the stairs, and you're good to go.

Steeper stairs might be easier with the bike on your right shoulder, provided that it doesn't feel uncomfortable and the drink cages don't poke you. Left hand holds the left handlebar and right hand helps carry some of the weight of the top tube.

There are also bike-carrying-specific accessories like leave-on handles and attach-when-necessary shoulder straps that you might find worth adding if you do a lot of bike hefting.

Always stay on the left side of your bike so you don't rub against your chain.

▰▰▰▰▰▰▰▰▰▰▰▰

› If you notice any problem with a rack, notify the bus operator and wait for the next bus—it's best for everyone's safety (as well as for the well-being of your bike!).
› Folding bikes should be folded and taken with you onto the bus. Not all

folding bikes fold small enough to fit under the seat—bikes with larger folded-up dimensions may be subject to the driver's discretion.

› If your bike has very small wheels (such as a children's bike) or very big wheels, check ahead to make sure it will fit on the rack. Most racks can only accommodate bikes with wheels between 20 and 29 inches.

› If you need help, the bus operator is not permitted to load your bike for you. However, they may offer you advice or directions while you mount your bike.

› Beware of forgetting your bike on the bus—it happens! Check ahead to see if there is a special phone number for lost and found bikes.

› Some bus stops are accessed by stairs or elevators (and escalators, but bikes are generally not allowed on escalators). Carry your bike upstairs (see sidebar) or walk it to the elevator. If either of these options seems more of a hassle than it's worth, choose the next bus stop up or down the line.

COMMUTER TRAIN

Like taking the bus with a bike, taking the train with a bike involves some extra rules and planning ahead. Again, rules vary from city to city, but many commuter trains do allow bikes on board. Some cities restrict bike usage to off-peak hours—for example, Chicago Transit Authority doesn't allow weekday travel on the "L" with full-size bikes between 7:00 a.m. and 9:00 a.m. or 4:00

p.m. and 6:00 p.m. And some cities don't allow bikes to use certain crowded stations during peak hours. Note: most of these rules apply to full-size bicycles only, not folding bikes.

PROS:
› Trains run often.
› Fast, rarely impacted by traffic
› Easy access to congested areas

CONS:
› Many trains aren't at street level and you must carry your bike up and down stairs or find the elevator.
› Bikes aren't allowed on escalators.
› Some trains may restrict bikes at certain hours.
› Train stations are often crowded and not easy to walk your bike through.
› Train cars are crowded and hard to cram into with a bike.
› You must remember to bring fare or transit pass.

LOADING YOUR BIKE

Commuter trains are quite a bit simpler than the bus since the bike travels inside with you, not exposed out front on a rack. Your biggest challenges will probably be navigating your way through a crowded field of bodies while walking your bike, trying not to trip anyone or bang your shin on your pedal, and carrying your bike up and down stairs if your station is not at ground level.

Check the website of your city's transit operator to see what bike facilities exist

Commuter train bike hook

CHANGE IS POSSIBLE

After a brief pilot program of testing bikes on trains during peak commute hours, Bay Area Rapid Transit (BART) changed its rules to allow bikes on all trains at all times. For people who wish to avoid bikes, the first three cars of any peak train (7:00 a.m. to 9:00 a.m., 4:30 p.m. to 6:30 p.m.) are bike-free.

in your train cars because there is more variability than for buses. You will probably enter the train through one of the doors with a bike symbol on it—provided the car is not too full to accommodate you and your bike, in which case you wait for the next train—and then either hang your bike vertically from a hook and sit down in a seat, or stand in a designated area with your bike. If you think something will fall off your bike while it's hanging, remove it first, but most things can stay put—panniers, lights, and water bottles shouldn't dislodge.

A SAMPLING OF RULES

› Walk your bike in the station.
› Do not ride the escalator with your bike.
› Bikes are not permitted in crowded cars.
› Only two bikes allowed per car.
› Do not block the aisle.
› Bikes may not be permitted on trains on holidays and during special events.

FERRY

Take your bike aboard a ferry to avoid the long way around a waterway. There is often no extra charge for bringing a bike aboard. Some ferries are equipped to carry many bikes—the Golden Gate Ferry to Sausalito can hold 715 passengers and 200 bikes, but smaller vessels, like the same system's Larkspur Ferry, which uses a high-speed catamaran on weekdays, can hold only 15 bikes.

PROS:
› Often limitless space for bikes
› Drastically cuts mileage on trips by skirting a body of water

CONS:
› Boarding is often farther out of the way than other transit options
› Must bring ferry fare or pass
› Less frequent trips compared to other transit options

LOADING YOUR BIKE

Ferries operate a little differently from one another so check the ferry system's website for loading instructions ahead of time. Some ferries load foot passengers and bicyclist passengers from the same area. Larger ferries might have a lane just for bikes, next to the car lanes.

Some ferries allow bicyclists to ride aboard; some require that you walk your bike on. Beware of metal plates and gaps, especially if you're riding. Shift down to your lowest gear as you traverse the deck in case there is a climb to get off the ferry. Bikes will board either before the cars or after all the cars, with a designated area with bike rack or railing or similar surface to lean the bike against or tie it up.

You don't have to stay with your bike during the journey. I usually hook my handlebar over the railing, tie the thin string around my top tube, give my saddle a little pat, and take off for the cafeteria.

If you notice other bike commuters stripping their bikes of belongings before entering the passenger area of the ferry, ask them if they worry about theft. I have yet to ride a ferry where everyone didn't leave everything on their bikes, but it's worthwhile to check the behavior of the more seasoned ferry riders.

TRANSIT BIKE

Some people who live close to transit, but can't use it to get all the way to their destination, leave a cheap bike with a very secure lock (or multiple locks) at the station. This can even be done with a bike on either side!

PROS:
› No hassle of bringing bike on transit

CONS:
› Exposure to theft
› Must bring transit fare or pass

BIKE LOCKERS

Bike lockers are provided at many transit facilities, such as bus stops, train stations, transit centers, and Park and Ride lots to facilitate multimodal travel, offering a safer way to leave a bike if you don't want to bring it with you on the bus or train. In Seattle, you can lease a specific locker for $50 annually, or an on-demand locker for five cents an hour. Here and in most cities, you phone or email to check availability; use the contact information provided on the transit website.

PROS:
› Secure, weatherproof bike parking

CONS:
› Not always available
› Added expense

/ / / / / / / / / / / /

FOLDING BIKES: THE QUINTESSENTIAL MULTIMODAL BIKE

Folding bikes make for excellent multimodal travel companions. Space rules generally apply just to full-sized nonfolding bikes, which means you can bring your folding bike along on any bus, train, or ferry. Check local rules—you are probably allowed to wheel your bike, unfolded, through the station, but will need to have it completely folded and ready to carry for boarding. I don't know if I'd want to tote a 25-pound folding bike for extended periods of time, but carrying a small form through a crowded station, over turnstiles, and up the stairway can be a lot easier than finding room for a full-size bike.

/ / / / / / / / / / / /

BIKE TRANSIT CENTERS

A step up from bike lockers, bike transit centers often combine secure bike parking with additional services, like bike repair and showers. Many operate as membership programs, although some offer free bike parking but require a membership purchase to use the other amenities. These are often located at transit centers for easy connecting to bus and train, or near the city center.

The Chicago Bike Station is a 300-space, climate-controlled indoor bicycle-parking facility that provides lockers, showers, bike repair mechanic service, bike rental, bicycle tours, and other amenities designed to encourage biking to Millennium Park and other downtown Chicago locations. Parking is free, but memberships and day passes can be purchased for access to showers and other services.

Portland's Go by Bike is a free bike valet connected to the Oregon Health & Science University aerial tram. Parked bikes are exposed to the elements, but free seat covers are provided. Rentals and bike repair are also offered on-site.

Bikestation is a network of bike transit centers with several locations in California (Covina, Long Beach, Palo Alto, and Santa Barbara) and one in Washington, DC. Each Bikestation is different, but many have showers and day-use lockers, discounts on retail products, and access to repair services. The Long Beach Bikestation currently offers free daytime bike parking to the public, but the others only provide access to members.

Sarah Tew

David Katzmaier

New York, New York

David Katzmaier is a born-again bike commuter in America's biggest city. He used to bike to work in the mid-2000s from Brooklyn to Lower Manhattan . . . until the day he got doored. Neither he nor the bike was hurt badly, but he decided to switch to subway commuting and walking. When Citi Bike launched in mid-2013, though, he joined.

Biking doesn't save David a lot of time—it takes six or seven minutes versus the fifteen minutes he used to walk from Penn Station to his office at CNET.com on the West Side—but it's better exercise and a lot of fun. And he was able to convince his employer to pay the $95 annual fee (although he says he would have joined even if he had to pay it himself, considering it an amazing bargain). He rides every weekday except in the worst weather, which so far has only been three or four days per year due to bad rain or snow. On nice mornings, he often takes a longer route for the joy and exercise. It takes about four times as long at 26 minutes, but he tends to do it a few times per week.

BIKES

Transporting his personal bike on the train he takes from Long Island to Penn Station would prove a major hassle, so Citi Bike is the perfect solution. He lauds the comfortable seat and handlebars, superb brakes, full fenders, easy seat adjustability, internal hub gearing (so you can shift during stops), and ingeniously designed cargo rack. Not having a high top tube to rest the bike against his leg when stopped at a light meant the step-through frame took David some getting used to, and he wishes there were more than three gears to combat the slowness and heaviness of the bikes.

David likes that he doesn't need to spend time and money maintaining a bike—the tires are always full, and rarely does a bike he takes out of the rack have any issue. If it does, he just bears with it for his short ride or grabs a new one.

CLOTHING

The biggest change in David's wardrobe is carrying around a helmet. While on foot and on the train, he simply straps the helmet to his backpack—a minor inconvenience he barely notices anymore. Otherwise, he hasn't made any clothing adjustments, wearing the same shoes and pants as ever, and the same jackets, gloves, and scarves when it's cold. In wintry weather he also adds the earflap-equipped winter insert to his Bern Allston bike helmet and is perfectly comfortable on even the chilliest days. During summer's hottest days he gets a little sweaty, but not bad enough to ruin a shirt or disturb coworkers or fellow train passengers (that he knows of).

BIKE SECURITY

With Citi Bike, locking up the bike isn't an issue. Using his annual passkey, David unlocks the bike from a "station," a large fancy rack with individual locking docks for each bike, at Penn Station. Then he locks it up at a different station near his office, and the bike is ready for another rider.

ROADSIDE REPAIR

While David keeps a repair kit on his home bike, it's not necessary with Citi Bike. He's never had a flat, but in the event of a problem, he says he'd walk the bike to the nearest station—if he didn't already know its location, he'd find it via any number of smartphone apps—dock the bike, and hit the red "Repair Needed" alert button on the dock.

COMMUTERBLOG

The train portion of David's commute takes two hours round-trip, during which he does a lot of reading, a little bit of people watching, and writes and produces *Commuterblog* (see Resources). A reviewer of TVs and home theater products by profession, David's talents easily transfer to reviews of commute-related gear and all aspects of Citi Bike—and bike shares in general. He shares a couple "pro tips" here:

› Pro tip 1: At a well-stocked station, look for a bike with the seat height already adjusted close to yours; you'll save a few seconds not having to adjust it.
› Pro tip 2: Sometimes it pays to walk the bike across the street so you can make the light, and then put on your helmet and adjust the seat.

I particularly like his tips for finding bikes during peak season when the racks near Penn Station, and other hot spots, empty out: "As Citi Bike continues to gain popularity and the weather warms, I expect occasional empty racks to crop up. When that happens I turn to my phone. The official Citi Bike app provides real-time counts of all of the stations in the system, so you know (a) what station is closest and (b) whether it has any bikes. The information is usually correct, but if there are only one or two left at a station during rush hour, chances are the bikes are broken. Or they'll be snapped up before you can get there."

And the bell tip: "Occasionally something will be broken on a bike you get. The most common issue I've found is the bell won't ring or is too soft. I've learned to ring the bell and make sure it works *before* I chose that bike. I've never encountered a flat tire, on the other hand, and the rest of the stuff usually works great, so the bell is the only thing I bother checking before I pull out a bike."

DAVID'S TIPS FOR NEW BIKE COMMUTERS

› In New York it pays to explore. If you have a couple of extra minutes, particularly in the morning before you have to be at work, check out different routes beyond the one that gets you there the fastest.
› Ride defensively, assume drivers and especially (in NYC) pedestrians are unaware of you, use your bell constantly, use a hand signal when moving in and out of traffic, and anticipate the doors opening on parked cars. Stick to bike lane streets when possible, and *never* ride the wrong way down a street, even for just one block.
› Obey traffic signals for the most part but if you decide to cross against the red (seriously, all NYC bikers do it) be extra careful of cars, and especially police (they will ticket unlucky bikers).
› Don't use headphones (two is illegal in New York, but even one severely impairs your awareness).

"Of course, always wear a helmet. In NYC, especially with Citi Bikers and novice bicyclists, helmets are being seen more as optional than necessary. That's a dangerous trend. Like many other things with riding, wearing a helmet not only keeps you safer, but shows that you know your stuff and belong on a bike in the city. It's also a fashion statement, so if you're commuting by bike every day go ahead and splurge. I don't regret paying extra for mine because, well, it's awesome."

PRESCRIBE-A-BIKE

In March 2014, Boston began a "Prescribe-a-Bike" program for its Hubway bike-share system. Boston Bikes and the Boston Public Health Commission offer subsidized annual memberships for just $5 to low-income Boston residents. Participants also get a free helmet and Bicycle Benefits sticker (see profile of Bicycle Benefits in Chapter 1).

PROS:
› Secure bike parking
› Often free
› Easy access to repair services

CONS:
› One location, might not be convenient

BIKE SHARE

Bike-share programs provide a number of self-serve bike stations throughout a city for point-to-point trips. They're designed for users who want to take short trips—akin to on-demand public transit since the bikes are docked at stations, ready when you are. When you've finished, you dock the bike at any station. There is no worry of theft as with a locked personal bike, nor any upkeep. Various subscriptions are available—day passes, multiday passes, monthly and annual memberships—and depending on the city, trips under 30 or 45 minutes are generally free, making it an affordable transportation option for both regular local users and out-of-town visitors. Bike share really shines when using it away from home and most trips are taken by people without annual passes.

I met a woman at a bike shop who said she used to bike commute before her child's school schedule made it too difficult, but now she leaves her car in the parking garage for the day and uses bike share on her lunch hour to run errands.

The bikes are sturdy and comfortable, with always-on front and rear lights, fenders, a front basket for your belongings, a soft saddle of adjustable height, a kickstand, and easy-to-use gears—with a range to match the terrain of the

given city: relatively flat New York's Citi Bike has three gears and hilly Seattle's Pronto has seven. The only thing you need to bring in most cities (other than your annual pass key or credit card) is a helmet. Seattle is an interesting exception, with its all-ages helmet law, and Pronto provides rental helmets for an additional fee (free for members).

Bike share is already available in over thirty large cities with a dozen more in the planning stages. The Pedestrian and Bicycle Information Center maintains a map and list of US bike-share systems with over seventy-five programs listed, which includes college campus systems and soon-to-be-opened programs.

Citi Bike in New York reported amazing numbers for its first year of operation: May 2013 through May 2014—over 8.75 million trips with over 14.7 million miles pedaled.

PROS:

› No lock necessary—when you're done, you dock the bike at a station.
› Many locations and bikes throughout participating cities.

› Smartphone apps make it easy to locate docking stations and available bikes and open spots.
› No hassle
› No fees for maintaining a personal bike
› Your company may provide a corporate membership.
› It's fun! The upright bikes are comfy and fun to ride.
› Community engagement—be prepared to answer questions about bike share.

CONS:
› Not available in all cities
› Sometimes hard to find a station with available bikes
› Sometimes hard to find a station with an available slot for returning a bike
› Must complete trip within 30 or 45 minutes to avoid a fee
› Will probably require walking a block or more than riding your own bike would

Bike share station

CHAPTER 11

Commuting with Kids

SHUTTLING SMALL KIDS TO and from daycare, school, activities, and routine errands is a major part of many commutes. Some assume this spells the end of bike commuting and so trade bike for minivan—but that doesn't have to be the case. Many liken the sense of euphoria of riding a bike as an adult to feeling like a kid again. Adding an *actual* kid to the mix further punctuates your day with a dose of joy. Plus, kids are small, light, and terrifically portable by bike.

My daily commute includes two small kids, and while the mad rush to get out the door on time feels similar to any other sort of commute, once we're sailing down the street on our big family bike, life slows down to an observable and enjoyable speed. We wave at the crossing guard, exchanging a few words as we turn left at his post; marvel at the progress the big machines are making at a construction site; take in the aromas of the Fremont Brewing Company and Theo Chocolate Factory; laugh at the rain in our faces; and celebrate beating the sailboats to our drawbridge crossing. We also sing songs and spell words, although this is often interrupted to chat with another bicyclist or motorist at a red light: "Yes, it's a great day for a bike ride—every day is!" "Ha ha, no, the kids don't realize how lucky they are. Someday they'll help with the pedaling."

SELECTING A BIKE, SEAT, OR TRAILER

Just like children transition from infant car seat to convertible car seat to booster seat to standard seat belt when they ride in cars, the growth of your child will require similar adjustments to the family bike. Sometimes this involves smaller changes, like seating systems attached to a cargo bike, but sometimes it calls for a different bike altogether. My own seven-years-and-counting biking-with-kids journey has followed this course:

› Front child seat on a bike we already owned (for six months)
› Front child seat on more accommodating new bike (for one year)
› Front child seat and trailer containing infant car seat (for one year)
› Front child seat and rear child seat (for one year)

> Longtail cargo bike (for three years)
> Longtail cargo bike with kids increasingly riding on their own (currently)

At some point in the future, I'd love to add a tandem bike with a trailer bike attached behind, but as our current system works fine, I'm in no rush to add another bike to my collection just yet.

Any number of combinations could have worked for my carrying one, then two kids, but I felt comfortable entering the family biking ranks by adding an affordable seat (unused, from an online auction site, in my case) to an underutilized bike in the garage. Had I looked at the big picture and immediately invested in a cargo bike, I know I would have loved that too.

Many parents balk at the cost of cargo bikes because often bikes are still seen as recreational "toys" even when they're used for replacing trips otherwise taken by a car or a bus. However, family bikes and family biking accessories resell well and cost much less than cars, probably less even than some fancy strollers. Since family biking is seeing a rise in America, demand will make for mass-produced, less expensive options and more used family bikes to be found.

And you don't have to choose just one thing—or choose one thing and then stick with only it. We've had a lot of overlap with our fleet. The beach cruiser is long gone, but I still have its replacement bike, though now only with the rear seat. This I use for multimodal trips—my younger son sits in the rear seat and my older son

rides his own bike, and it's perfect for getting all of us to the bus.

If you have the space and budget to get a trailer *and* add a seat to your bike, or to get an entirely new cargo bike, get them both, get them all! They all have advantages—the trailer is enclosed and cozy and can also be used for carrying nonkid cargo for years and years to come . . . in fact, your kids can carry stuff with it *for* you down the road. Not to mention the peace of mind of having backup family biking systems. Flat tire on your regular rig? Hook the trailer up to your mountain bike and you're good to go! At one point I had three bikes with which I could carry two kids.

There's a bit more to it than just attaching a seat or trailer, sticking the kid in it, and pedaling off into the sunset, but the basic components are these: selecting a kid-carrying bike or accessory, probably making a few adjustments to your riding style and route, and encouraging the kid to come along willingly. And as with regular bikes, there are a range of bikes and kid seats with hopefully a price point for everyone.

BIKE RIDING BREAKDOWN BY AGE
> *Ages zero to eleven months:* The American Academy of Pediatrics states that infants under twelve months old should not be carried on a bicycle. (See Babies on Bikes.)
> *Ages one to three:* Once they are a year old, children are strong enough to support the weight of a helmet and

BABIES ON BIKES

The American Academy of Pediatrics warns that babies under one should not be carried on bikes. However, this doesn't mean you won't see infants on bikes. There are numerous families whose research and preference for a car-lite or car-free lifestyle has led them to emulate methods used in other countries, such as the Netherlands, for transporting babies on bikes. In the Netherlands it is common practice to carry babies in infant car seats secured in *bakfietsen* (Dutch-style long john cargo bikes).

An issue in America is that car seats are not designed to contain helmet-wearing infants, but helmets are required by law for all children when on bikes.

Since *bakfietsen* are not as ubiquitous in the Unites States as in their homeland, you may also see infants in car seats transported in trailers. This is how I chose to carry my second child. I did this by opting for the safety of the infant car seat to act as a roll cage and considered him more protected in its cocoon than he would have been with a helmet. I also kept the trailer's wheels underinflated, biked slower than normal, and stuck to smooth roads and paths. He loved it from ten weeks old to a bit over a year, when he outgrew the car seat and graduated to wearing a helmet in the trailer or in the front bike seat. Granted, he spent much of that time sleeping, lulled by the gentle ride that seemed even less jostling than being pushed in a stroller.

sit up in a seat (at the front or the rear of the bike) or in a trailer or on/in a cargo bike.

› *Ages four to seven:* Kids may begin outgrowing the trailer—or prefer being up and out of it. New options for this reality: rear seats, trailer bikes, and cargo bikes.

› *Ages five to ten:* Rear seats with higher weight limits (up to 77 pounds), trailer bikes, cargo bikes, and tandem bikes are great for this age range.

› *Age eight and up:* Ideally, a city's bicycle infrastructure supports bicyclists starting at age eight. If this isn't the case for your city, many of the options

Baby Wylie loves his front seat.

above still work for commuting with a larger kid: cargo bikes, trailer bikes, and tandem bikes.

FAMILY BIKES

Any bike carrying an adult and one or more kids is a family bike. There is a wide variety of family bikes, from a regular bike with an added front child seat to an enormous motorized tricycle with a box and canopy large enough to hold eight kids. There are also many things a family bike is *not*. Maybe you've seen someone riding a bike while babywearing an infant using a sling or backpack, with a second child propped on the handlebars or top tube, or standing on the rear rack. These scenarios fall outside the typical definition of "family bike" and also fall outside of what is considered safe family biking practice in America.

Bikes and add-ons for carrying kids vary by size, age, and rider preference. Many seats are rated for certain weight ranges—a distinction that roughly correlates to age and ability. Age recommendations are just estimates—some children ride successfully much earlier than the ages suggested. Do what feels safe and comfortable, and discuss any concerns with your trusted pediatrician.

Read on for special equipment and bikes for safely carrying your family on two—and sometimes three—wheels.

FRONT SEATS

Ages: one to three years

Front seats are fun for small kids, as they're encompassed in the rider's arms and can easily communicate with you. Napping is possible, although only some front seats come with a nap bar accessory and even then, naps are often taken on your arm. Most bikes can accommodate front seats—they usually attach to the stem—but upright bikes, where there is more room to stick an extra person between your torso and the bike's handlebars, are the most comfortable option.

Pros:

> Your child is in front of you and is easy to communicate with.
> Many front child seats are easy to take off when not in use or can be swapped between multiple bikes.
> It's an affordable option.
> Most bikes can accommodate a front seat.
> Steering isn't much different with a front-mounted seat.

Cons:

> Weight limits range from 33 to 40 pounds and some tots will outgrow them very quickly.
> On bikes that aren't fully upright, you will probably need to stick your knees out to the side a bit to avoid striking the seat while pedaling.
> Kids are exposed to the elements, although some brands have optional windscreens that block wind and some rain.
> It's not usually compatible with a front basket or bag.
> Child can reach and thus interfere ("help") with shifting and braking.

Some front seats come with kid handlebars to dissuade them from this.

FRONT SEATS FOR BIGGER KIDS
Ages: four to seven years

Front seats for larger kids take the form of saddles, many of which attach to the top tube, therefore requiring a flat top tube. They generally come with foot pegs and the child can share the rider's handlebars.

One unique system in this category is the Brompton folding bike with Pere (formerly IT Chair) child seat. The bike has an overall weight limit (rider and cargo) of 240 pounds, so the simple seat can accommodate big children or smaller riders.

Pros:
> Front seat saddles are an affordable way to carry a bigger kid on a regular bike.
> The position of the seat allows room for rear baskets or panniers to hold a lot of cargo.

Cons:
> Kids are exposed to the elements.
> It's a tight fit having a bigger kid in front so it's usually only comfortable for short trips.

REAR SEATS
Ages: one to five years

Rear seats are easy to add to most bikes and work well for small kids, although communication isn't quite as easy as with front seats. The higher back cradles short passengers' heads and makes naps easy, with some rear seats equipped with a recline setting.

Rear seats either attach to the seat post or to the rear rack. A kid is strapped in with a three- or five-point harness and has foot rests (some include feet buckles) and wheel guards—keeping small feet from getting caught up in the spokes. This makes it hard to fit baskets or panniers, although there are some extended racks that fit with certain rear seats. Rear seats are often used on longtail and midtail cargo bikes (covered below).

Pros:
> Rear seats fit on regular bikes.
> Napping is possible.
> Weight limit is higher than for front seats—around 50 pounds.

Cons:
> Kids are exposed to the elements, although DIY weather covers are fairly easy to make.
> Added weight at the back of the bike

makes maneuvering the bike, especially at slow speeds, more difficult.

› Baskets or panniers are hard to fit on the rear rack without an extended rack.

› Communication isn't as easy as with front seats.

REAR SEATS FOR BIGGER KIDS
Ages: five to ten years

Several lower-profile rear seats can carry kids up to 75 pounds. They're equipped with only a lap belt but do have foot pegs and wheel skirts. Some have seat backs that will fold down when not in use.

Pros:

› Regular bikes accommodate rear seats for larger kids.

› Lower-profile foot rests usually don't interfere with baskets or panniers as much as rear seats for smaller kids.

Cons:

› Kids are exposed to the elements, although there are options for fairly easy to make DIY weather covers.

› More difficult maneuvering of the bike (especially at low speeds) due to added weight at the back of the bike.

TRAILERS
Ages: under one to six years

Trailers can connect to almost any bike. Most trailers have a hitch that stays on your bicycle, connected to the axle through your rear hub. Some older trailers have a clamp that attaches to the chain stay. Both versions usually have a backup safety strap that wraps around part of your bike frame (chain stay or seat stay) and hooks onto the trailer arm. The arm then connects to the passenger compartment, which rests upon two wheels.

Trailers are popular for babies and toddlers, especially for travel during naptime. Some trailers boast recessed head pockets to comfortably accommodate helmeted heads, but smaller, shorter children often don't sit high enough to reach these pockets. Rounded rather than pointy-at-the-back helmets work best in trailers especially for this reason. But some parents will get creative with padding or pillows to make their children fit well. A small back pillow that still allows the harness to buckle securely, but makes for an extra inch of space between helmet and backrest, can keep a one-year-old's helmet from getting pushed forward over her eyes, thus avoiding a miserable ride.

Weight, rather than age, will probably determine how long your child rides in

Trailer

the trailer because many of us hit a point at which they're too heavy to be fun to haul around regularly, especially for long stretches. Taller, adaptive trailers exist for hauling passengers up to 150 pounds, and custom trailers can carry even heavier loads.

Pros:

› Affordable
› Longevity, accommodating children up to age six
› Provide shelter from the rain, the cold, and the sun
› Keep objects thrown or dropped by children en route contained
› Flexible, since different bikes can hook up to the trailer so you're able to leave the trailer locked up at daycare to later be retrieved by a different caregiver who also has a trailer-hitch-equipped bike
› Remove the trailer and you're on a regular bike.
› Some models can convert to strollers, making multimodal travel feasible. Put the bike on the bus rack, and wheel (or fold and carry, depending on your local transit rules) the stroller inside.
› The wide wheelbase makes trailers stable: you fall, but your trailer will remain upright.
› Great for naptime riding or for lulling your child to sleep anytime
› Versatile for nonhuman cargo conveyance. Single trailers haul up to around 75 pounds and double trailers up to 100 pounds.

Cons:

› The distance between you and your kids makes it hard to see and hear them.
› The footprint to maneuver (and worry about) is wide.
› The long bike setup's extra length is behind you and out of your line of sight.
› The low profile of a trailer is not as visible to others, even with a bright safety flag, as a system that is higher off the ground.
› Heavy loads create drag and are harder to carry up hills.
› Heavy trailers push you down hills, even the slight incline of curb cuts and driveways, making for a jolty ride.

THE JAPANESE MAMACHARI

The *mamachari* is the ubiquitous Japanese family bike. Many have made their way to America and they're quite popular. It's a city bike with an integrated front child seat that can double as a cargo basket, and an add-on rear child seat. Many come standard with electric assist.

Child's bike coupled to adult bike

TRAILER BIKES AND COUPLED KID BIKES

Ages: four to ten years

Trailer bikes are a popular way to add a kid to any bike. An arm hitches a sort of half-bike to the parent bike; the half-bike has a regular saddle, handlebars, pedals, and rear wheel. Children are free to coast along, but are also able to pedal and participate in the ride. Some trailer bikes have gears for the child to learn shifting and if so inclined, help more effectively.

The most affordable trailer bikes attach at the seat post, but this makes them prone to listing to the side, making the ride a bit uncomfortable for both adult and child—the adult has to work harder to keep the bikes steady and the child has to deal with riding at a cant. Other trailer bikes include a specific rear rack that attaches to a regular bike's eyelets. This of course requires a

bike that can accommodate a rear rack, which is standard for many commute-friendly bikes. This setup doesn't have the leaning problem experienced with seat-post-connecting trailer bikes.

Trailer bikes can be created using regular kids bikes too (with wheels from 12 inches to 20 inches). A device attaches the adult bike to the kid's—either from the adult bike seat post to the kid bike head tube, or from the adult bike rear hub to the kid bike front hub.

Note that when kids have access to pedal power, communication is vital to alert them to cease pedaling when approaching a stop, lest you get pushed farther forward than you'd intended— or likely need to squeeze your brakes marginally harder than otherwise necessary to counteract kid propulsion. And in the case of coupled bikes, kids may need to be periodically reminded of "no braking" while becoming acclimated to biking together.

Pros:
› Kid is exposed to the elements, but can pedal to keep warm (recumbent models have optional weather shield).
› Adult may receive some propulsion help.
› They're easy to remove and switch from bike to bike.
› Some models have gears for children to learn and practice shifting.
› Some come in tandem models to carry two kids.
› Some have add-on back rests.
› Recumbent models allow for napping.
› Recumbent models have storage for snacks and gear.
› Kid feels like she's participating in the ride.

Cons:
› They're heavy, and kids usually don't do much pedaling.
› Communication is vital to let kids know when to stop pedaling when approaching a stop.
› The bike's length makes maneuvering more difficult—although a kid can help walk the bike through tricky spots and communicate distances when negotiating tight turns.

LONGTAILS
Ages: one year to adult
Longtail cargo bikes feature a longer wheelbase, with rear wheel extended about an extra foot. This provides room for

Longtail cargo bike

a long deck behind the rider on which to attach one or two seats or other kid-toting accessories. Foot pegs and handlebars attached to the seat post ("stoker bars") work for some toddlers as young as two and a half. Roll cages that surround the deck also provide containment for small kids. As of this writing, there is no mass-produced weather cover for longtail bikes, so kids are more exposed to the elements.

Pros:
› Napping is easy in a rear seat, possible in roll cages.
› The deck can carry two or three kids.
› It's easy to carry long cargo.

Cons:
› Kids are exposed to the elements
› Kids are behind you, out of sight.
› Longer bike is harder to maneuver at slow speeds.

> Longer bikes are harder to transport by car—their length is wider than most vehicles—but they can ride in a roof-rack tandem tray.

MIDTAILS
Ages: one year to adult

Midtail cargo bikes are in between the length of a regular bike and a longtail cargo bike. There is room for a rear seat and extra cargo. The midtail's main appeal is the added cargo capacity compared to a regular bike (although less than that of a longtail) while still fitting in most of the places a regular bike can go—like bus racks and car racks.

Pros:
> The deck can accommodate two kids old enough and simpatico enough to share stoker bars (this is usually only OK for short trips).
> They can accommodate larger cargo bags than regular bikes.
> They fit on car racks, bus bike racks, and in trains for multimodal travel.

Cons:
> Kids are exposed to the elements.
> Kids are behind you, out of sight.

LONG JOHNS
Ages: all ages

Bikes with a large cargo area—usually defined by a big wooden box attached to the bike's metal frame—in front, like the iconic Dutch *bakfiets* (which translates to "box bike"), are called long johns. Long johns carry infants to adults and everything in between.

Long john cargo bike with weather canopy

Rear bucket bike

There are a variety of long johns nowadays, but the original Dutch *bakfiets* is designed for the flat terrain of the Netherlands. This means not only that it's hard to pedal these sturdy, heavy bikes up hills, but also that they are not equipped with adequate brakes for reducing their speed when coming down big hills. I love long johns, especially the heavy *bakfietsen*, and enjoy using them when visiting flat cities. If you don't live in a flat area, consider a long john designed for working in a hilly city.

Pros:
› Longevity: they last for a long time.
› Hold kids of all sizes—the long boxes hold four kids and the shorter boxes hold two kids.
› Children are in front, so are easy to see and hear.
› Babies can ride in front, where they are rearfacing and easily visible.

› The box can easily accommodate a weather cover.

Cons:
› They're more expensive than a regular bike-plus-trailer setup.
› Most are very heavy, necessitating ground-level storage.
› They're long and hard to maneuver into tight spots.
› Some are limited to flat cities, not designed for riding up and down hills.

REAR-BUCKET BIKES
Ages: all ages
Rear-bucket bikes are the opposite of larger long johns: the cargo area consists of a four-kid-holding bucket behind the saddle.

Pros:
› The bucket is big enough for four kids.
› Removable benches make it possible

to put an infant car seat low in the bucket.

› The bucket can easily accommodate a weather cover.
› They're cheaper than long johns.

Cons:
› The weight of the bike makes for more difficult maneuvering.
› Kids are behind you, out of sight.

CARGO TRIKES
Ages: all ages

Cargo trikes are similar to long johns but have three wheels, one on either side of the large cargo box. Most cargo trikes feature the box in front, but some delta-style trikes have the cargo box in the rear. Trikes are slow, heavy vehicles and therefore not for all riders, but they're incredibly stable—the third wheel makes for a balanced platform, meaning you don't have to put a foot to the ground when coming to a stop. It's a great feeling to stay in the saddle at all times, stopped or in motion. However, the need to keep three wheels on the ground does introduce some new challenges. Trikes must be turned slowly and kept away from anything on a slant, like riding down a curb at an angle or on a sideways slope, lest you risk a tip-over.

Pros:
› Hold kids of all sizes—their big boxes usually hold up to four.
› Children are in front, easy to see and hear.
› Babies can ride in front, where they are rearfacing and easily visible.

Cargo trike

› The box can easily accommodate a weather cover.
› The third wheel makes cargo bikes very stable.

Cons:
› They're more expensive than a regular bike-plus-trailer setup.
› They're heavy and slow.
› They're not designed for riding up and down hills—best suited to flat cities.
› They're unstable when not used properly, such as on tilted surfaces or riding down curbs.

TANDEM BIKES
Ages: four years to adult

Tandem bikes are quite different from trailer bikes since the pedals are synchronized in most cases. Kids can choose how much effort they apply to the pedals, or even remove their feet from the pedals and rest them on the frame, but I've found

Semi-recumbent tandem (plus rear seat!)

they most often are compelled to keep their feet on the pedals and help propel the bike.

There are tandem bikes specifically designed for adult and child, but any tandem can be made to work by adding a kidback to raise the pedals up close enough for a child to reach. For taller kids, crank shorteners or pedal blocks are smaller accessories that make a slight adjustment for fit. Tandem bikes with an upright position similar to commute bikes are most comfortable for riding with kids and gear. A racing tandem won't have braze-ons to accept a rack and panniers, and the aggressive body position won't be as city-friendly as a slower, upright tandem.

Most tandems feature the captain (adult) in front with the stoker behind, although there are some with the positions reversed, such as the semi-recumbent tandems (see below) and some tandems designed specifically for use with kids. Having the child up front is nice for communication—not to mention being able to monitor when to put her resting feet into action when you need the extra force! However, these small-stoker-in-the-front bikes are specifically designed as such, so they come at a higher price than converting any regular tandem into a family bike.

Pros:
› Kid participates in the ride too.
› Most can fit two adults and a family for many years.

Cons:
› They're heavier than a regular bike when riding without a helpful stoker.
› The much longer wheelbase makes maneuvering in tight areas hard.

SEMI-RECUMBENT TANDEMS
Ages: all ages

Tandem bikes are a popular choice for family biking with bigger kids; certain tandem bikes even work well with infant car seats. Semi-recumbent tandems have the parent/captain in back, in a regular, upright type of saddle and pedal configuration. The child/stoker is in front in a recumbent chair-type seat with pedals directly in front. The large seat provides enough room to place and attach an infant car seat.

It is amazing how versatile these bikes are, from infant in car seat to pedaling child to pedaling adult.

Pros:
› Babies can ride in front, where they are rearfacing and easily visible.
› Adjustable so they can also accommodate two adults or an adult and pedaling kid.
› Kids can nap on this sort of tandem.

Cons:
› They're longer and heavier than a regular bike, making for more difficult maneuvering.
› There's no box or bucket for holding extra cargo, although they can be fitted with baskets or panniers.

Dorie Apollonio

Dorie Apollonio

San Francisco, California

Dorie Apollonio traded a life of on-and-off bike commuting for a minivan after having kids, but a work trip to Copenhagen and an introduction to cargo bikes in 2011 changed everything. She and her husband, Matt, got family bikes after returning from their eye-opening trip, sold the minivan in 2012, and have been biking ever since—in the world's second hilliest city.

Dorie's weekday commute to the University of California, San Francisco, where she's a professor of health policy, is usually 7.5 to 9 miles round-trip, broken into pieces: 3 miles from home to her son's school, another few blocks to her daughter's preschool, and then 1.5 miles to her office.

BIKES

Dorie and her husband have several bikes. The main two-kid hauler is a BionX-assisted Bullitt, a front-loading box bike. It's nimble and stable, has excellent weather protection for passengers, and can handle most San Francisco hills, even fully loaded, with the electric assist. If Dorie is carrying only one kid, she typically rides her "ancient, battered," pedal-assisted Bridgestone Japanese *mamachari* with a rear child seat that she found on Craigslist a few years ago. Like many *mamacharis* in America, it was brought over by a Japanese family when they moved to the States and passed along when their children outgrew it. Dorie calls her *mamachari* "pretty much a piece of junk," but admits it's fun to ride and unlikely to be stolen, which is a big issue in San Francisco. If Matt is carrying only one kid, he rides their Kona MinUte midtail, a cargo bike with a rear deck long enough that one kid (or two amicable kids for a short trip) can sit upon it while holding "stoker bars": small handlebars that are attached to the rider's seatpost. And if they're going somewhere that involves a bus ride, Dorie takes their Brompton folding bike, which has a child seat. She imagines they'll probably add another Brompton to their collection, and maybe a longtail cargo bike as well.

CLOTHING

Dorie was a self-proclaimed sloppy dresser until a promotion at work and exposure to some of the bicycling fashion blogs (*Bike Pretty* and *One Woman Many Bicycles*) made for a dressier wardrobe, such as skirts and flats. The biggest changes dictated by bike commuting are that she now wears merino wool long underwear under her clothes in colder months and no longer wears pencil skirts, as they don't allow enough leg movement for pedaling a bike.

BIKE SECURITY

Dorie's security level varies by bike. For the *mamachari*, which looks goofy and has Japanese parts—and is thus wildly unattractive to thieves—she typically only locks up with a rear wheel lock and an Abus Bordo Granit-X folding lock through the front wheel and frame. The battery is always automatically locked to the frame, by design. The Bullitt, their most valuable bike, has Pitlock locking skewers on all moving parts except the pedals, as well as on the seat post and saddle. When it's parked, they lock it with an Abus folding lock through the frame and a rear wheel lock and remove the controller to disable the electric assist. Like the *mamachari*, its battery is automatically locked to the frame by design. They also carry separate insurance for the Bullitt. The Kona MinUte is Pitlocked as well, and they lock up with an Abus through the frame and rear wheel and a cable lock through the front wheel (which Dorie admits is overkill given that the front wheel is Pitlocked, but their first MinUte was stolen). She carries the Brompton inside rather than lock it.

At home they use the rear wheel locks and disable the controllers on the assisted bikes, but don't worry much about theft because their neighbor keeps twenty expensive road bikes in the front of the garage—more attractive theft targets.

ROADSIDE REPAIR

Dorie doesn't carry a repair kit since the chances of being able to do anything useful to repair a bike while supervising her kids are basically nil. When their bikes break down, they load them on a bus rack (if normal-size) or call for a ride (taxi, car share, or bicycle roadside assistance); as a last resort, one of them will pick up the other in a rental car. They always carry mobile phones.

HUM OF THE CITY

Dorie's blog, *Hum of the City* (see Resources), is the go-to source for all things cargo bike and electric assist. A prolific bike test rider and reviewer, she provides bike comparisons not found anywhere else. Dorie's reviews also taught me the importance of good brakes: yes, it's great to have a bike designed to get up a big hill, but that doesn't matter if it's not also designed to have the braking power for coming back down. Of course this isn't an issue for residents of flat cities, but riders from Cincinnati or Pittsburgh can learn a lot from a knowledgeable San Franciscan. Dorie's blog also covers bike insurance; car share; and sadly, stories of her recuperation from a shattered leg after she was rear-ended by a driver in Golden Gate Park.

DORIE'S TIPS FOR NEW BIKE COMMUTERS

"I think sometimes people expect too much of themselves. Any change takes time and practice."

HELMETS

The only piece of equipment you *need* to buy besides your child-carrying system of choice is a helmet. Just like adult helmets, some helmet styles fit some kids better than others. Some have brims and some have magnetic clasps that won't pinch tender skin, but the most important thing is a comfortable fit so your child will want to wear the helmet.

HELMET ACCEPTANCE

The methods you employ to ensure helmet acceptance should follow your style of parenting for any necessary evil, but there are some tried and true tricks.

Practice in the house—you too! The more your child wears his helmet, the less foreign it should feel. Seeing you wearing your helmet should also help ameliorate helmet hesitancy. In a worst-case situation, be prepared to be the only one wearing your helmet around the house for a while.

Practice with toys. Fashioning a helmet out of paper, a bowl, or something more creative to model on a favorite doll or stuffed animal might be even more enticing for a child than seeing her parents wearing helmets in the house.

Practice with ride-on toys. Four months before I started riding with my first son, he received a ride-on toy we kept inside. We also got a helmet around this time and got into the habit of putting on the helmet as a fun accessory that went with the ride-on toy. The toy had buttons, sounds, and lights and made for an exciting baby experience, rendering the helmet unnoticed.

Decorate helmets. Art-loving kids might enjoy personalizing their helmet with stickers. Bicycling-specific reflective stickers will hold up well to the weather while adding visibility, but any stickers will work.

Sometimes there's nothing to be done to appease helmet hatred, but know that once you start moving, the helmet will likely be forgotten as the exciting changing scenery takes center stage.

HELMETS FOR TRAILERS

Look at the shape of the various helmets you try on: notice some are flatter in the back and some have a more pointed aerodynamic shape. The smoother ones will be more comfortable for kids in trailers—especially for shorter kids who don't yet reach high enough to make use of recessed areas for helmets (usually a mesh area that allows some give for the helmet to cradle into).

METHODS, TIPS, AND TRICKS

A good defense is the best offense when it comes to any foray away from home with children in tow. Just like travel by car, bus, train, ferryboat, or airplane, travel by bike should be smooth sailing as long as no one is overly tired, there are plenty of snacks, and there is sufficient entertainment. Down the road, you'll likely take your tired kid out on the bike, but when you are just getting started, having an eager, rested kid will be easier—for everyone. Your parenting techniques for any disruption will translate well to biking, but here are a few extra tips to inspire happy bicycling with kids.

PRACTICE SOLO

Practice without your child first. Try mounting and dismounting multiple times. If you have a rear child seat, you will need to get used to contorting your leg up and over the top tube if you're used to swinging your leg over the back of your bike. If you have a front child seat, practice getting on and off your saddle—you might not be able to slide forward off your saddle anymore with the child seat in the way. Put a bag of rice or potatoes in the seat and see how the bike starts to lean as you shift your weight while getting on and off. Ride your cargo bike unladen and then mimic the kid weight with your bag of rice or potatoes. Some bikes, like long johns, are easier to maneuver with weight in the box.

LOWER YOUR SEAT

Biking with a small passenger for the first time is quite different from riding alone. It's important for everyone's safety to provide a comfortable environment for the passenger, but what about you? A very easy way to feel more in control of your bike now that its weight is altered is to lower your seat. Much like learning to ride a bike for the first time, being able to put a flat foot down while still on the saddle will make you confident you can maneuver this possibly unwieldy load. Long-term riding with one's seat too low can result in knee pain, but it's common for family bikers to start—if not remain—with their seats a bit on the low side. In time (perhaps two weeks of regular riding), the different weight distribution will feel normal and you can slowly raise your seat back to its former position.

GIVE YOURSELF TIME TO FEEL COMFORTABLE

Most children take to riding on family bikes immediately—what's not to love, after all? But *you* are adjusting from solo bicycling to being responsible for an extra being, all while getting used to a new bike or one that suddenly feels quite different. This might take some time. Your first rides should be short and close to home so you can quit if either of you declares it's time to stop. Hopefully,

you'll both have fun from the get-go, but even so, your new bike—whether it's a trailer added to your regular bike or a completely new vehicle—will take quite a bit of getting used to before it feels like an extension of yourself. With each family biking change I've gone through, it's taken two weeks before I felt completely comfortable on the bike and two months before I felt like a pro.

BIKING IN A FISHBOWL

Kids don't always like riding in cars—in fact my firstborn could only tolerate the car if I played a staticky radio station at high volume and kept his window completely rolled down—year-round—for his first two years of life. But at least his discomfort was hidden from the public in our cocoon of a car. Aboard a bike, every wail and sibling strike is on display for public consumption. It's hard not to worry about onlookers watching my unhappy kids. I'd like to shout, "It's OK! He just realized he left that perfectly round rock at a picnic table when we had discussed bringing it home for his collection. We're going to find the same or at least a replacement rock tomorrow!" at every curious passerby, but instead I remind myself that 99 percent of the time the kids are happy campers.

I work hard to keep my passengers engaged in the ride—and less interested in fighting or fussing—with a steady flow of conversation: "Let's all look to the left to see if a car is coming out of that alley" or "Look! Double dump truck!"

But the occasional on-bike incident is unavoidable. The most important thing is to keep calm and stay focused on the task at hand—something I'll admit I find much easier on my bike than when driving a car. A calm bike pilot will get kids calmer faster and make it easier to ride safely. Distraction in the form of a little dose of reality often works for me: "Hey, let's all be quiet while I navigate this tricky intersection and then we'll figure out what's wrong in a minute." Often the quick pause of the ruckus is enough to dissipate the problem, but at least I've made it through an intersection before having to work harder at intervening.

LISTEN TO MUSIC

Most of the time just being out on the bike is enough to make any ride joyous, rain or shine. My usual failsafe item for a successful trip is plenty of snacks that can be munched on the bike. Also handy is a chosen toy to accompany us. Finally, just the usual distraction of pointing out sights and sounds, asking questions, and singing songs together works well. But one fun thing that isn't as easily correlated to other aspects of parenting (because can't everything be solved with snacks, toys, and distraction?) is music. Some solo riders wear earphones to listen to music while they ride and this can work for kids as well, but many family bikers find it easiest to use speakers to play music for the whole crew. If you don't need to worry about rain, any portable speaker will do, but waterproof bike-specific speakers are just great. Many mount to handlebars, and it's common to connect them to a smartphone or portable music player with Bluetooth because no wires means more weather resistance. We sing along to songs by local kiddie rock bands, and while sometimes the music selections of my children embarrasses me, it keeps things copacetic and we can still converse over the music if necessary.

PREPARE FOR WEATHER

In cold weather, kids who aren't pedaling and aren't protected by a weather shield can get very cold. It's hard for a parent who is busily overheating to appreciate the relative difference. When it's cold, make sure your nonpedaling passengers always have one more layer than you need for yourself. For smaller kids in trailers, cargo bikes, and on-bike seats, it is relatively easy to fashion a sun shade or a rain cover when a mass-produced solution doesn't exist. But for exposed kids, the clothing and gear for nonideal conditions covered in Chapter 8 applies to kids just as well as adults. Kids are sometimes even easier to bundle up if they're not involved in the pedaling and can therefore have bulkier, looser layers on their legs.

For all weather extremes—and for all riding, for that matter—if conditions get too unpleasant, find somewhere to take a break. It's often tempting to rush home, but a brief stop to warm up or cool down can often (and easily) change a miserable ride into an exciting (if short) adventure.

For the Cold:
› Base layer of wool or silk
› Shoe covers
› Snow gear: snow suits, snow boots, balaclavas, snow mittens, ski helmets, and goggles
› Blankets: as long as they can be securely fastened to the child so there's no danger of getting loose and tangling in the spokes
› Oversized jackets (your extra snow jacket) over the child's regular jacket: This also covers or partially covers legs. Kids sitting on decks or benches can wear the extra jacket in the normal style. Kids in bike seats can wear jackets several ways: zipped up around their body and bike seat; forward with their arms through sleeves; or backward with the arms tied in a knot for more of a blanket feel. To better cover just legs, tie the jacket sleeves around your kid's waist, with the jacket draped over their legs like an apron.

I sometimes have to make compromises on kid outfits, such as starting with sunglasses instead of goggles, wool socks on hands instead of gloves, or balaclavas pulled down below mouths. But I still bring the goggles and gloves along and make sure they're within easy reach when the kids are ready to let me augment their outfits.

For the Rain:
› One-piece rain suits, rain pants and jacket, or rain poncho
› Rain boots
› Gloves
› Waterproof bags for holding exposed kid gear (backpacks, lunch boxes, artwork)

When my children were in preschool, I liked having a rain suit to cover up their outfits for the day. The rain suit hang-dried at preschool, plus I had time at check-in to help with removing rain boots and suit. But with the quicker elementary school drop-off, an outer layer that requires shoe removal to get off—not to mention gets soaked en route and has to stay with the child all day—isn't as convenient, so I prefer a rain poncho (or adult rain jacket that sufficiently covers legs). I can quickly remove it and keep it with me on the bike while a dry kid runs into the school building.

For the Heat and Sun:
› Sunscreen
› Extra water
› Sun hats
› Loose, light-colored long sleeves to cover bare arms
› DIY sun shades—often easily made from stroller parts for bike seats and wagon parts for cargo bikes.

RIDING WITH BICYCLING KIDS

Most city streets aren't designed for small, slow riders. Even if you think you've been riding quiet routes, once your child starts riding separately, your opinion of your routes might change. A mostly quiet route with one tricky intersection may no longer be acceptable when an eight-year-old is riding beside you.

SAFE ROUTES TO SCHOOL

See if your city has a Safe Routes to School (SRTS) program. Your child's school may have a bike train or funds for safety improvements. Also find resources, like safety videos for kids, on the website of the National Center for Safe Routes to School: www.saferoutesinfo.org.

LOOK FOR EVEN QUIETER ROUTES

See if you can find the quietest route possible. The routes I take when riding alone are different than the routes I take when riding my family bike. I thought my "family-friendly routes" were as good as it got until my children started riding their own bikes. After a few days of despair during which I thought there was no kid-friendly bike route between home and preschool, I realized that by adding two circuitous sections—which only increased the distance from 2.1 miles to 2.9 miles—I felt OK riding it with my preschooler.

KIDS ON THE SIDEWALK

Even in cities where it is not legal for adults to bicycle on the sidewalk, it's usually legal for children under eighteen to do so. Sidewalks are a dangerous place to bike and a street-adjacent parent forced to travel the very slow speed of a sidewalk-bound kid isn't in the safest position either. Still, many parents find that quiet streets where they can place a kid on the sidewalk makes the most sense for their commute. Make the best of it by reviewing the sidewalk-riding techniques section in Chapter 6 and take extra caution.

KIDS IN THE FRONT OR IN THE BACK

It's OK to ride either in front or in back of your child—experiment to see which feels most comfortable to you. I liked starting out with my kids in front of me so I could keep an eye on them and shout reminders about staying clear of the door zone and checking for cross traffic as needed . . . which was very often. As soon as they became more practiced riders and I got more comfortable being out with them on their own bikes, I put them behind me so I could lead the way. Nowadays I like to let them go ahead of me when we're on multi-use trails so they can zoom ahead if they choose—and know to wait for me to catch up at intersections—but on the road, I still like being in front. I figure I'm a bigger shape for drivers to notice and I like being able to check intersections as we pass through rather than have the kids come to a complete stop while I pull ahead to check for all of us.

CHAPTER 12

Laws, Theft, and Collisions

WE'VE ALREADY COVERED a lot of safety material—riding safely, keeping your bike in safe working order, and wearing safety gear. Knowing your rights and responsibilities under the law is just as important. It's also important to know what to do in worst-case scenarios such as theft and crashes.

BIKE LAWS

You don't *need* to know all the laws surrounding bicycling in your city, but the more you know, the safer you'll be. Sadly, sometimes this only comes in handy for knowing not to comply when a driver yells, "Get on the sidewalk!" Ideally, knowing where your bike is legally welcome, as well as legally unwelcome, should aid in predictable behavior and contribute to an overall safe coexistence between bikers and other roadway and sidewalk users.

All laws have various levels of implementation and interpretation. Some laws are cut-and-dried ("It is illegal to ride on the sidewalk") and some rely upon your discretion ("Ride as far to the right *as is safe*") Opinions even differ on clear-cut laws, though: some people disapprove of helmet laws because they think they discourage biking by making it look like an unsafe activity requiring safety gear. Meanwhile people who opt not to wear helmets in cities where it's not required by law for adults may regularly have "Helmet!!" yelled at them by other (read: helmeted) people on bikes. Your opinions may change over time, but being confident in your choices and maybe even having a bit of legal rationale to share with peers who want advice (or question your choices) may keep ill will at a minimum. It could even recruit a new urban biker, if not educate a motorist and turn him into a more understanding road sharer.

Every city is different, but most bike laws are found within the vehicle code. To find the latest local laws pertaining to bicycling, start by checking your city government's website or the Department of Transportation of your city, county, or state.

The League of American Bicyclists maintains a resource called Bike Law University with bicycle-related traffic laws organized by topic and by state. Sources are cited for most of the laws, so always verify with your local municipality that you have the latest information, although the League does make every effort to stay up to date.

The Bicycle Helmet Safety Institute (BHSI) at www.helmets.org maintains a *Helmet Laws for Bicycle Riders* webpage with, helmet requirements organized by state, and, if applicable, broken out by city and by ages. The list may be out of date, however, so it's best to confirm with your local organization—and alert the BHSI with the updated information.

Look specifically for laws concerning helmet and light/reflector requirements and where to ride—sidewalk usage, any wording for keeping right.

To serve as an example, the following is the *Washington State Bicycle Laws*, from the Washington State Department of Transportation website:

› *Bicycle Helmets.* Currently, there is no state law requiring helmet use. However, some cities and counties do require helmets.
› *Riding on the Road.* When riding on a roadway, a bicyclist has all the rights and responsibilities of a vehicle driver (RCW 46.61.755). Cyclists who violate traffic laws may be ticketed (RCW 46.61.750).
› *Roads Closed to Bicycles.* Some designated sections of the state's limited access highway system may be closed

to bicycles for safety reasons .... In addition, local governments may adopt ordinances banning cycling on specific roads or on sidewalks within business districts.

› *Children Bicycling.* Parents or guardians may not knowingly permit bicycle traffic violations by their ward (RCW 46.61.700).
› *Riding Side by Side.* Cyclists may ride side by side, but not more than two abreast (RCW 46.61.770).
› *Riding at Night.* For night bicycle riding, a white front light (not a reflector) visible for 500 feet and a red rear reflector are required. A red rear light may be used in addition to the required reflector (RCW 46.61.780).
› *Shoulder vs. Bike Lane.* Cyclists may choose to ride on the path, bike lane, shoulder, or travel lane as suits their safety needs (RCW 46.61.770).

And from California Vehicle Code 21202(a), here is the wording for bicyclists keeping right:

Any person operating a bicycle upon a roadway at a speed less than the normal speed of traffic moving in the same direction at that time shall ride as close as practicable to the right-hand curb or edge of the roadway except under any of the following situations:

1. When overtaking and passing another bicycle or vehicle proceeding in the same direction.
2. When preparing for a left turn at an intersection or into a private road or driveway.

3. When reasonably necessary to avoid conditions (including, but not limited to, fixed or moving objects, vehicles, bicycles, pedestrians, animals, surface hazards, or substandard width lanes) that make it unsafe to continue along the right-hand curb or edge, subject to the provisions of Section 21656. For purposes of this section, a "substandard width lane" is a lane that is too narrow for a bicycle and a vehicle to travel safely side by side within the lane.
4. When approaching a place where a right turn is authorized.

While there are numerous recent studies revealing that helmet laws may not increase safety and in fact result in less ridership, the important thing to know is that if you are in an area where you are required to wear a helmet, you should *wear a helmet*. Some anti-helmet proponents worry that focusing on helmets leads to a false sense of security and detracts from learning safe riding skills.

And some go even further to suggest that helmets give drivers a false sense of bicyclist security: a 2006 study by the University of Bath concluded that "probably the main negative impact of helmets is that drivers pass helmeted bicyclists more closely than unhelmeted bicyclists (because unhelmeted bicyclists seem more vulnerable), and so helmeted bicyclists are more likely to get hit." But while safe riding skills are important, and safe bicycling infrastructure is even more important for riders of all ages and abilities, there is a lot of attention given to helmets; if you are involved in any collision or infraction, your use of a helmet will be noted by medical personnel, in a police report, and in any news coverage.

VULNERABLE USER LAWS

Vulnerable User Laws protect bicyclists and pedestrians—the "vulnerable" road users who aren't protected by automobile safety features. More US states are starting to adopt these stringent laws and it's helpful to know your local version. Many

Governing Body	Regulation
District of Columbia (district law)	Under 16
City of Chicago (city law)	All bike messengers
Massachusetts (state law)	Passengers under 5
	Riders under 17
Pennsylvania (state law)	Riders under 12

Helmet laws vary from state to state—and even within states. (Source: Bicycle Helmet Safety Institute)

first responders don't know the Vulnerable User Laws, even though they're not a recent development. If you witness any accident, ascertain whether the police on the scene are aware of the law (if you are able to interact with them).

Currently only six states—Delaware, Hawaii, Oregon, Utah, Vermont, and Washington—have Vulnerable User Laws. In Washington State a driver committing a traffic infraction—such as speeding, texting while driving, or running a red light—that results in the serious injury or death of a vulnerable roadway user will face an automatic fine of up to $5,000 and a ninety-day suspension of driving privileges. Before the law, a small traffic fine was the end of it.

BIKE SECURITY

So you have your U-lock—two, in fact—and you're always careful to lock your bike to something that's bolted to the ground, your frame and each wheel within the hug of a U-lock and anything removable removed.

But still! For extra bike security, record your bike's serial number, take a few photos of your bike, and register it. It's better to be prepared than heartbroken when your unregistered bike disappears without a trace.

SERIAL NUMBER

Bikes built after 2000 have serial numbers, usually stamped into the bottom bracket—the part the pedals connect to. Your bike shop probably recorded the number along with your name, but you should do this too.

If your bike doesn't have a serial number, you can engrave your own (if your bike is not carbon fiber). Your driver's license number is a popular makeshift serial number, but you can make up any number so long as you record it—and you should plug the number into the Bike Index and make sure a similar bike doesn't come up with the same number. Hardware stores sell small engravers, if you can't find one to borrow. Engrave your serial number of choice in the standard position on the bottom bracket to make it easy for bike shops/authorities to find it. Some people also engrave a second number (even some people with bikes that have serial numbers do this) in case a thief files off the first number and doesn't think to look for a second. And if visible, the presence of that second number might make the bike appear less worth stealing.

PHOTOS OF YOUR BIKE

A photo of your bike is a good visual aid if you have to run an ad listing it as stolen. A photo of you with your bike—ideally date stamped—is useful for showing the authorities when attempting to reclaim your stolen property. You could even take a photo of yourself with your bike while holding a sign with the serial number printed on it to fully cover all your bases. I keep my bike photos on my phone and backed up on my computer, but have never had cause to use them.

REGISTER YOUR BIKE

You can register your bike for free at Bike Index (https://bikeindex.org) and Bike Shepherd (www.bikeshepherd.org). The National Bike Registry (http://national bikeregistry.com) requires a fee (currently starting at $10 for ten years) and will send you a sticker to affix to your bike. Bike Shepherd also sells tamper-proof stickers. A registration sticker may deter theft.

See if there are other places to register your bike's serial number, such as at your university or with the manufacturer of your bike.

It's possible to input your bike after it's been stolen too. Currently you can register your stolen bike with the National Bike Registry for only 99 cents. Bike registries are checked by police when they've recovered stolen bikes as do shops—including pawn shops—when attempts are made to sell them a bike. Register your lock too!

MARK YOUR BIKE

In general, the more identifying features your bike displays, the less likely it is be stolen. If you're not sticker averse, tamper-proof registry stickers are an attractive way to mark your bike. Permanent marker works too. Write your name or something witty on your tires or on your frame and then cover it with clear packing tape.

If you prefer less visible markings, there are some sneakier methods. I love the idea of keeping a photo of you with your bike or a note of some sort hidden in your seat tube. Or get high tech with a GPS bike security product, many of which are just now entering the market. These are hidden on your bike and provide the ability to track its movements if stolen, often with an associated small monthly service fee.

INSURE YOUR BIKE

Your bike is likely insured against theft to some degree under your homeowner's insurance or renter's insurance. In many cases, the theft payout is subject to depreciation and your deductible might be greater than that—so check and see what your coverage entails. Just as GPS tracking devices are new to the market, we're in the early days of bicycle insurance policies. Markel Insurance offers policies under both the Markel name and Velosurance. These both cover more than homeowner's and renter's insurance policies. Velosurance policies start at $100 and average between $250 and $300 per year. There is no depreciation, so in the event of theft, the price to replace the same bike is paid, minus the deductible.

For both types of insurance, your bike must be securely locked to qualify for theft reimbursement. Your lock manufacturer will probably pay the deductible if your lock is registered.

Your insurance probably covers partial theft as well—if a thief makes off with one of your wheels or your saddle, say, but check the details of your coverage to be sure.

Alliance for Biking & Walking

Washington, DC

Do you want to help create safe streets in your community? Then connect with the Alliance for Biking & Walking. Over 200 bicycling and walking advocacy organizations in North America are members of the alliance, and searching the membership directory is the best way to find your local advocacy group.

The alliance works in several ways, from providing training, giving annual Advocacy Awards, and supplying grants—$100,000 in 2014—to compiling valuable data.

Every two years, the alliance publishes a Benchmarking Report. The report combines the alliance's own research with that of over twenty government sources for data on bicycling and walking levels and demographics, safety, funding, policies, infrastructure, education, public health indicators, and economic impacts. It's free to download.

Here are the "8 Fascinating Facts about Bicycling and Walking" from the 2014 report:

1. We're seeing small but steady increases in the number of people biking and walking to work.
2. There are lower bicyclist and pedestrian fatality rates where there are more people biking and walking.
3. More people tend to bike or walk to work when a city has strong biking and walking advocacy.
4. People are healthier in states where more people bike and walk.
5. A large percentage of commuters bike and walk to work in Alaska, Oregon, Montana, New York, and Vermont. Not so much in Alabama, Georgia, Mississippi, Tennessee, and Texas.
6. Biking and walking fatality rates have been decreasing for decades—but are seeing a recent uptick.
7. Few federal dollars go toward bicycling and walking, compared to trips taken and fatality rates.
8. More and more cities are setting goals to increase biking and walking and improve safety.

One of the major initiatives of the alliance is the Open Streets Project, a collaboration with the Street Plans Collaborative. Open Streets are festive events where streets are temporarily closed to cars so people can use them for walking, biking, seeing public art, listening to live music, and socializing. Examples are Los Angeles' CicLAvia, New York City's Summer Streets, Portland's Sunday Parkways, and San Francisco's Car-Free Sundays in Golden Gate Park. The project shares best practices for holding an Open Streets event, holds a national summit, and helps organizations launch their own Open Streets initiatives.

As for using alliance resources as an individual, check out the group's webinars. Most have a small fee (currently $15) for nonmembers. These mean that anyone passionate about creating safe and healthy streets—even without access to a local advocacy groups—can benefit from ongoing education through the alliance.

WHAT TO DO IF YOU SPOT YOUR STOLEN BIKE

I've heard quite a few stories from friends about confronting thieves and regaining possession of their stolen bikes. Getting a bike back is great, but confronting a thief is a bad idea. Even with favorable outcomes, most bike rescuers will admit that it was a risky endeavor and they should have let the police handle the matter. It's frustrating to wait for the police to arrive and worry about your bike leaving the scene with its captor, but it's not worth the risk to engage the bike thief. Instead, get a description, take a photo of the thief, and call the police.

If the bike is locked and unattended, add your U-lock so it stays put until the police can help. If your bike was recently stolen, it's not a bad idea to travel around with an extra U-lock in the hopes you'll encounter just this situation.

For example, I've seen my stolen trailer around town a couple times, and while it didn't occur to me to lock it up—primarily because the trailer is in pretty scary condition now and I didn't want it back—the bike it was attached to looked brand new, so I took a picture to show others in case that bike had been stolen, too, hoping to help crack a bike-theft ring. Nothing came of it, but recovering one bike often leads to others.

COLLISIONS

I have never been hit by a car while on my bike. Once, a slow-moving, out-of-control guy out for his first spin on his road bike in clipless pedals bumped into the side of my stopped cargo bike and bounced off me while the kids and I slowly tipped over into the grass while trying not to laugh (at the situation, not at him!). I have been in six car-car collisions of varying degrees of severity, as probably mirrors the experience of many Americans. None of this has led to an especially high or especially low degree of anxiety over collisions on my part, although I guess it may be a small part of why I prefer biking to driving.

I do have a healthy fear of collisions. This fear is always more pronounced when I'm bicycling on my own in a new city (following a friend seems to mitigate this) or even in an unfamiliar neighborhood close to home. The degree to which I am fearful in these particular situations has gradually lessened the more hundreds of miles I've pedaled, and is probably more of an "overly cautious" feeling than "healthy fear" now. For me, it's second nature to ride around in a good mood, feeling carefree, yet still practicing caution and being prepared for the unexpected. On a zippy bike this feels a bit like a dance, but at my everyday slow pace it's more of a calculated—yet carefree, remember!—circuit through obstacles.

COMMON CAUSES OF DRIVERS HITTING BICYCLISTS

In May 2014, the League of American Bicyclists released the *Every Bicyclist Counts* report, a study of 628 fatal bike crashes that discovered some unexpected results: for decades, rear-endings have been considered very rare yet it turns out an alarmingly high 40 percent of the studied fatalities were just that.

The most common driver-caused collisions happen in intersections—a good reminder to be your most cautious in intersections. From Commute by Bike, there are three mistakes drivers make that cause the most collisions with bike commuters:

1. Not obeying stop signs
2. Passing a bicyclist and immediately turning right across a bicyclist's path, "right hook"
3. Turning left in front of a bicyclist who is going straight through an intersection, "left cross"

Other common causes of collisions due to bicyclist mistakes are:

1. Riding too far to the right. This puts the bicyclist at risk of being hit by an opening parked car door or being right hooked.
2. Riding on the sidewalk
3. Riding the wrong way on the street ("salmoning")
4. Stopping in a driver's blind spot
5. Passing a car on the right. Note: If the car in front of you slows, you should slow too. Don't assume the driver is preparing to turn left; he may be preparing to pull into a parking spot on the right. You can wait.

Not all crashes end in a fatality, but according to the Law of Gross Tonnage, the unprotected bicyclist always gets the worst of it. The New York State Department of Motor Vehicles cites that:

› If someone is hit by a car going 40 mph, there is a 70 percent chance that person will die.
› If someone is hit by a car going 30 mph, there is a 20 percent chance that person will die.
› If someone is hit by a car going 20 mph, there is a 2 percent chance that person will die.

Advocating for protected bike lanes, lower speed limits, traffic-calming devices like speed humps and diverters, and enforcement of Vulnerable User Laws will lower these fatalities in the future. For your immediate safety, stick to streets with lower speeds of traffic (posted and observed), position yourself where you can easily be seen, and signal all turns and lane changes. You will still encounter the unexpected, like a person speeding through a stop sign or turning right in front of you without signaling or checking his mirrors, but you'll catch this with plenty of time to react in your normal course of observing each intersection as your approach. That doesn't mean you have to like it or (hopefully) worry about seeing things like this on a daily basis, but you'll have sufficient time to predict the fast-moving driver blowing through a stop sign that it won't result in a scary miss, and you can proceed with your trip unruffled. Also stay rubber-side down by always following the safe riding techniques covered in Chapter 6.

▰▰▰▰▰▰▰▰▰▰▰▰

INSURANCE FOR COLLISIONS

If you own a car, your car insurance will cover your medical expenses in the event of a collision. It's wise to make sure you have the maximum Uninsured/Underinsured Motorist (UI/UIM) coverage. This is a good idea in general, not just because you ride a bike around cars.

If you don't own a car and therefore don't have car insurance, the bicycle insurers mentioned in Insure Your Bike (earlier in this chapter) offer optional Medical Payments and Vehicle Contact Protection.

▰▰▰▰▰▰▰▰▰▰▰▰

WHAT TO DO IF YOU ARE IN OR WITNESS A COLLISION

When I witnessed a crash at the end of Bike Month on a multi-use trail, I felt a bit helpless and wished I had thought beforehand what to do to help in such a situation. A woman cycled past me and declared, "Wow, you must be strong!" as she checked out my cargo bike with kids aboard, and moments later we saw her collide with a jogger. We were among the first on the scene and found both women on the ground and in pain. I quickly dialed 911.

My surprisingly calm children sat on the bike as we related our location to the 911 operator. Having a rough idea of named streets near sections of multi-use trails is now on my safety list, as I learned that the first responders' maps couldn't resolve the trail name into an ambulance-friendly address. Another bicyclist stopped beside the fallen biker, and the jogger was with a friend, so I didn't have to do more than just relay information on the phone. Once off the phone I noticed both women were still on the trail—near the edges, but in danger of getting hit again. It appeared both were fine to move—the jogger with scraped legs and the bicyclist with an injured wrist—so I encouraged them to scoot to the grassy shoulder on either side of the trail.

We left once the fire engine arrived on the scene—again, the kids much more relaxed than I would have expected. By this point the bicyclist who stopped to keep the woman company had aided her in making a phone call. More to add to my checklist of Things to Help with in the Event of Witnessing a Collision.

While it's no fun to talk or think about collisions, it's important to know what to do in the event of one. Here is a list of steps to take if you've witnessed a collision or if you've been in one.

Immediately After a Collision:
› Stay calm.
› Move off the street, trail, or bike path if you're able.
› Check yourself for injuries.
› Call 911 for medical assistance and/or to file a police report.
› Get the other person's information (name, address, phone number, insurance info, license plate).
› If the other person left the scene, ask if witnesses took down the license plate number (if the other person was driving a car) or any other pertinent information (car/bike make or color).
› Get contact information of witnesses.
› Wait for help—don't assume you're OK and don't assure the driver that you or your bike are OK.
› Take pictures of everything: your bike, your injuries, the car, the street.

Once You've Left the Scene:
› Get medical treatment if you weren't treated at the scene.
› Have your bike checked by a mechanic.
› Replace your helmet—and save your receipt.
› File a police report if you didn't do so at the scene.
› Consider consulting an attorney.

CHAPTER 13

Next Steps

KUDOS FOR SAVING THE world, pocketing massive amounts of saved money, and prolonging your life by biking for transportation. On top of this, you've probably also experienced the joy bicycling brings to the daily grind of commuting, grocery shopping, and even shuttling around kids.

If you want to add to your repertoire, there are countless options to explore—and your regular city cycling has prepared you for all of it. Want to go faster? Try racing. Want to go farther? Join a cycling club. Want to go *much* farther? Become a *randonneur*. Want to fix bikes? Find a wrenching party or take a series of bike maintenance classes. Want to fix your city? Become a bicycle advocate. Hopefully you've noticed hints of a bicycling culture—maybe in the form of a tweed-costumed pedaling party, a flyer for a lecture about bike touring, or a crowd gathered to watch a bike polo match—as you pedal home from work. You can easily join one of them—or even all of them.

GO ON GROUP RIDES

In Chapter 7, I mentioned group rides as a means for practicing urban riding skills and a way to discover new routes and route-resourceful people. These are my personal favorite reasons for attending group rides, but for many they're simply a way to get out and go for a long ride with company. You can find group rides for anyone and everyone—beginners, families, racers, and more.

LOCAL ADVOCACY GROUPS

If your city has a local advocacy organization, it may run a free group rides program. If not, they can probably direct you to a local organization that does.

CYCLING CLUBS

There are often many cycling clubs to choose from, some with a general audience and some quite specific. Chicago has the Chicago Cycling Club for all and the Windy City Cycling Club, a lesbian, gay, bisexual, and transgender (LGBT) club.

ONLINE RESOURCES

Web searches should turn up any organization-run rides programs, but some groups are a bit harder to find if they exist only on Facebook, Meetup, or a local bulletin board. There's definitely a trick to finding groups, and even after living in Seattle for six years, I still learn of longstanding groups and see new groups form. Once you're actively looking, you're bound to find something, but ask around too—a friendly bike mechanic, other bicycle commuters—or scan the various stickers on the bike racks for group logos and their URLs.

Meetup.com

Meetup is a great place to find local group rides, especially if they're not affiliated with an organization that already has a calendar . . . and even if they are. Club ride leaders might put their rides into Meetup as well as list them in the club calendar. Examples of popular Meetup groups are San Diego's Urban Bike and Social Club and Boston Area Cycling.

Online Communities

Online communities provide much more than just group rides. Usually discussion forums comprise the main content of the site, but their calendar sections tend to have the best listing of all bicycle goings-on for their given city. Check out The Chainlink in Chicago and SHIFT in Portland (see Resources for more information).

CRITICAL MASS

Critical Mass is a monthly, worldwide group ride. It occurs on the last Friday of the month in most host cities. It began in San Francisco in 1992 as a protest to reclaim the streets. In some cities it's still a protest-oriented ride, demonstrating that bikes are traffic, too, but elsewhere it has evolved into a regularly scheduled group ride. Visit the webpage for Critical Mass in your city to get a sense of its vibe.

Having heard our local ride was family friendly, I brought my kids to one, accompanied by a friend who is a long-time participant and had his kid in tow as well. Our small gathering ended with everyone stopping for snacks on a multi-use trail. It felt a lot like the Kidical Mass family group rides I lead, which is only akin to Critical Mass in name, with nothing but smiles, waves, and cheery bell dinging. In contrast, the large group on our twentieth anniversary of Critical Mass felt more like the original rides must have been, with a bit of yelling and going through corked red lights to keep the group together and to make a spectacle—and a statement.

LEAD GROUP RIDES

Participating in group rides is a blast, but maybe you want to be the one in charge! Most group rides are led by volunteers, and your city's club would love to have your help. Some clubs even provide training. To become a Cascade Bicycle Club ride leader I signed up for a two-hour class (that came with free pizza!), paid my annual club dues, participated in at least five group rides, and then helped lead two rides with a mentor. Of course I could lead my rides off-book, but I like knowing I have the liability insurance of the big club behind me. Fortunately I've never had an incident and am unaware if my required safety spiel has scared off any would-be participants.

My two regular group rides are Kidical Mass, a family-friendly ride, and Critical Lass, a social women's group ride. Kidical Masses and Critical Lasses existed in other cities before ours so the catchy names aren't my own creation. Note: although their names evoke Critical Mass, there is nothing protest-oriented about either ride. Especially in the case of Kidical Mass, there is a statement to be made: *Kids are Traffic Too*. Plus, the rides are certainly a bit of a spectacle when there's a large group, demonstrating a type of bike ride that many people sharing the road with us may not regularly get to see. In addition to the waiver, I get to list the rides on the club calendar, reaching thousands of eyes that a nonendorsed ride would miss.

LEAGUE CYCLING INSTRUCTOR

The League of American Bicyclists offers instructor training. League Cycling Instructors (LCIs) complete an intense 3-day seminar training, which certifies them to teach the League's Smart Cycling class series. Instructors are covered by the League's liability insurance. The Smart Cycling classes taught by LCIs are:

› Traffic Skills 101
› Traffic Skills 201
› Group Riding
› Commuting
› Bicycling Skills 123 Youth
› Bicycling Skills 123
› Safe Routes to School

BIKE TRAIN CONDUCTOR

Turn your commute into a train! Bike trains, the commute-specific recurring group rides mentioned in Chapter 7, are often in search of new conductors. There might be specific routes in need of a train, or you can suggest a route not already in service that fits your needs.

START A GROUP

Can't find a group or the right group? Start one! Many groups were started by an individual or a small group of people and have grown over time. Create a web presence of some sort (free website, Facebook page, Twitter account, Meetup group) and hang flyers where you think you'll find your group members—bike shops often have community boards, as do coffee shops, libraries, and recreation centers. Does another city have a ride of the same sort you want to start? It's not a mandate that you contact them about using the name, but it's a nice gesture. Kidical Mass is held in the United States and Canada, with different leaders in each city. Anyone can start a group, no notice

Loaded bike camping rig

necessary, although contacting Shane MacRhodes of Eugene, Oregon's original Kidical Mass is necessary to get information about new groups onto the main website. Critical Lass existed in Chicago and Edmonton, Alberta before Seattle, but when one of the Edmonton organizers moved to the Pacific Northwest, she checked with her cohorts on growing the movement and they readily agreed.

RACE

You've probably seen (or been blown past by) people who turn their bike commutes into races. It might be a woman on a cycling team in her race kit (Lycra cycling outfit printed with team name and sponsors) who only knows how to ride one speed, or a competitive man who records every trip to work with a cycling GPS tracker on his smartphone and strives to move up in the ranks of those who record their times with the same app. If you can resist the urge to turn your commute into a race, get your racing in on the side instead.

The same clubs that offer group rides often have fast-paced rides of varying degrees, but there are also clubs entirely focused on speed, like San Francisco Cycling as well as racing teams.

USA Cycling is the official governing body for all disciplines of competitive

CycloFemme

Nationwide

For all the women out there (and the men, too—tell the women you know!): put Mother's Day on your calendar. Not just to celebrate your mom, but to *bike* with your mom, and all the other women in your life that you can gather, at CycloFemme. A socially driven, grassroots celebration of women on bikes, CycloFemme's annual Mother's Day ride unites riders regardless of gender, age, ethnicity, or bicycle preference to share in the joy of bicycling.

CycloFemme was founded by Sarai Snyder of the *Girl Bike Love* blog in 2012, in collaboration with Tanya Quick and Jenn Cash of the design firm Language Dept, and fiscally sponsored by the League of American Bicyclists. The goal? To honor the past, celebrate the present, and empower the future of women: "Encourage women to ride," CycloFemme says, "and they will change the world. It's grown fast, from 163 rides in 14 countries in 2012 to 303 rides in 25 countries in 2014."

Two friends and I founded Seattle's Critical Lass social ride to coincide with the first CycloFemme ride, and being part of the large national movement made for a tremendous turnout. The ride attracted women of all manner: a young woman new to Seattle and in search of a racing team, women who hadn't bicycled in years and never in a city as large as Seattle, mothers with young children in tow, and many local bicycling advocates.

Our ride has grown over the years too. In 2014 we met in Flo Ware Park, named for a local activist, and invited women from many local organizations, such as CoolMom—a local nonprofit that advocates for lifestyle choices that promote a healthy planet—to ride with us through the city to a picnic lunch donated by Seattle Neighborhood Greenways. Part of the beauty of the ride's coinciding with Mother's Day is that there is often a visiting mother along on a borrowed bike, on her first ride in decades. Even if she doesn't incorporate regular bicycling into her life going forward (though hopefully she does!), it makes for a wonderful and memorable day.

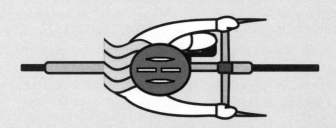

cycling in the United States and provides a listing of clubs, searchable by state.

Bike racing doesn't take place only on the road . . . although you'll feel most like you're in the Tour de France if you pursue road bike racing. If you like competing but aren't keen on long miles on the open road, look into mountain bike racing, track racing in a velodrome, BMX, and my favorite: cyclocross racing.

For the handful of cyclocross races and one road race I have taken part in, it's not necessary to be part of a team. Just sign up if you want to get started—although it's nice to have a support group. USA Cycling also keeps listings of events searchable by state or event name.

GO ON A BIKE TOUR

It's a blast getting to the office, school, or grocery store by bike, but what about getting somewhere even farther? Check out the Adventure Cycling Association for maps, guided tours, and tons of tips and resources.

We take an annual family bike camping trip with a large group and it's amazingly fun; as a regular kid-carrying cargo biker, adding half of our camping gear to my rig doesn't feel all that different from a day trip to the beach. However, when I set out solo on a somewhat-too-big, borrowed touring-cum-commuter bike to visit my aunt and uncle on a small Canadian island, I felt like I was conquering the world. Granted, ferries did most of the mileage, but my small contribution: five miles to the ferry terminal downtown before dawn, a two-hour race between

ferry terminals on Vancouver Island, and an hour of the hilliest riding I have ever done, left me feeling exhausted yet powerful. For most, bike touring involves camping—and carrying that camping gear—so overnighting on my aunt's couch didn't feel entirely on par with the hard-core bike tourers, but it was the experience of a lifetime for me.

WARM SHOWERS

I mentioned bike camping as the usual means of overnighting while bike touring, but that's not always true. Many bike travelers utilize hospitality sites like Warm Showers to access a community of hosts with couch, room, or yes, also places to camp.

Warm Showers describes itself as "a free worldwide hospitality exchange for touring bicyclists. People who are willing to host touring bicyclists sign up and provide their contact information, and may occasionally have someone stay with them and share great stories and a drink."

If you've been bitten by the bike touring bug, but aren't quite ready to set off, sign up as a host and listen to the inspiring stories of your guests until you're ready to follow suit.

SUB-24 HOUR OVERNIGHT (S24O)

The S24O, invented by Grant Peterson of Rivendell Bicycle Works, is a popular mini-bike-tour concept. The idea is to head somewhere close enough to home that you still have time to enjoy your destination, yet at the same time escape the city . . . and then be back in less than 24 hours.

An S24O can even be done midweek! Aldan Shank recaps a great trip from Seattle to Whidbey Island:

"We met downtown after work on a Tuesday afternoon and took the Sounder commuter train to the Mukilteo ferry terminal. We hopped on the ferry and then rode our bikes a few miles on the island to a farmhouse where our friends were staying. We built a fire, made dinner, and hung out before camping for the night. The next morning we caught an early ferry and an early train back to the city, and all of us were at work by 9:00 a.m. The trip was a blast, and it's one of my fondest bike memories."

RANDONNEUR

For long-distance bicycling with a lot of hills, a set route and checkpoints, and only a race against the clock to arrive before the cut-off time, try *randonneuring*. *Randonneuring* is unsupported, which means riders are required to be self-sufficient—and they pride themselves on being so.

There are "brevets," the term for *randonneuring* events, of various lengths and cut-off times:

> 200 km—within 13.5 hours
> 300 km—within 20 hours
> 400 km—within 27 hours
> 600 km—within 40 hours
> 1000 km—within 75 hours
> 1200 km (also called Grand Randonnées)—within 90 hours

The original *Grand Randonnée* is the Paris-Brest-Paris (PBP), older even than the Tour de France. Many cities or states have *randonneuring* clubs, such as Iowa Randonneurs, Lone Star Randonneurs of North Texas, Oregon Randonneurs, and Seattle International Randonneurs.

The Audax Club Parisien (ACP) keeps the official calendar of all brevets, hopefully with something near you, as you work your way up to the Paris-Brest-Paris.

USE BIKES WHEN TRAVELING

You love biking for transportation—and know that seeing a city by bike is the best way to experience that city—so what about those destinations where you don't use your bike to get there and you don't bring it along?

There are several ways to keep your favorite mode of travel going when you're in a different city without your usual bike. Bike share (see Chapter 10) is terrific for travel, with no need to worry about overnight storage or locking up between destinations. If you're lucky, your hotel or vacation home comes with bikes—try choosing hotels based on bike availability. But if not, check bike shops for rental bikes, or investigate peer-to-peer rental programs like worldwide Spinlister or Austin's Spokefly. (Think about putting your extra bike on Spinlister to enable more bicycling in your city. And to reap the monetary benefits.)

For the right price, and especially for weeklong stays, you might even buy a used bike through online classifieds, like

Eric Abbott

Barb Chamberlain

Seattle, Washington

Barb Chamberlain, the executive director of Washington Bikes (formerly the Bicycle Alliance of Washington), commutes ten to fourteen miles each way, depending on which route she chooses. She rides the one-hour round trip three to five days each week; for the other days, she buses with her bike one way. She also uses her bike to attend meetings, which are sometimes even farther away than her regular commute.

Barb's different routes allow her to observe—and avoid—different things. By using a multi-use trail, she skips out on some hill climbing, but since it adds three miles, it's better for the way home when she has fewer time constraints. A different multi-use trail spins her by stunning views of the Space Needle and the jammed interstate, reinforcing her appreciation of the true mobility her bike gives her.

BIKES

Barb's current commute bike is a Specialized Dolce road bike, customized to work for urban commuting with added rear rack, fenders, stem extender (to raise the handlebars to a more upright position), and hybrid pedals that are clipless (for riding with cycling shoes) on one side and regular platform (for wearing work shoes) on the other. She doesn't see it as the perfect bike for her long commute, but it's very light for lifting onto the bus bike rack. She also has—and loves—an eight-speed step-through upright city bike, but it isn't up to the task of hilly Seattle.

Barb thinks her perfect commuter might be a mix of the two with wider tires, disc brakes, generator hub lighting, front basket, and rear rack. I have to agree.

CLOTHING

Barb has made far fewer wardrobe changes for her ride to work than you might think would be necessary. She makes sure her straight skirts are made out of stretchy fabric and avoids long flowing skirts because they'd get caught in her spokes. She primarily wears skirts or the Outlier Women's Riding Pant, which she loves for its stretchy fabric

and gusseted crotch because that translates to more comfort in the saddle. Her former three-and-a-half-mile commute didn't require much thought about fabric, but her current twenty-mile round-trip dictates wearing a wicking fabric as a base layer. She stays away from clothes that will require her to fiddle with them to be ready to ride, like pants with wide legs, preferring to just hop on her bike and go. She stopped buying clothes that wrinkle easily, but admits that's more about the ironing than the bicycling.

Barb has some great advice for trying on cycling clothes: mimic your bike moves in the dressing room. She throws her leg over the top tube of an invisible bike and assumes an on-bike position to check how far a skirt will ride up.

BIKE SECURITY

Barb's bikes live inside the house—in the bedroom, on a stand, since she doesn't have a garage—and inside the office at work.

Around town, in high-theft areas where she'll be inside for a long time, she asks to bring her bike inside. Otherwise she uses a thick cable lock to lock her bike to a rack or tall pole. She doesn't like U-locks because they don't fit all parking scenarios, like tree trunks.

ROADSIDE REPAIR

Barb carries a repair kit and can fix a flat tire, but is out of practice thanks to her flat-resistant tires. She is a master—thanks to her husband—of pedaling a dropped chain back onto her bike and diagnosing odd sounds.

BIKE STYLE LIFE

On her blog, *Bike Style Life* (see Resources), Barb shares lessons learned from her policy and advocacy work, gear and clothing tips, and tricks like the aforementioned how to pedal a dropped chain back onto your bike. She also maintains an amazing list of over 500 women's bike blogs.

BARB'S TIPS FOR NEW BIKE COMMUTERS

"Tell people you're going to do it. One of the things we know about behavioral change is that you're more apt to follow through if you make a public commitment. You'll also find support from friends who already ride.

"Downsize the stuff you carry! If you're like I was, you've allowed your purse or laptop bag to accumulate all kinds of odds and ends. These all represent weight you have to carry personally—and you have a lower horsepower rating than your car or the bus. You may want to leave some things at the office to have them on hand in case you need them, but you most likely don't need to haul them back and forth every day."

Craigslist. However, reselling the bike when you're done with it might be more than you want to deal with while on vacation so look for a local bicycle nonprofit that accepts bike donations or donate it to the closest thrift store.

BE AN ADVOCATE AND VOLUNTEER

It's hard to bike regularly and not become an advocate for city cycling. Even fielding questions at a red light about your bike or your cool bike bag, or giving bike directions to the library, makes you an advocate. Join your local bike advocacy group to learn more about the changes proposed for your city and what you can personally do to help them come to fruition.

The League of American Bicyclists keeps report cards for each state that list state advocacy groups. Even fiftieth-ranked Alabama has the Alabama Bicycle Coalition, working to promote cycling, safety, education, and access. State organizations will have links to local organizations that will help you find a group in or near your city.

Use PeopleForBikes' "Get Local" map to see what's going on in your state and find a local group to join.

SAFE ROUTES TO SCHOOL (SRTS)

If you have school-age children, you might be particularly interested in joining or starting a Safe Routes to School program. These programs are run by parent volunteers with help from the school; community programs; and local, state, and federal governments. The aim is to get more kids walking and biking to school by setting up bike trains (group rides), walking school buses (group walks), and studying and improving road and sidewalk conditions around the school. Safe routes to schools provide safe routes for all road users.

A Safe Routes to School program at our local school resulted in a new crosswalk, curb ramps, and bright yellow signs for crossing a very busy street two blocks from school—a start to making that particular area safer for kids. The National Center for Safe Routes to School has resources, webinars, grants, and much more.

COMMUNITY COUNCIL MEETINGS

If you can't find a group to join, advocate for change on your own. Attend your local community council meeting and speak out about changes that have meaning to you—such as advocating for a stoplight at the busiest intersection along your commute if you experience frequent near misses there or proposing that the community come together to paint a street mural (pretty *and* good for traffic calming!) near the library. Anyone can attend these meetings and voice concerns, so let your voice be heard.

I've spoken at meetings about the need for a safe way to cross a major street in our neighborhood, and it was invigorating to see it move up from a neighborhood level to a district level to a Department of Transportation presentation. Without advocates helping each step of the way, change might never happen.

BICYCLE REPAIR PARTIES

If you've become a bike repair expert, what better way to keep your skills nimble than to take part in a nonprofit wrenching session? Brooklyn's Recycle-a-Bicycle has a weekly volunteer night. Seattle's Bike Works, in addition to offering many repair classes, has twice-weekly Volunteer Repair Parties. No experience is necessary for either organization, so you can even start your volunteering gig before (or instead of) your first repair course. Disassembling, cleaning, and repacking wheel hubs on kid bikes at Bike Works one Super Bowl Sunday left me covered in grease and surrounded by new friends and purpose.

WORK IN THE INDUSTRY

If bike commuting to your nonbike-related job has blossomed into a love of all things bike and, further, has convinced you that a change of employment is needed to better match your passion, there are many avenues to pursue.

Ride the City's free job listings cover all areas of bike-related employment. Or explore the specific ideas listed below.

ADVOCACY

Advocacy isn't only a volunteer activity. The Alliance for Biking & Walking has a job board with job listings from its member organizations across North America. Also look directly to your local advocacy club.

START A BIKE-BASED BUSINESS

Why bike *to* work when your bike can *be* your work? Bike messengers are just the tip of the iceberg. With the right bike, many professions can become bike based: food carts, lawn maintenance, sperm-bank delivery (in a sperm-shaped cargo bike, of course), beekeeping, traveling notary public—OK, I can't find a bike-based notary, but I think it's a great idea. Many bike-based business proposals appear on crowdfunding websites (and successfully launch!) because their start-up costs are modest.

My own bike-based business dream is to pedal bike-share bikes to the empty docking stations, and although I've pitched this idea to a couple bike-share board members, they seem set on sticking with the gas-guzzling cars to do the rebalancing. I imagine I'll eventually come up with a more lucrative, and acceptable, bike-based business.

Resources

Throughout this book, I've named names and cited resources but have collected my favorites here. This is by no means comprehensive, as I am always finding new sources of information.

BOOKS

Bailey, Dennis and Keith Gates. *Bike Repair and Maintenance for Dummies.* Hoboken, NJ: John Wiley and Sons, 2009.

Birk, Mia. *Joyride: Pedaling Toward A Healthier Planet.* Seattle: Mountaineers Books, 2012.

Blue, Elly. *Bikenomics: How Bicycling Can Save the Economy.* Portland, OR: Microcosm Publishing, 2013.

___Everyday Bicycling: *How to Ride a Bike for Transportation (Whatever Your Lifestyle).* Microcosm Publishing, 2012.

Jones, Calvin. *Big Blue Book of Bicycle Repair,* 3rd edition. St. Paul, MN: Park Tool Company, 2013.

National Association of City Transportation Officials (NACTO), *Urban Bikeway Design Guide,* 2nd edition. Washington, DC: Island Press, 2014.

Refer, Kelli. *Pedal, Stretch, Breath: The Yoga of Bicycling.* Portland, OR: Microcosm Publishing, 2013.

Zinn, Lennerd. *Zinn & the Art of Road Bike Maintenance*, 4th edition. Boulder, CO: Velo Press, 2013.

Zinn, Lennard and Todd Telander, *Zinn & the Art of Mountain Bike Maintenance*, 5th edition. Boulder, CO: Velo Press, 2010.

MAGAZINES

Bicycling
www.bicycling.com

Momentum Mag
http://momentummag.com

WEB PORTALS

Bicycle Benefits
www.bicyclebenefits.org

Commute by Bike
commutebybike.com

Elly Blue Publishing
http://takingthelane.com

Girl Bike Love
http://girlbikelove.com

Sheldon Brown's Bicycle Technical Info
http://sheldonbrown.com

BLOGS
Bike Style Life
http://bikestylespokane.com

Commuter Blog
http://commuterblog.com

Ding Ding Let's Ride
http://dingdingletsride.com

Hum of the City
http://humofthecity.com

30 Days of Biking
http://30daysofbiking.com

BIKE REGISTRIES
Bike Index
https://bikeindex.org

Bike Shepherd
www.bikeshepherd.org

The National Bike Registry
http://nationalbikeregistry.com

BICYCLING ADVOCACY ORGANIZATIONS
Alliance for Biking & Walking
www.bikewalkalliance.org

Bicycle Culture Institute
http://bicycleculture.org

CycloFemme
http://cyclofemme.com

The League of American Bicyclists
www.bikeleague.org

Seattle Neighborhood Greenways
http://seattlegreenways.org

ROUTE MAPPING WEBSITES
Bikely
www.bikely.com

MapMyRide
www.mapmyride.com

Open Street Map
www.openstreetmap.org

Ride the City
http://ridethecity.com

Ride with GPS
http://ridewithgps.com

SMARTPHONE APPS
Bike Doctor
Bike Repair
Ride the City

NONPROFIT BIKE CLUBS, CITY-SPECIFIC
Bikes Not Bombs, Boston
https://bikesnotbombs.org

Bike Works, Seattle
http://bikeworks.org

Cascade Bicycle Club, Seattle
www.cascade.org

Cycles for Change, Saint Paul, Minnesota
www.cyclesforchange.org

The Recyclery Collective, Chicago
www.therecyclery.org

San Francisco Bike Coalition,
San Francisco
http://sfbike.org

Time's Up, New York City
http://times-up.org

BIKE TRAINS, CITY-SPECIFIC
Bike Train, New York City
www.nycbiketrain.org/

Cyclelicious, Bay Area, CA
www.cyclelicio.us/silicon
-valley-bike-trains

Los Angeles Bike Trains
http://labiketrains.com/

SD Bike Train, San Diego
http://sdbiketrain.com/

Seattle Bike Train
http://seattlebiketrain.wordpress.com/

RACING
USA Cycling
www.usacycling.org/clubs
www.usacycling.org/events

BIKE INSURANCE PROVIDERS
Markel Insurance Company
www.markelinsurance.com

Velosurance
https://velosurance.com

Index

A

accessories and gear, 65–91
accidents, 229–232
age, bike riding breakdown by, 200–201, 203
air pumps, 86
air quality while biking, 17–18
Alliance for Biking & Walking, 228–229
Apollonio, Dorie, 214–216
Arnold, Samantha, 40–42, 149, 150
automatic shifting, 57

B

babies on bikes, 201
backpacks, 82
bags, 82–85
Balish, Chris, 15
Basics and Benefits of Bicycle Commuting (Balish), 15
baskets, 84, 85
batteries for e-bikes, 33
bells, 90, 124
belt drives, 57
Bicycle Benefits programs, 20
Bicycle Culture Institute, 137
bicycle-specific traffic lights, 104–106
bicycling infrastructure, 93–99, 101–106
bike boxes, 101–102
bike check, basic, 162
bike clubs, 177, 233, 247
bike commute mentor programs, 132
bike commuting
    benefits of, 13–22
    IRS reimbursement for, 16
    multimodal, 181–191
Bike Doctor app, 180
bike equity, 81–82
bike lanes, 95–98
bike lockers, 190–191
bike maintenance, 177–178
bike maps, 129
bike materials, 44

bike shops, 176–177
bike tours, 238–239
bike trains, 132, 134
bike transit centers, 191
bike-based businesses,
    starting, 244
bikes
    anatomy of (fig.), 24
    basic maintenance, 161–178
    buying, 23–39
    buying used, 42–43
    carrying your, 187
    commuter, 25–34
    for different sized people, 39
    gear and accessories, 65–91
    locking your, 67–68
    parts and components, 24, 47–63
    rain, weather accessories, 143–153
    riding techniques, 107–117, 119–126
    roadside repair, 41, 59
    route, having good bicycle, 127–141
    snow, ice equipment, 148–151
    testing and adjusting fit, 43–45
    tuning up old, 27
    types of, 23, 25–39, 62
Bikes Not Bombs (BNB), 179
bike-share programs, 195–197
Biking Portland (Wozniak), 131
blowouts, 167–168
Blue, Elly, 25, 58–59
"bonking," 153
box store bikes, 38
brakes, 51–52, 170–172
Brown, Sheldon, 71
buffered bike lanes, 98
buses and bikes, 184–188
buying
    bikes, 23–39
    used bikes, 42–43

C

cable locks, 68, 69–70
café locks, 70
car bike racks, 183–184
carbon dioxide, 21
carbon monoxide, 21

cargo bikes, 37, 209, 211
carrying your bike, 187
cars
    transporting bikes using, 181–184
    getting rides with your bike, 138–139
Cascade Bicycle Club, 133
Cash, Jenn, 237
cell-phone mounts, 89, 92
chain guards, 88, 90
chain locks, 69
chains, maintaining, 172–174
Chamberlain, Barb, 240–242
children, commuting with, 199–221
cleaning your bike, 176–177
clipless pedals, 54
clothing
    for bad weather, 144–148
    for bike commutes, 75–79
    for biking, 41, 59, 137, 155, 193, 215, 241
    men's, 78–79
    women's, 76–78, 81
collisions, 229–232
Colville-Andersen, Mikael, 76
commuter bikes, 25–34
commuter trains, 188–189
commuting
    benefits of cycling, 13–22
    with kids, 199–221
contra-flow bike lanes, 97–98
"Copenhagen Left," 102–104, 117
cost
    electric bikes (e-bikes), 33
    folding bikes, 31
    trikes, 38
    upright city bikes, 29
    urban commute bikes, 30
Critical Lass, 235–236, 237
Critical Mass, 234
crossing rails, obstacles, 121–122
cup holders, 91–92
"cycle chic," 76
cycling infrastructure/bicycle facilities, 93–99,
    101–106
cycling lanes, infrastructure, 93–99, 101–106
CycloFemme, 237

D
Datzmaier, David, 192–194
defensive riding, 108–109
Delfs, Juliette, 76
disc brakes, 52
door zone, avoiding, 119–120
drink cages, 91–92
drinking water, 153
Dutch bikes, 28

E
earbuds, 91
education
    bike maintenance classes, 176
    urban riding skills classes, 108
electric bikes (e-bikes), 32–33
environment, saving by bike commuting, 19, 21
exercise intensity, 16

F
family bikes, 203–213
fenders, 85–86, 144, 149
ferries, 189–190
fitness websites, 131
fixed-gear bikes, 62
flat (handle)bars, 62
flat-resistant tires, 49–50
flats, fixing, 168–170
folding bikes, 30–31, 191
foot pumps, 86
frame bags, 85
front baskets, 84
front seats, 202–204
front-wheel stabilizers, 87

G
gear and accessories, 65–91
gears, 55–57
gloves, 145–146
Google Maps, 130, 141
GPS devices, 135, 138
grippy pedals, 53
group rides, 132, 233–236

H

hair styles for helmets, 74–75
handlebars
    adjusting, 45
    type, and scanning, 116
    types of, 62
happiness, benefit from bike commuting, 19
health, benefits of bike commuting, 16–19
Heart Opener yoga pose, 157, 159
heat and humidity, 151–153
helmet covers, 144
helmets
    fitting, 74–75
    heat, humidity and, 151
    for kids, 216–217
    laws on, 223–225
    styles, 72
hills, 139
hubs, externally and internally geared, 56–57
hydrocarbons, 21
hypoglycemia (bonking), 153

I

ice and snow, 150–151
Idaho Stop Law, 113
illness, 156
infinite gearing, 57
inflating your tires, 163–164
infrastructure, urban bicycling, 93–99, 101–106
injuries, 156–157, 159
inner tubes, tires, 47–51, 162–170
insuring your bike, 227, 231, 247
intersections, traversing, 117, 119
IRS reimbursement for bike commuting, 16

J

Japanese mamachari bikes, 206, 215

K

kickstands, 87
Kidical Mass, 235–236
kids, commuting with, 199–221
King, Anne and Tim, 17
Klepetar, Ian, 20

L

lane splitting, 121
lanes, bike, 95–98, 114, 115–116
Law of Gross Tonnage, 110, 230
laws, bike, 66, 223–226
League Cycling Instructors (LCIs), 118
League of American Bicyclists, 242
    Equity Advisory Council, 81
    League Cycling Instructors (LCIs), 108, 235
    overview of, 118
left-turn boxes, 102–104
LeMond, Greg, 139
lights, 66
locking skewers, 70
locks, 67–71
longtrails, long johns, 208–210
Lugo, Adonia, 80–82

M

maintaining your bike, 161–178
maintenance toolkits, 162
mamachari bikes, 206, 215
maps, bike, 129
mental acuity, benefit from bike commuting, 18–19
messenger bags, 82–83
mirrors, 87–88
mixing zones, 97
Momentum Mag magazine, 73
money saved by bike commuting, 15–16
motorists, dealing with aggressive, unsafe, 125–126
mountain bikes, 35
mud flaps, 144
multimodal bike commuting, 181–191
multi-use trails, 99, 124–125
music, 90–91, 219

N

Neighborhood Greenways, 99–101
nitrogen oxides, 21
noise pollution, 21–22

P

panniers, 83–84
park and ride, 184
passing, 120–121

patch kits, 175
Pedal, Stretch, Breathe: The Yoga of Bicycling (Refer), 159
pedal assists, 32–33
Pedaling to Prosperity (Sierra Club), 16
pedals, 52–54
PeopleForBikes' Green Lane Project, 109
phone mounts, 89, 92
platform pedals, 53–54
practice runs for routes, 140–141
Prescribe-a-Bike Program, Boston, 195
Presta valves, 48
professional bike fits, 45
protected bike lanes, 98
pumps, 86, 174
punctures, 167

Q
Quick, Tanya, 237
quick releases of wheels, 165–166

R
racing, 236, 247
racks, 83
Rails-to-Trails Conservancy, 101
rain, riding in, 143–153, 220
randonneuring, 239
rear baskets, 84
rear racks, 83
rear seats, 204–205
recumbent bikes, 36–37
red lights, 113
Refer, Kelli, 159
reflectors, 65–66
registering your bike, 227
repair, roadside, 41, 59, 155, 176, 193, 216, 242, 243
repair kits, 174–176
resources
    books, magazines, online, 245–247
    online, 234
Ride Smart program (League of American Bicyclists), 125
riding
    defensively, 108–109
    predictably, 110–112
    on sidewalks, 122–123

riding techniques, 107–117, 119–126
rim brakes, 51–52
road bikes, 26, 34–35
roadside repair, 41, 59, 137, 155, 176, 193, 216, 242, 243
route planning, 127–141

S
saddle covers, 146–147
saddle sores, 156–157
saddles
    adjusting, 44–45
    types and materials, 54–55
Safe Routes to School (SRTS), 221, 243
Safe Routes to School: Steps to a Greener Future, 22
safety
    perceived, of protected bike lanes, 109
    traffic-crash fatalities involving bikes, 107
    of upright city bikes, 26
salmoning, 123–124
scanning, 116
Schrader valves, 48, 50
sealants, tire, 50
seat bags, 85
Seattle's Neighborhood Greenways, 100
security
    bike, 41, 81, 137, 155, 193, 215–216, 226–227, 229, 241–242
    locks, 67–71
sensors, bicycle, 104–106
Shank, Aidan, 76, 78, 83
sharing bikes, 195–197
sharrows (Shared Lane Markings), 94–95
shifters and gears, 55–57, 60–61
shoe covers, booties, 147
sickness, 156
sidewalks, riding on, 122–123
signaling and turning, 114–117
signs, wayfinding, 106
single-speed bikes, 60
Smart Cycling program, 108
smartphone apps, 180, 246
snow and ice, 150–151
Snyder, Sarai, 237
speakers, 90–91

speed of bike commuting vs. other means, 14–15
sprung saddles, 55
Stephenson, Patrick, 154–155
stolen bikes, 229
sweatbands, 151–152
swept-back (handle)bars, 62

T
tandem bikes, 211–213
tandem commute bike with front & rear fenders
   (ill.), 85
testing and adjusting bike fit, 43–45
time, saving by bike commuting, 14–15
tires, inner tubes, 47–51, 162–170
toe clips, toe straps, 54
tools for planning bike route, 129–131
top-tube bags, 85
touring bikes, 35, 37
traction tires, 148–149
traffic lights, 104–106
traffic-crash fatalities involving bikes, 107
trailers, 205–208
trails, multi-use, 99, 124–125
trains, commuter, 188–189
transit bikes, 190
travel time by bike, 14
trikes, 37–38
tubeless tires, 49
tubes and tires, 47–51, 162–170
tuning up
   old bikes, 27
   your bike, 161

Turnaround Twist yoga pose, 158, 159
turning and signaling, 114–117

U
U-locks, 68, 69
unsafe drivers, 125–126
upright city bikes, 26–30
urban bicycling infrastructure, 93–99, 101–106
urban commute bikes, 30
used bikes, buying, 42–43

V
valves for inner tubes, 48
Varnado, Nona, 136–138
vehicular cycling, 112, 114
Vulnerable User Laws, 225–226

W
washcloths, 152
water, drinking, 153
waterproofing raingear, 147–148
wayfinding signs, 106
wear and debris, 164–165
weather, preparing for bad, 143–153, 219–220
weight of upright city bikes, 29
wheel locks, 70
Women Bike and Equity Initiative, 118
women's clothing for biking, 76–78, 81
women-specific bikes, 38
WorkCycles Omafiets Dutch bike, 41
Wozniak, Owen, 131

About the Author

MADI CARLSON is the board president of Familybike, a nonprofit organization dedicated to promoting bicycling as a means for moving toward sustainable lifestyles and communities. She is the cofounder and ride leader of Critical Lass Seattle, an easy, social, ladies' group ride for new and experienced bicyclists; and director of Seattle's Kidical Mass organization, a monthly ride for families. While primarily a transportation bicyclist, Madi also enjoys racing cyclocross, cargo bikes, and all-women alleycats.

Madi bikes all over the Emerald City, both alone and with her two small children, and has been profiled by the Associated Press, *OutdoorsNW*, CoolMom, and *ParentMap*, and she contributed to *Everyday Bicycling* by Elly Blue. When not busy pedaling or encouraging others to pedal, she writes for *Seattle Bike Blog* as a Staff Family Cycling Expert and works with Seattle Neighborhood Greenways to advocate for safe and healthy streets. Visit Madi at www.madicarlson.com.

Greta Meyer-Arendt

ABOUT SKIPSTONE

Skipstone is an imprint of Seattle-based nonprofit publisher Mountaineers Books. It features thematically related titles that promote a deeper connection to our natural world through sustainable practice and backyard activism. Our readers live smart, play well, and typically engage with the community around them. Skipstone guides explore healthy lifestyles and how an outdoor life relates to the well-being of our planet, as well as of our own neighborhoods. Sustainable foods and gardens; healthful living; realistic and doable conservation at home; modern aspirations for community—Skipstone tries to address such topics in ways that emphasize active living, local and grassroots practices, and a small footprint.

Our hope is that Skipstone books will inspire you to effect change without losing your sense of humor, to celebrate the freedom and generosity of a life outdoors, and to move forward with gentle leaps or breathtaking bounds.

All of our publications, as part of our 501(c)(3) nonprofit program, are made possible through the generosity of donors and through sales of more than 600 titles on outdoor recreation, sustainable lifestyle, and conservation. To donate, purchase books, or learn more, visit us online:

SKIPSTONE

LIVE LIFE

MAKE RIPPLES

www.skipstonebooks.org
www.mountaineersbooks.org